Contents

TO M. EUGÈNE LAMBERT.

MY DEAR CHILD,—As you like to hear me relate the tales told by the peasants at our *veillées*,—I mean the watch-nights of my youth, when I had time to listen to them,—I shall try to recall the story of Étienne Depardieu, and piece together the scattered fragments of it still remaining in my memory. It was told to me by the man himself during several of the *breyage* evenings,—a name given, as you know, to the late hours of the night spent in grinding hemp, when those present relate their village chronicles. It is long since Père Depardieu slept the sleep of the just, and he was quite old when he told me this story of the naïve adventures of his youth. For this reason I shall try to let him speak for himself, imitating his manner as closely as I can. You will not blame me for insisting on so doing, because you know from experience that the thoughts and emotions of a peasant cannot be rendered in our own style of language without making them unnatural and giving them a tone of even shocking affectation.

You also know by experience, that the peasantry guess or comprehend much more than we believe them capable of understanding; and you have often been struck with their sudden insight, which, even in matters of art, has an appearance of revelation. If I were to tell you in my language and yours certain things which you have heard and understood in theirs, you would find those very things so unlike what is natural to these people that you would accuse me of unconsciously putting something of my own into the relation, and of attributing to the peasantry reflections and feelings which they could not have. It suffices to introduce into the expression of their ideas a single word that is not in their vocabulary to raise a doubt as to whether the idea itself emanated from them. But when we listen to their speech, we at once observe that although they may not have, like us, a choice of words suited to every shade of thought, yet they assuredly have words enough to formulate what they think and to describe what strikes their senses.

Therefore it is not, as some have reproachfully declared, for the petty pleasure of producing a style hitherto unused in literature, and still less to revive ancient forms of speech and old expressions which all the world knows and is familiar with, that I have bound myself to the humble task of preserving to Étienne Depardieu's tale the local color that belongs to it. It is, rather, because I find it impossible to make him speak as we do without distorting the methods by which his mind worked when he expressed himself on points with which he was not familiar, and as to which he evidently had a strong desire both to understand and to make himself understood.

If, in spite of the care and conscientiousness which I shall put into this task, you find that my narrator sometimes sees too clearly or too deeply into the subjects he takes up, you must blame the weakness of my presentation. Forced as I am to choose among our familiar terms of speech such only as all classes can understand, I voluntarily deprive myself of those that are most original and most expressive; but, at any rate, I shall endeavor to employ none which would be unknown to the peasant who tells the tale, and who (far superior in this to the peasant of to-day) did not pride himself on using words that were unintelligible to both his hearers and himself.

I dedicate this novel to you, my dear Eugène, not to give you a proof of motherly affection, which you do not need to make you feel at home in my family, but to leave with you, after I am gone, a point of contact for your recollections of Berry, which has now become, in a way, the land of your adoption. You will hereafter recall that you said, at the time I was writing it: "By the bye, it will soon be ten years since I came here, intending to spend a month. I must be thinking of leaving." And as I did not see the why and the wherefore, you explained to me that, being a painter, you had worked ten years among us to observe and feel nature, and that it was now necessary you should go to Paris and seek discipline of thought and the experience of others. I let you go; but on condition that you would return to us every summer. Do not forget your promise. I send this book, a distant echo of our bagpipes, to remind you that the trees are budding, the nightingales have come, and the great spring-tide festival of nature is beginning in the fields.

GEORGE SAND.

NOHANT, April, 1853.

FIRST EVENING.

I was not born yesterday, said Père Étienne in 1828. I came into the world, as near as I can make out, in the year 54 or 55 of the last century. But not remembering much of my earlier years, I shall only tell you about myself from the time of my first communion, which took place in '70 in the parish church of Saint-Chartier, then in charge of the Abbé Montpéron, who is now very deaf and broken down.

This was not because our own parish of Nohant was suppressed in those days; but our curate having died, the two churches were united for a time under the ministry of the priest of Saint-Chartier, and we went every day to be catechised,—that is, I and my little cousin and a lad named Joseph, who lived in the same house with my uncle, with a dozen other children of the neighborhood.

I say "my uncle" for short, but he was really my great-uncle, the brother of my grandmother, and was named Brulet; hence his little granddaughter and only heir was called Brulette, without any mention whatever of her Christian name, which was Catherine.

Now, to tell you at once about things as they were, I soon felt that I loved Brulette better than I was obliged to do as a cousin; and I was jealous because Joseph lived in the same house, which stood about a stone's throw distant from the last houses in the village and rather more than three quarters of a mile from mine,—so that he could see her at all times, while I saw her only now and then, till the time when we met to be catechised.

I will tell you how it happened that Brulette's grandfather and Joseph's mother lived under the same roof. The house belonged to the old man, and he let a small part of it to the woman, who was a widow with only one child. Her name was Marie Picot, and she was still marriageable, being little over thirty, and bearing traces in her face and figure of having been in her day a very pretty woman. She was still called by some people "handsome Mariton,"—which pleased her very much, for she would have liked to marry again. But possessing nothing except her bright eyes and her honest tongue, she thought herself lucky to pay a low price for her lodging and get a worthy and helpful old man for a landlord and neighbor,—one too who wouldn't worry her, but might sometimes help her.

Père Brulet and the widow Picot, called Mariton, had thus lived in each other's good graces for about a dozen years; that is, ever since the day when Brulette's mother died in giving birth to her, and Mariton had taken charge of the infant with as much love and care as if it had been her own.

Joseph, who was three years older than Brulette, remembered being rocked in the same cradle; and the baby was the first burden ever trusted to his little arms. Later, Père Brulet, noticing that his neighbor had her hands full with the care of the two as they grew stronger, took Joseph into his part of the house; and so it came to pass that the little girl slept with the widow, and the little boy with the old man.

All four, however, ate together. Mariton cooked the meals, kept the house, made over and darned the clothes, while the old man, who was still sturdy enough to work, went out by the day and paid the greater part of the household expenses. He did not do this because he was well-off and his living was bound to be good accordingly, but because the widow was kind and amiable, and excellent company; and Brulette considered her so much like a mother that my uncle grew to treat her as a daughter, or at any rate as a daughter-in-law.

Nothing in the world was ever prettier or sweeter than the little girl under Mariton's bringing up. The woman loved cleanliness, and kept herself as spick and span as her means allowed; and she had early taught Brulette to do the same. At the age, therefore, when children usually roll in the dirt like little animals, the darling was so clean and dainty in all her ways that everybody wanted to kiss her; but she was already very chary of her favors, and would never be familiar unless quite sure of her company.

When she was twelve years old she was really, at times, like a little woman; and if, carried away by the liveliness of her years, she did forget herself so far as to play while being catechised, she soon caught herself up, even more, it seemed to me, out of self-respect than for the sake of religion.

I don't know if any of us could have told why, but all of us lads, unlike enough when it came to catechising, felt the difference that there was between Brulette and the other little girls.

I must own that some in the class were rather big boys. Joseph was fifteen and I was sixteen, which our parents and the curate declared was a disgrace to us. Such backwardness certainly did prove that Joseph was too lazy to study, and I too lively to give my mind to it. In fact, for three years he and I had been rejected from the class; and if it had not been for the Abbé Montpéron, who was less particular than our old curate, I suppose we might have continued so to this day.

However, it is only fair to confess that boys are always younger in mind than girls; and you will find in every Confirmation class just this difference between the two species,—the males being already strong, grown lads, and the females still small, hardly old enough to wear the coif.

As for knowledge, we were all about alike; none of us knew how to read, still less to write, and we only learned what we did just as the little birds learn to sing, without knowing either notes or Latin, by dint only of using their ears. But all the same, Monsieur le curé knew very well which of the flock had the quickest minds, and which of them remembered what he said. The cleverest head among the girls was little Brulette's, and the stupidest of all the stupid boys was Joseph.

Not that he was really duller than the rest, but he was quite unable to listen and so get a smattering of things he did not understand; and he showed so little liking for instruction that I was surprised at him,—I who could take hold of my lessons fast enough when I managed to keep still, and quiet down my lively spirits.

Though Brulette scolded him for it sometimes, she never got anything out of him but tears of vexation.

"I am not worse than others," he would say; "I don't want to offend God; but words don't come right in my memory, and I can't help it."

"Yes, you can," replied the little one, who already took a tone of ordering him about; "you can if you choose. You can do whatever you like; but you let your mind run after all sorts of things,—it is no wonder Monsieur l'abbé calls you 'Joseph the absent-minded.'"

"He can call me so if he likes," answered Joseph. "I don't understand what it means."

But the rest of us understood very well, and turned it into our own childish language by calling him José l'ébervigé [literally, the bewildered, the staring-eyed]; a name which stuck to him, to his great disgust.

Joseph was a melancholy child, with a puny body and a mind turned inward. He never left Brulette, and was very submissive to her; nevertheless, she said he was as obstinate as a mule, and found fault with him all the time. Though she did not say much to me about my lawless, do-nothing ways, I often wished she would take as much notice of me as she did of him. However, in spite of the jealousy he caused me, I cared more for José than for my other comrades, because he was one of the weakest, and I one of the strongest. Besides, if I had not stood up for him, Brulette would have blamed me. When I told her that she loved him more than she did me, who was her cousin, she would say,—

"It is not on his account; it is because of his mother, whom I love better than I do either of you. If anything happened to him, I should not dare go home; for as he never thinks of what he is about, she charged me to think for both, and I try not to forget it."

I often hear our betters say: "I went to school with such a one; he was my college companion." We peasants, who never went to school in my young days, we say, "I was catechised with such a one; that's my communion comrade." Then is the time we make our youthful friendships, and sometimes, too, the hatreds that last a lifetime. In the fields, at work, or at the festivals, we talk and laugh together, and meet and part; but at the catechism classes, which last a year, and often two, we must put up with each other's company, and even help each other five or six hours a day. We always started off together in a body every morning across the fields and meadows, beside the coverts and fences, and along the foot-paths; and we came back in the evening anyhow, as it pleased the good God, for we took advantage of our liberty to run where we chose, like frolicking birds. Those who liked each other's company stayed together; the disagreeable ones went alone, or banded in twos and threes to tease and frighten the rest.

Joseph had his ways; they were neither horrid nor sulky, and yet they were not amiable. I never remember seeing him really enjoying himself, nor really frightened, nor really contented, nor really annoyed with anything that ever happened to us. In our fights he never got out of the way, and he usually received blows which he did not know how to return; but he made no complaint. You might have supposed he did not feel them.

When we loitered to play some game, he would sit or lie down at a little distance and say nothing, answering wide of the mark if we spoke to him. He seemed to be listening or looking at something which the others could not perceive; that's why he was thought to be one of those who "see the wind." Sometimes, when Brulette, who knew his crotchets, but would not explain them, called him, he did not answer. Then she would begin to sing,—that was sure to wake him up, as a whistle is sure to stop people from snoring.

To tell you why I attached myself to a fellow who was such poor company is more than I am able to do; for I was just the opposite myself. I could not do without companions, and I was always listening and observing others; I liked to talk and question, felt dull when I was alone, and went about looking for fun and friendship. Perhaps that was the reason why, pitying the serious, reserved boy, I imitated Brulette, who would shake him up sometimes,—which did him more good than it did her, for in fact she indulged his whims much more than she controlled them. As far as words went she ordered him about finely, but as he never obeyed her it was she (and I through her) who followed in his wake and had patience with him.

The day of our first communion came at last; and, returning from church, I made such strong resolutions not to give way to my lawlessness any more that I followed Brulette home to her grandfather's house, as the best example I could lay hold of to guide me.

While she went, at Mariton's bidding, to milk the goat, Joseph and I stayed talking with his mother in my uncle's room.

We were looking at the devotional images which the curate had given us in remembrance of the sacrament,—or rather I was, for Joseph was thinking of something else, and fingered them without seeing what they were. So the others paid no attention to us; and presently Mariton said to her old neighbor, alluding to our first communion,—

"Well, it is a good thing done, and now I can hire my lad out to work. I have decided to do what I told you I should."

My uncle shook his head sadly, and she continued:

"Just listen to one thing, neighbor. My José has got no mind. I know that, worse luck! He takes after his poor deceased father, who hadn't two ideas a week, but who was a well-to-do and well-behaved man, for all that. Still, it is an infirmity to have so little faculty in your head, because if ill-luck has it that a man marries a silly wife, everything goes to the bad in a hurry. That's why I said to myself, when I saw my boy growing so long in the legs, that his brain would never feed him; and that if I could only leave him a little sum of money I should die happy. You know the good a few savings can do. In our poor homes it is everything. Now, I have never been able to lay by a penny, and I do suppose I'm not young enough to please a man, for I have not remarried. Well, if that's so, God's will be done! I am still young enough to work; and so I may as well tell you, neighbor, that the innkeeper at Chartier wants a servant. He pays good wages,—thirty crowns a year! besides perquisites, which come to half as much again. With all that, strong and lively as I know I am, I shall have made my fortune in ten years. I can take my ease in my old days, and leave a little something to my poor boy. What do you say to that?"

Père Brulet thought a little, and then replied,—

"You are wrong, neighbor; indeed you are wrong!"

Mariton thought too; and then, understanding what the old man meant, she said,—

"No doubt, no doubt. A woman is exposed to blame in a country inn; even if she behaves properly, people won't believe it. That's what you meant, isn't it? Well, but what am I to do? Of course it deprives me of all chance of re-marrying; but we don't regret what we suffer for our children,—indeed, sometimes we rejoice in it."

"There is something worse than suffering," said my uncle,—"there is shame; and that recoils upon the children."

Mariton sighed.

"Yes," she said, "a woman is exposed to daily insults in a house of that kind. She must always be on the look-out to defend herself. If she gets angry, that injures the custom, and her masters don't like it."

"Some of them," said the old man, "try to find handsome and good-humored women like you to help sell their liquors; a saucy maid is often all an inn-keeper needs to do a better business than his neighbors."

"I know that," said Mariton; "but a woman can be gay and lively, and quick to serve the guests, without allowing herself to be insulted."

"Bad language is always insulting," said Père Brulet; "and it ought to cost an honest woman dear to get accustomed to such ways. Think how mortified your son will be when he hears the carters and the bagmen joking with his mother."

"Luckily he's simple," said Mariton, looking at Joseph.

I looked at him too, and I was surprised that he did not hear a word of what his mother was saying in a voice loud enough for me to catch every word. I gathered from that that he was "hearing thick," as we said in those days, meaning one who was hard of hearing.

Joseph got up presently and went after Brulette, who was in her little goat-pen, which was nothing more than a shed made of planks stuffed with straw, where she kept about a dozen animals.

He flung himself on a pile of brushwood; and having followed him (for fear of being thought inquisitive if I stayed behind), I saw that he was crying inside of him, though there were no tears in his eyes.

"Are you asleep, José?" said Brulette; "if not, why are you lying there like a sick sheep? Come, give me those sticks you are lying on; I want the leaves for my goats."

So saying, she began to sing,—but very softly, because it wasn't the thing to make a racket on the day of her first communion.

I fancied her song had the usual effect of drawing Joseph from his dreams, for he rose, and went away. Then Brulette said to me,—

"What is the matter? He seems worse than usual."

"I think he must have heard that he is to be hired out and leave his mother," I replied.

"He expected it," said Brulette; "isn't it the custom for all of us to go out to service as soon as we have received the sacrament? If I were not lucky enough to be my grandfather's only child, I should have to leave home and earn my living as others do."

Brulette did not seem much distressed at the thought of parting from Joseph; but when I told her that Mariton was also going to hire herself out and live far away, she began to sob, and rushing into the house, she flung herself on Mariton's neck, drying out,—

"Is it true, darling, that you are going to leave me?"

"Who told you that?" asked Mariton. "It is not decided."

"Yes, it is," cried Brulette; "you said so, and you want to hide it from me."

"As some inquisitive boys don't know how to hold their tongue," said Mariton, with a severe glance at me, "I must tell you all. Yes, my child, you must bear it like a brave and sensible girl who has given her soul to the good God this very day."

"Papa," said Brulette, turning to her grandfather, "how can you consent to let her go? Who is to take care of you?"

"You, my child," replied Mariton; "you are now old enough to do your duty. Listen to me,—and you too, neighbor; for here is something I have not yet told you."

Taking the little girl on her knee, while I stood between my uncle's legs (for his grieved look drew me to him), Mariton continued to reason, first with one, and then with the other.

"If it had not been for the friendship I owe you," she said, "I ought long ago to have left Joseph here and paid his board while I went out to service and laid by a little money. But I felt I was bound to bring you up, my Brulette, till you made your first communion, because you are the youngest, and because a girl wants a mother longer than a boy. I hadn't the heart to leave you as long as you couldn't do without me. But now, you see, the time has come; and if anything can reconcile you to losing me, it is that you will soon feel useful to your grandfather. I have taught you how to manage a household and all that a good girl ought to know for the service of her parents and family. You'll practise it for my sake and to do credit to my teaching. It will be my pride and consolation to hear people tell how my Brulette takes good care of her grandfather, and manages his money like a little woman. Come, be brave, and don't deprive me of the little courage that I have got; for if you feel badly at my departure, I feel worse than you. Remember that I am leaving Père Brulet, who has been the best of friends to me, and my poor José, who will hear hard things said of his mother and his home. But my duty bids me do it, and you wouldn't wish me to go against that?"

Brulette cried till evening, and could not help Mariton in anything; but when she saw her hiding her tears as she cooked the supper, the girl flung her arms round her foster-mother's neck and vowed to do as she had taught her; and thereupon set to work with a will.

They sent me to find Joseph, who had forgotten (not for the first time, nor for the last either) that he ought to come home and get his supper like other people.

I found him in a corner all alone, dreaming and gazing at the ground as if his eyes would take root in it. Contrary to his usual custom, he did let me drag a few words out of him, in which, as I thought, there was more annoyance than grief. He was not surprised at having to go out to service, knowing that he was now old enough, and could not do otherwise; but without showing that he had overheard his mother's plans, he complained that nobody loved him or thought him capable of doing good work.

I could not get him to explain himself any farther; and all that evening—for I stayed to say my prayers with him and with Brulette—he seemed to sulk, while Brulette, on the contrary, was full of kindness and caresses for everybody.

Soon after this, Joseph was hired out as a laborer to Père Michel on the estate of Aulnières.

Mariton went to work at an inn called the Bœuf Couronné, kept by Benoit at Saint-Chartier.

Brulette remained with her grandfather, and I with my parents, who had a small property and kept me at home to help them cultivate it.

The day of my first communion affected my spirits. I had made great efforts to bring myself into thoughts that were suitable to my age; and the catechising with Brulette had also changed me. Thoughts of her were always mixed up, I don't know how, with those I tried to give to the good God; and all the while that I was growing in grace as to my behavior, my head was running on follies of love which were beyond her years, and even for mine they were a little ahead of the proper season.

About this time my father took me to the fair at Orval, near Saint-Armand, to sell a brood-mare; and for the first time in my life I was away from home. My mother observed that I did not sleep or eat enough to support my growth, which was faster than customary in our part of the country, and my father thought a little amusement would do me good. But

I did not find as much in seeing the world and new places as I should have done six months earlier. I had a foolish, languishing desire to look at the girls, without daring to say a word to them; then I thought of Brulette, whom I fancied I could marry, for the sole reason that she was the only one I was not afraid of, and I reckoned her age and mine over and over again,—which didn't make the time go any faster than the good God had marked it on his clock.

As I rode back on the crupper behind my father on another mare which we had bought at the fair, we met, in a dip of the road, a middle-aged man who was driving a little cart laden with furniture, the which, being drawn by nothing better than a donkey, had stuck fast in the mud, and couldn't go on. The man was beginning to lighten the load by taking off part of it; and my father, seeing this, said to me,—

"Let us get down, and help a neighbor out of his trouble."

The man thanked us; and then, as if speaking to his cart, he said,—

"Come, little one, wake up; I shouldn't like to upset you."

When he said that, I saw, rising from a mattress, a pretty little girl, apparently about fifteen or sixteen years old, who rubbed her eyes, and asked what had happened.

"The road is bad, daughter," said the man, taking her up in his arms. "Come, I can't let you get your feet wet,—for you must know," he added, turning to my father, "she is ill with fever from having grown so fast. Just see what a rampant vine she is for a girl of eleven and a half!"

"True as God," said my father; "she is a fine sprig of a girl, and pretty as the sunshine, though the fever has rather paled her. But that will go off; feed her up, and she won't sell the worse for it."

When my father said this his head was still full of the talk of the horse-dealers at the fair. But seeing that the girl had left her sabots in the cart, and that it would be no easy matter to find them, he said to me,—

"Here! you are strong enough to hold the little girl for a while."

Then, putting her into my arms, he harnessed our mare into the place of the useless donkey, and pulled the cart out of the mud-hole. But there was another quagmire farther on, as my father knew, having gone that road several times; so calling to me to come on, he walked in front with the peasant, who was twisting his ass's ears.

I carried the great girl and looked at her with amazement; for though she was a head taller than Brulette, I could see by her figure that she was no older.

She was white and slender as a wax taper, and her black hair, breaking loose from a little cap made in the fashion of other parts, which had been rumpled as she slept, fell over my breast and almost down to my knees. I had never seen anything so perfect as her pale face, her clear blue eyes fringed with thick lashes, her gentle, tired air, and even a perfectly black mark at one corner of her mouth, which made her beauty something strange and never to be forgotten.

She seemed so young that my heart said nothing to me, though it was close to hers; yet it was not so much her want of years, perhaps, as the languor of her illness that made her appear so childish. I did not speak to her, and walked along without thinking her heavy; but I took pleasure in looking at her, the same pleasure that one feels at the sight of any fine thing, whether it be a girl or a woman, a flower or a fruit.

As we neared the second mud-hole, where her father and mine began, the one to urge his horse, the other to shove the wheel, the little girl spoke to me in a language which made me laugh, for I did not understand a word of it. She was surprised at my surprise, and then she spoke in the language we all speak.

"Don't strain yourself carrying me," she said; "I can walk very well without sabots; I am as much used to it as others."

"Yes, but you are ill," said I; "and I could carry four like you. What country do you belong to? That was a queer language you spoke just now."

"What country?" she said. "I don't belong to any country; I come from the woods, that's all. And you, where do you come from?"

"Ah! my little fairy, if you belong to the woods, I belong to the fields," I answered, laughing.

I was going to question her further, when her father came and took her from me.

"Well," he said, shaking hands with my father, "I thank you, my good people. And you, little one, kiss the kind lad who has carried you like a load of game."

The child did as she was bid; she was not old enough to be coy, and thinking no harm, she made no difficulty. She kissed me on both cheeks, saving: "Thanks to you, my fine carrier;" then, passing into her father's arms, she was laid on her mattress, and seemed about to go to sleep again, without minding the jolts or thinking about the risks of the journey.

"Good-bye again!" said her father, taking me by the knee, to mount me on the mare's crupper. "A fine lad!" he remarked to my father, looking me over, "and as forward for the age you say he is as my little girl is for hers."

"He is a little the worse for it in the way of health," answered my father; "but, God willing, work will soon cure him. Excuse us if we go on before you; we have far to go, and I want to get home before night."

Thereupon my father struck his heels into the mare, which trotted off, while I, looking back, saw the man turn his cart to the right, and go off in another direction.

I was soon thinking of something else, but a recollection of Brulette coming into my head, I remembered the free kisses the little girl had given me, and wondered why Brulette always slapped me when I tried to get a kiss from her; then, as the ride was long, and I had got up before daylight, I fell asleep behind my father, mixing up in my tired head, I'm sure I don't know how, the faces of the two little girls.

My father pinched me to wake up, for he felt my weight on his shoulders, and was afraid I should tumble off. I asked him who those people we had met were.

"Which of them do you mean?" he said, laughing at my sleepy way. "We have met more than five hundred since morning."

"Those with the cart and donkey," I replied.

"Oh!" said he, "well, faith, I don't know; I never thought to ask. Probably they come from either La Marche or Champagne, for they speak with a foreign accent; but I was so busy watching to see if the mare was good at the collar that I didn't take notice of much else. She does pull very well, and didn't hang back at all; I think she will prove serviceable, and that I have not paid too dear for her."

From that time on (the trip having certainly done me good) I got better and better, and took a liking for work. My father gave me first the care of the mare, then that of the garden, and finally that of the field; and, little by little, I came to take pleasure in digging, planting, and harvesting.

By that time my father was a widower, and seemed anxious to let me benefit by the property my mother had left me. So he gave me a share in all our little profits, and wished for nothing so much as to see me turn out a good farmer. It was not long before he found I had a relish for the life; for if youth needs courage to deprive itself of pleasure in the service of others, it needs none at all to work for its own interests, above all when they are in common with those of a worthy family, honest in the division of profits, and agreeing well as to the work.

I still continued rather fond of gossiping and amusing myself on Sundays. But no one blamed me for that at home, because I was a good worker during the week. Such a life brought me health of body and good-humor, and a little more sense in my head than I gave promise of at first. I forgot all the vaporings of love, for nothing keeps you so quiet as to sweat with a spade from sunrise to sunset; and when night comes, those who have had to do with the heavy, rich soil of our parts (the hardest mistress there is), amuse themselves best by going to sleep, to be ready for the morrow.

That is how I peacefully reached the age when it is allowable to think, not of little girls, but of grown-up ones; and at the very first stirring of such ideas, I found my cousin Brulette still fixed, above all others, in my inclinations.

Living alone with her grandfather, Brulette had done her best to be older than her years in sense and courage. But some children are born with the gift or the fate of being always petted and cared for. Mariton's former lodging was let to Mère Lamouche, of Vieilleville, who was poor, and was therefore ready to serve the Brulets as though they paid her wages, hoping thereby to get a hearing when she declared herself unable to pay the rent. It so turned out; and Brulette, finding that the new neighbor helped her, forestalled her, and made things comfortable for her, had time and ease to grow in mind and beauty without much effort of soul or body.

SECOND EVENING.

Little Brulette was now called "handsome Brulette," and was much talked of in our country-side; for within the memory of man no prettier girl or finer eyes or slimmer waist or rosier cheek or hair of brighter gold had ever been seen; her hand was like satin, and her foot as dainty as a young lady's.

All that tells you plain enough that my cousin did not work very hard; she never went out in bad weather, took care to shade herself from the sun, did not wash the clothes, and made no use of her limbs to tire them.

Perhaps you will think she was idle? Not at all. She did everything that she could not help doing fast and well. She had too much good sense not to keep order and neatness in the household and take the best care of her grandfather, as in duty bound. Moreover, she liked finery too well not to do a good bit of sewing; but as to hard work, she never so much as heard of it. There was no occasion that she should, and therefore it can't be said she was to blame.

There are some families where toil and nothing else comes early to warn young people that life is not so much a question of amusement in this low world as of earning a living among their fellows. But in Père Brulet's home there was little to do to make both ends meet. The old man was only in the seventies, and being a good workman, very clever at cutting stone (which, you know, is quite a science in these parts), steady, and much in demand by every one, he earned a good living; and, thanks to the fact of being a widower with no one to support but his granddaughter, he had laid by quite a little sum against illness or accident. Fortunately he kept his health, so that, without riches, he was never in want.

My father, however, declared that Brulette loved ease and comfort too well; meaning by that, that she might have to come down to other things when it was time for her to marry. He agreed with me that she was as sweet and amiable in her ways as in her person; but he would not encourage me to court her in marriage. She was too poor, he said, to be a lady, and he often declared that a wife should be either rich or very full of energy. "At first sight, I like one as well as the other," he would say; "though perhaps, on second thoughts, I would rather have the energy than the money. But Brulette has not enough of either to tempt a wise man."

I knew my father was right; but my cousin's sweet eyes and gentle speech had more influence over me than he could have, and over other young fellows too,—for you must know that I was not the only one. From the time she was fifteen she was surrounded with striplings like me, whom she knew how to restrain and order about as she had done in her childish days. You might say she was born proud, and knew her value long before compliments had given her an idea of it. She loved praise and submission, and while she never allowed any one to make free with her, she was very willing they should love her timidly. I, like a good many others, was filled with the strongest desire to please her, and at the same time I was often annoyed to find myself only one of a crowd.

Two of us, however, were privileged to talk to her rather more intimately, and to walk home with her when we met at a dance, or after church. I mean Joseph Picot and I. But we gained little or nothing by that; and perhaps, without saying so, we laid the blame to each other.

Joseph was still on the farm at Aulnières, about a mile and a half from Brulette's house, and half that distance from mine. He was a mere laborer. Though he was not really handsome, some, who did not object to a melancholy face, might think him so. His face was lean and yellow, and his brown hair, falling straight from his head and down his cheeks, made him even more puny in appearance. Nevertheless, he was not ill-made, nor ungraceful in body, and there was something in his closed jaw which always seemed to me the reverse of weakness. He was thought ill because he moved slowly and had none of the gayety of youth; but seeing him often, as I did, I knew it was his nature to be so, and that he really was not suffering at all.

He was, however, a very poor laborer of the soil, not over careful with cattle, and far from agreeable in temper. His wages were the lowest that were ever paid to a plough-boy, and people were surprised that his master still kept him; for nothing prospered with him, either in the stable or the fields, and he was so sullen when reproved that no one could do anything with him. But Père Michel declared that he never gave any angry answer, and he preferred those who submitted without a word, even if they did have sulky looks, to those who deceived you with flattery.

His faithfulness and the contempt he showed at all times for injustice made his master respect him, though he often remarked what a pity it was that an honest, upright lad had such soft muscles and a mind so indifferent to his work. But he kept him for what he was worth, from habit, and also out of consideration for Père Brulet, who was one of Père Michel's earliest friends.

In what I have said of Joseph you will readily see that he could not please the girls. Indeed, they never looked at him, except to wonder why they never caught his eye, which was large and clear as an owl's and never seemed to see anything.

Yet I was always jealous of him, because Brulette paid him more attention than she gave to any one else, and obliged me to do the same. She no longer lectured him, and openly accepted his temper as God made it, without getting angry or seeming at all annoyed. She forgave him his want of gallantry, and even politeness,—two things which she exacted from the rest of us. He might do all sorts of stupid things,—such as sit down on a chair if she left it for a moment, and oblige her to find another; or neglect to pick up her balls of wool when they rolled away; or break a bodkin or some other sewing utensil,—he might do all such things, and she would never say an impatient word to him; whereas she scolded and ridiculed me if I did a tenth part of them.

Then, she took care of him as if he were a brother. She kept a bit of meat put by for him when he came to see her, and made him eat it whether he was hungry or not, telling him he ought to strengthen his stomach and make blood. She had an eye to his clothes just like Mariton, and even took upon herself to make him new ones, saying that his mother had not time to cut and sew them. Sometimes she would lead her cattle to pasture over where he was at work, and talked to him; though he talked very little, and very badly when he tried to do so.

Besides all this, she would not allow any one to treat him with contempt, or to make fun of his melancholy face and his staring eyes. To all such remarks she replied that his health was not good; also that he was not more stupid than other people; if he talked little, it was not that he did not think; and, in short, that it was better to be silent than to talk a great deal with nothing to say.

Sometimes I was tempted to contradict her; but she quickly cut me short by saying,—

"You must have a very bad heart, Tiennet, to abandon that poor lad to the jeers of others, instead of defending him when they torment him. I thought better of you than that."

Then of course I did her will, and defended Joseph; though for my part I could not see what illness or affliction he had, unless laziness and distrust were infirmities of nature,—which might be possible; though it certainly seemed to me in the power of man to subdue them.

On his side, Joseph, without showing an aversion for me, treated me just as coldly as he did the rest, and never appeared to remember the assistance he got from me in his various encounters. Whether he cared for Brulette, like all the others, or whether he cared only for himself, he smiled in a strange manner and with an air of contempt whenever she gave me the most trifling mark of friendship.

One day, when he had pushed the thing so far as to shrug his shoulders, I resolved to have an explanation with him,—as quietly as possible, so as not to displease my cousin, but frankly enough to make him feel that if I put up with him in her presence with great patience, I expected him to treat me in the same way. But as on that occasion a number of Brulette's other lovers were present, I put off doing this until the first time I should find him alone. Accordingly, I went the next day to join him in a field where he was at work.

I was a good deal surprised to find Brulette with him, sitting on the roots of a big tree by the side of a ditch, where he was supposed to be cutting brush to make pegs. But in fact he was cutting nothing at all; though by way of work he was whittling something which he quickly put in his pocket as soon as he saw me, closing his knife and beginning to talk as if I had been his master and had caught him in a fault, or as if he had been saying secret things to my cousin which I had interrupted.

I was so troubled and vexed that I was going away without a word, when Brulette called to me, and beginning to knit (for she too had laid aside her work while talking to him), she told me to sit down beside her.

It struck me it was only a sop to soothe my vexation, so I refused, saying that the weather was not pleasant enough to sit about in ditches. And truly, though not cold, it was very damp; the thaw had made the brook full and the grass muddy. There was still a little snow in the furrows, and the wind was disagreeable. According to my notions, Brulette must have thought Joseph very interesting to make her lead her flock out there in such weather—she who so often and so readily turned them over to the care of her neighbor.

"José," said Brulette, "our friend Tiennet is sulky because he sees we have a secret between us. Won't you let me tell it to him? His advice will do no harm, and he will tell you just what he thinks of your idea."

"He!" said Joseph, beginning to shrug his shoulders just as had done the night before.

"Does your back itch whenever you see me?" I said to him, spitefully. "I can scratch you in a way that will cure you once for all."

He looked at me from under his lids as if ready to bite me; but Brulette touched him gently on the shoulder with the end of her distaff, and calling him to her, she whispered in his ear.

"No, no!" he answered, without taking the trouble to hide his answer. "Tiennet is no good at all to advise me,—he knows no more than your goat; and if you tell him the least thing, I won't tell you anything more."

Thereupon he picked up his shears and his chopper, and went to work at some distance.

"There!" said Brulette, rising to call in her flock, "now he is cross. But never mind, Tiennet, it is nothing serious,—I know his fancies; there is nothing to be done, and indeed the best way is to let him alone. He's a lad who has had a bee in his bonnet ever since he came into the world. He doesn't know how to express what he feels, and he really can't. It is better, therefore, to leave him to himself; for if one worries him with questions, he only cries, and then we have hurt his feelings for nothing."

"It is my opinion, though," I said to Brulette, "that you know how to make him confess himself."

"I was mistaken," she answered; "I thought he had some much worse trouble. It would make you laugh if I could tell you what the trouble really is; but as he chooses to tell no one but me, let us think no more about it."

"If it is such a little thing," I persisted, "you would not take so much interest in it."

"Do you think I take too much?" she said. "Don't I owe it to the woman who brought him into the world and who brought me up with more care and kindness than she gave to her own child?"

"That's a good reason, Brulette. If it is Mariton you love in her son, very good; in that case, I wish Mariton was my mother,—it would be better for me than being your cousin."

"Leave that sort of nonsense to my other sweethearts," answered Brulette, blushing a little. But no compliments ever came amiss to her, though she pretended to laugh at them.

As we left the fields just opposite to my house she came in with me to say good-evening to my sister.

But my sister was out, and Brulette could not wait, because her sheep were in the road. In order to keep her a moment, I bethought me of taking off her sabots, to remove the lumps of snow, and drying them. And so, holding her as it were by the paws,—for she was obliged to sit down while she waited for me to finish,—I tried to tell her, better than I had ever yet dared to do, the trouble my love for her was piling up in my heart.

But there! see the devilish thing,—I couldn't get out the crowning word of it. I managed the second and the third, but the first wouldn't come. My forehead was sweating. The girl could have helped me out, if she only would, for she knew the tune of my song well enough; others had sung it to her already. But with Brulette, one had to have patience and discretion; and though I was not altogether new at gallant speeches, those I had exchanged with others who were less difficult than Brulette (just by way of getting my hand in) had taught me nothing that was proper to say to a high-priced young girl like my cousin.

All that I could manage was to hark back to the subject of her favorite, Joseph. At first she laughed; then, little by little, seeing that I was seriously finding fault with him, she became herself serious. "Let the poor lad alone," she said; "he is much to be pitied."

"But why and wherefore? Is he consumptive, or crazy, that you are so afraid of his being meddled with?"

"He is worse than that," answered Brulette; "he is an egotist."

"Egotist" was one of the curate's words which Brulette had picked up, though it was not used among us in my day. Brulette had a wonderful memory; and that was how she sometimes came out with words which I might have recollected too, only I did not, and consequently I could not understand them.

I was too shy to ask her for an explanation and admit my ignorance. Besides, I imagined it was a mortal illness; and I felt that such a great affliction convicted me of injustice. I begged Brulette's pardon for having annoyed her, adding,—

"If I had known what you tell me sooner, I shouldn't have felt any bitterness or rancor for the poor fellow."

"How came you never to notice it?" she said. "Don't you see how he makes every one give way to him and oblige him, without ever dreaming of thanking them; how the least neglect affronts him, and the slightest joke angers him; how he sulks and suffers about things nobody else would ever notice; and how one must put one's best self into a friendship with him without his ever comprehending that it is not his due, but an offering made to God of love to our neighbor?"

"Is that the effect of illness?" I asked, a little puzzled by Brulette's explanation.

"Isn't it the very worst thing he can have in his heart?" she replied.

"Does his mother know he has something the matter with his heart?"

"She guesses at it; but, you see, I can't talk to her about it for fear of grieving her."

"Has no one tried to cure him?"

"I have done, and I mean to do, my best," she answered, continuing a topic on which we didn't understand each other; "but I think my way of managing him only makes him worse."

"It is true," I said, after reflecting awhile, "that the fellow always did have something queer about him. My grandmother, who is dead,—and you know how she piqued herself on foretelling the future,—said he had misfortune written on his face; that he was doomed to live in misery or to die in the flower of his age, because of a line he has on his forehead. Ever since then, I declare to you that when Joseph is gloomy I see that line of ill-luck, though I never knew where my grandmother saw it. At such times I'm afraid of him, or rather of his fate, and I feel led to spare him blame and annoyance as if he was not long for this world."

"Bah!" said Brulette, laughing, "nothing but my great-aunt's fancies! I remember them very well. Didn't she also tell you that light eyes, like Joseph's, can see spirits and hidden things? As for me, I don't believe a word of it, neither do I think he is in danger of dying. People live a long time with a mind like his; they take their comfort in worrying others, though perhaps, while threatening to die, they will live to bury all about them."

I could not understand what she said, and I was going to question her further, when she asked for her sabots and slipped her feet easily into them, though they were so small I couldn't get my hand in. Then, calling to her dog and shortening her petticoat, she left me, quite anxious and puzzled by all she said, and as little advanced as ever in my courtship.

The following Sunday, as she was starting for mass at Saint-Chartier, where she liked better to go than to our own parish church, because there was dancing in the market-place between mass and vespers, I asked if I could go with her.

"No," she said. "I am going with my grandfather; and he does not like a crowd of sweethearts after me along the roads."

"I am not a crowd of sweethearts," I said. "I am your cousin, and my uncle never wanted me out of his way."

"Well, keep out of mine now," she said,—"only for to-day. My father and I want to talk with José, who is in the house and is going to mass with us."

"Then he has come to propose marriage; and you are glad enough to listen to him."

"Are you crazy, Tiennet? After all I told you about José!"

"You told me he had an illness that would make him live longer than other people; and I don't see what there is in that to quiet me."

"Quiet you for what?" exclaimed Brulette, astonished. "What illness? Where are your wits? Upon my word, I think all the men are crazy!"

Then, taking her grandfather's arm, who just then came out of the house with José, she started, as light as a feather and gay as a fawn, while my good uncle, who thought there was nothing like her, smiled at the passers-by as much as to say, "You have no such girl as that to show!"

I followed them at a distance, to see if Joseph drew any closer to her on the way, and whether she took his arm, and whether the old man left them together. Nothing of the kind. Joseph walked all the time at my uncle's left, and Brulette on his right, and they seemed to be talking gravely.

After the service I asked Brulette to dance with me.

"Oh, you are too late!" she said; "I have promised at least fifteen dances. You must come back about vesper time."

This annoyance did not include Joseph, for he never danced; and to avoid seeing Brulette surrounded by her other swains, I followed him into the inn of the "Bœuf Couronné," where he went to see his mother, and I to kill time with a few friends.

I was rather a frequenter of wine-shops, as I have already told you,— not because of the bottle, which never got the better of my senses, but from a liking for company and talk and songs. I found several lads and lasses whom I knew and with whom I sat down to table, while Joseph sat in a corner, not drinking a drop or saying a word,—sitting there to please his mother, who liked to look at him and throw him a word now and then as she passed and repassed. I don't know if it ever occurred to Joseph to help her in the hard work of serving so many people, but Benoit wouldn't have allowed such an absent-minded fellow to stumble about among his dishes and bottles.

You have heard tell of the late Benoit? He was a fat man with a topping air, rather rough in speech, but a good liver and a fine talker when occasion served. He was upright enough to treat Mariton with the respect she deserved; for she was, to tell the truth, the queen of servants, and Benoit's house had never had so much custom as while she reigned over it.

The thing Père Brulet warned her of never happened. The danger of the business cured her of coquetry, and she kept her own person as safe as she did the property of her master. The truth is, it was chiefly for her son's sake that she had brought herself down to harder work and greater discretion than was natural to her. In that she was seen to be so good a mother that instead of losing the respect of others, she had gained more since she served at the inn; and that's a thing which seldom happens in our country villages,—nor elsewhere, as I've heard tell.

Seeing that Joseph was paler and gloomier than usual, the thought of what my grandmother had said of him, together with the illness (very queer, it seemed to me) which Brulette imputed to him, somehow struck my mind and touched my heart. No doubt he was still angry with me for the harsh words I had used to him. I wanted to make him forget them, and to force him to sit at our table, thinking I could unawares make him a trifle drunk; for, like others of my age, I thought the fumes of a little good white wine a sovereign cure for low spirits.

Joseph, who paid little attention to what was going on around him, let us fill his glass and nudge his elbow so often that any one but he would soon have felt the effects. Those who were inciting him to drink, and thoughtlessly setting him the example, soon had too much; but I, who wanted my legs for the dance, stopped short as soon as I felt that I had had enough. Joseph fell into a deep cogitation, leaned his two elbows on the table, and seemed to me neither brighter nor duller than he was before.

No one paid any attention to him; everybody laughed and chattered on their own account. Some began to sing, just as folks sing when they have been drinking, each in his own key and his own time, one fellow trolling his chorus beside another who trolls his, the whole together making a racket fit to split your head, while the whole company laughed and shouted so that nobody could hear anything at all.

Joseph sat still without flinching, and looked at us in his staring way for quite a time. Then he got up and went away, without saying anything.

I thought he might be ill, and I followed him. But he walked straight and fast, like a man who was none the worse for wine; and he went so far up the slope of the hill above the town of Saint-Chartier that I lost sight of time, and came back again, for fear I should miss my dance with Brulette.

She danced so prettily, my dear Brulette, that every eye was upon her. She adored dancing and dress and compliments, but she never encouraged any one to make serious love to her; and when the bell rang for vespers, she would walk away, dignified and serious, into church, where she certainly prayed a little, though she never forgot that all eyes were on her.

As for me, I remembered that I had not paid my score at the Bœuf Couronné, and I went back to settle with Mariton, who took occasion to ask me where her son had gone.

"You made him drink," she said; "and that's not his habit. You might at least not have let him wander off alone; accidents happen so easily."

THIRD EVENING.

I went back to the slope and followed the road Joseph had taken, inquiring for him as I went along, but could hear nothing except that he had been seen to pass, and had not returned. The road led me to the right of the forest, and I went in to question the forester, whose house, a very ancient building, stands at the top of a large tract of heathland lying on the hillside. It is a melancholy place, though you can see from there to a great distance; and nothing grows there at the edge of the oak-copses but brake and furze.

The forester of those days was Jarvois, a relation of mine, born in Verneuil. As soon as he saw me, and because I did not often walk that way, he was so friendly and hospitable that I could not get away.

"Your comrade, Joseph, was here about an hour ago," he said, "and asked if the charcoal-burners were in the woods; his master probably told him to inquire. He spoke clear enough and was steady on his legs, and he went on up to the big oak; you need not be uneasy. And now you are here, you must drink a bottle with me, and wait till my wife comes back with the cows, for she will be hurt if you go away without seeing her."

Thinking there was no reason to worry, I stayed with my relations till sunset. It was about the middle of February; and when it got to be nearly dark I said good-night, and took the upper road, intending to cross to Verneuil and go home by the straight road, without returning to Saint-Chartier, where I had nothing further to do.

My relative explained the road, as I had never been in the forest more than once or twice in my life. You know that in these parts we seldom go far from home, especially those of us who till the ground, and keep near our dwellings like chicks round a coop.

So, in spite of a warning, I kept too far to the left; and instead of striking a great avenue of oaks, I got among the birches, at least a mile and a half from where I ought to have been.

The night was dark, and I could not see a thing; for in those days the forest of Saint-Chartier was still a fine one,—not as to size, for it was never very large, but from the age of the trees, which allowed no light from the sky to get through them. What it thus gained in grandeur and greenery it made you pay for in other ways. Below it was all roots and brambles, sunken paths and gullies full of spongy black mud, out of which you could hardly draw your feet, and where you sank knee-deep if you got even a little way off the track. Presently, getting lost in the forest and scratched and muddied in the opens, I began to curse the luckless time and the luckless place.

After struggling and wading till I was overheated, though the night was chilly, I got among some dry brake which were up to my chin; and looking straight before me, I saw in the gray of the night something like a huge black mass in the middle of an open tract. I felt sure it was the big oak, and that I had reached the end of the forest. I had never seen the tree, but I had heard tell of it, for it was famous as one of the oldest in the country; and from the talk of others I knew pretty well how it was shaped. You must surely have seen it. It is a gnarled tree, topped in its youth by some accident so that it grew in breadth and thickness; its foliage, shrivelled by the winter, still clung to it, and it stood up there like a rock looking to heaven.

I was about to go towards it, thinking I should find the path, which made a straight line through the woods, when I heard a sound of music that was something like bagpipes, but so loud you might think it thunder.

Don't ask me why a thing which ought to have comforted me, by showing the presence of a human being, did actually frighten me like a child. I must honestly tell you that in spite of my nineteen years and a good pair of fists, I had not felt easy after I found I had lost my way. It was not because wolves do come down sometimes into that forest from the great woods of Saint-Aoust that I lost heart, nor yet that I feared any evil-intentioned Christian; but I was chilled through with the kind of fear that you can't explain to your own self, because you don't really know the cause of it. The dark night; the wintry fog; a jumble of noises heard in the woods, with others coming from the plain; a crowd of foolish stories which you have heard, and which now start up in your head; and finally the idea of being all alone far from your own belongings,—there's enough in all that to upset your mind when you are young, and, indeed, when you are old.

You can laugh at me if you like; but that music, in that lonely place, seemed to me devilish. It was too loud and strong to be natural, and the tune was so sad and strange that it was not like any other known music on this Christian earth. I quickened my steps; then I stopped, amazed at another sound. While the music clashed on one side, a bell chimed on the other; and the two sounds came at me, as if to prevent me from going forward or back.

I jumped to one side and hid in the brake; and as I did so, there was a flash of light about four feet from me, and I saw a large black animal, that I couldn't make out distinctly, spring up and disappear at a run.

Instantly from all parts of the undergrowth a crowd of the same animals sprang out, stamping, and running towards the bell and towards the music, which now seemed to be getting nearer to each other. There might have been two hundred of these animals, but I saw at least thirty thousand; for terror got hold of me, and I began to see sparks and white specks in my eyes, such as fear produces in those who can't defend themselves.

I don't know whose legs carried me to the oak; I seemed to have none of my own. But I got there, quite astonished to have crossed that bit of ground like a whirlwind; and when I recovered breath I heard nothing, neither far nor near, and could see nothing under the tree nor yet in the brake, and was not quite sure that I hadn't dreamed a pandemonium of crazy music and evil beasts.

I began to look about me and find out where I was. The oak-branches overhung a large piece of grassy ground; it was so dark under them that I could not see my feet, and I stumbled over a big root and fell, hands forward, upon the body of a man who was lying there as if asleep or dead. I don't know what fear made me say or shout, but at any rate my voice was recognized, and that of Joseph replied, saying,—

"Is that you, Tiennet? What are you doing here at this time of night?"

"And you yourself, what are you doing, old fellow?" I replied, much pleased and comforted to have found him. "I have looked everywhere for you. Your mother was worrying, and I hoped you had got back to her long ago."

"I had business over here," he replied, "and before starting back I wanted to rest, that's all."

"Were not you afraid of being here alone at night in this hideous, gloomy place?"

"Afraid of what? Why should I be afraid, Tiennet? I don't understand you."

I was ashamed to confess what a fool I had been. Still, I did venture to ask if he hadn't seen people and animals in the open.

"Yes, yes," he said, "I have seen plenty of animals, and people too; but they are not mischievous, and we can go away together without their harming us."

I fancied from his voice that he was sneering at my fears. I left the oak as he did; but when we got out of its shadow, I fancied that José's face and figure were not the same as usual. He seemed to me taller, and carried his head higher, walking quickly, and speaking with more energy than naturally belonged to him. This did not ease my mind, for all sorts of queer recollections crossed it. It was not from my grandmother only that I had heard tell that folks with white faces and green eyes, gloomy tempers and speech that you couldn't understand, were apt to consort with evil spirits; and in all countries, as you know, old trees are said to be haunted by sorcerers and *other such*.

I hardly dared to breathe as long as we were in the undergrowth. I kept expecting to see the same things I had either dreamed in my brain or seen with my senses. But all was still; there was no sound except the breaking of the dried branches as we went along, or the crunching of the remains of ice under our feet.

Joseph, who walked in front, did not follow the main path, but cut across the covert. You would have thought he was a hare, well acquainted with the ins and outs, and he led me so quickly to the ford of the Igneraie, without crossing the potter's village, that it seemed as if I got there by magic. Then he left me, without having opened his lips, except to say that he wished to show himself to his mother, as she was worried about him; and he followed the road to Saint-Chartier, while I took a short cut through the two parishes to my own house.

I no sooner found myself in the places I was familiar with than my terror left me, and I was very much ashamed not to have conquered it. Joseph would no doubt have told me the things I wanted to know if I had only asked him; for, for once in his life, he had lost his sleepy air, and I had even detected for an instant a sort of laugh in his voice, and something in his behavior like a wish to give assistance.

However, when I had slept upon the adventure, and my senses were calmer, I was convinced that I had not dreamed what I had seen in the undergrowth, and I began to think there was something queer about Joseph's tranquillity under the oak. The animals that I had seen in such number were certainly not an ordinary sight. In our part of the country we have no flocks, except sheep, and those I had seen were animals of another color and another shape. They were neither horses nor cattle nor sheep nor goats; besides, no animals were allowed to pasture in the forest.

Now, as I tell you all this, I think I was a great fool. And yet there's a deal that's unknown in the affairs of this world into which a man sticks his nose, and more still in God's affairs, which He chooses to keep secret. Anyhow, I did not venture to question Joseph; for though you may be inquisitive about good things, you ought not to be so about evil ones; and, indeed, a wise man feels reluctant to poke into matters where he may find a good deal more than he looks for.

FOURTH EVENING.

One thing gave me still more to think about in the following days. It was discovered in Aulnières that Joseph every now and then stayed out at night.

People joked about it, thinking he had a love-affair; but it was no use following and watching him, no one ever saw him turn to inhabited parts, or speak to a living person. He went away across the fields into the open country so quickly and slyly that it was impossible to find out his secret. He returned about dawn, and went to work like the rest; but instead of being weary, he seemed livelier and more contented than usual.

This was noticed three times in the course of the winter, which was very long and very severe that year. But neither the snow nor the north wind was able to keep Joseph from going off at night when the fancy took him. People imagined he was one of those who walk or work in their sleep; but it was nothing of the kind, as you will see.

On Christmas Eve, as Véret, the sabot-maker, was on his way to keep the midnight feast with his parents at Ourouer, he saw under the big elm Râteau, not the giant who is said to walk under it with a rake on his shoulder, but a tall dark man who did not have a good face, and who was whispering quite low to another man not so tall, and who had a more Christian kind of look. Véret was not actually afraid, and he passed near enough to listen to what they were saying. But as soon as the other two saw him, they separated. The dark man made off, nobody knows where, and his comrade, coming up to Véret, said to him in a strangled sort of voice,—

"Where are you going, Denis Véret?"

The shoemaker began to be uneasy; and knowing that you must not speak to the things of darkness, especially near an evil tree, he continued his way without looking round; but he was followed by the being he took to be a spirit, who walked behind, keeping step with him.

When they reached the end of the open ground the pursuer turned to the left, saying, "Good-night, Denis Véret!"

And then for the first time Véret recognized Joseph, and laughed at his own fears; but still without being able to imagine for what purpose and in whose company Joseph had come to the big elm between one and two o'clock in the morning.

When this last affair came to my knowledge I felt very sorry, and reproached myself for not trying to turn Joseph from the evil ways he seemed to be taking. But I had let so much time elapse I did not like to take the matter up then. I spoke to Brulette, who only made fun of it; from which I began to believe they had a secret love for each other of which I had been the dupe, like other folks who tried to see magic in it and only saw fire.

I was more grieved than angry. Joseph, so slack at his work and so cranky, seemed to me a weak stay and a poor companion for Brulette. I could have told her that (putting myself entirely out of the question) she could have played a better game with her cards; but I was afraid to say it, thinking I might make her angry, and so lose her friendship, which seemed to me very sweet, even without her other favors.

One night, coming home, I found Joseph sitting on the edge of the fountain which is called the Font de Fond. My house, then known by the name of "God's crossing," because it was built where two roads, since altered, crossed each other, looked out upon that fine greensward which you saw not long ago sold and cut up as waste land,—a great misfortune for the poor, who used it as a common to feed their beasts, but hadn't enough money to buy it. It was a wide bit of pasture-land, very green, and watered here and there by the brook, which was not kept within bounds but ran as it pleased through the grass, cropped short by the flocks, and always pleasing to the eye as it stretched away in the distance.

I contented myself with bidding Joseph good-evening; but he rose and walked beside me, as if seeking a conversation, and seemed so agitated that I was quite uneasy about him.

"What's the matter with you?" I said at last, seeing that he was talking at random, and twisting his body and groaning as though he had stepped on an ant-hill.

"How can you ask me?" he said, impatiently. "Is it nothing to you? Are you deaf?"

"Who? why? what is it?" I cried, thinking he must see some vision, and not very anxious to share it.

Then I listened, and heard in the distance the sound of a bagpipe, which seemed to me natural enough.

"Well," I said, "that's only some musician returning from a wedding over at Berthenoux. Why should that annoy you?"

Joseph answered with an air of decision,—

"That is Carnat's bagpipe, but he is not playing it; it is some one more clumsy even than he."

"Clumsy? Do you call Carnat clumsy with the bagpipe?"

"Not clumsy with his hands, but clumsy in his ideas, Tiennet. Poor man, he is not worthy of the blessing of a bagpipe! and that fellow who is trying it now deserves that the good God should stop his breath."

"That's very strange talk, and I don't know where you have picked it up. How do you know that is Carnat's bagpipe? It seems to me that bagpipes are all alike, and grunt in the same way. I do hear that the one down there is not properly played, and the tune is rather choked off; but that doesn't trouble me, for I couldn't do as well. Do you think you could do any better?"

"I don't know; but there are certainly some who can play better than that fellow and better than Carnat, his master. There are some who have got at the truth of the thing."

"Do you know them? Where are the people that you are talking about?"

"I don't know. But somewhere truth must be, and when one has neither time nor means to search for it, one's only chance is to meet it."

"So your head is running on music, is it, José? I never should have thought it. I have always known you as mute as a fish, never catching nor humming a tune. When you used to practise on the cornstalks like the herd-boys, you made such a jumble of the tunes that nobody recognized them. In the matter of music we all thought you more simple than children, who fancy they can play the bagpipes with reeds; if you are not satisfied with Carnat, who keeps such good time for dancing, and manages his fingers so skilfully, I am more than ever sure your ear can't be good."

"Yes, yes," said Joseph, "you are right to reprove me, for I say foolish things and talk of what I know nothing about. Well, good-night, Tiennet; forget what I said, for it is not what I wanted to say; but I will think it over and try to tell you better another time."

And off he went, quickly, as if sorry for having spoken; but Brulette, who came out of our house just then with my sister, called to him and brought him back to me, saying,—

"It is time to put an end to these tales. Here is my cousin, who has heard so much gossip about Joseph that she begins to think he is a werewolf; the thing must be cleared up, once for all."

"Let it be as you say," said Joseph, "for I am tired of being taken for a sorcerer; I would rather be thought an idiot."

"You are neither an idiot nor crazy," returned Brulette; "but you are very obstinate, my poor José. You must know, Tiennet, that the lad has nothing wrong in his head, except a fancy for music, which is not so unreasonable as it is dangerous."

"Then," answered I, "I understand what he was saying to me just now. But where the devil did he pick up these ideas?"

"Wait a minute!" said Brulette; "we must not irritate him unjustly. Don't be in a hurry to say he can't make music; though perhaps you think, like his mother and my grandfather, that his mind is as dense to that as it used to be to the catechism. But I can tell you that Mariton, and grandfather, and you are the ones who know nothing about it. Joseph can't sing,—not that he is short of breath, but because he can't make his throat do as he wants it; and as he isn't able to satisfy himself he prefers not to use a voice he doesn't know how to manage. Therefore, naturally enough, he wants to play upon some instrument which has a voice in place of his own, and which can sing for him whatever comes in his head. It is because he has failed to get this borrowed voice that our poor lad is so sad and dreamy and wrapped up in himself."

"It is exactly as she tells you," remarked Joseph, who seemed comforted to hear the young girl lift his thoughts out of his heart and make me comprehend them. "But she does not tell you that she has a voice for me, so sweet, so clear, which repeats so correctly the music she hears that ever since I was a child my greatest pleasure is to listen to her."

"Yes," said Brulette, "but we always had a crow to pick with each other. I liked to do as all the other little girls who kept their flocks did; that is, sing at the top of my voice so that I could be heard a long distance. Screaming like that, I outdid my strength and spoilt all, and hurt José's ears. Then, after I settled down to singing reasonably, he thought I had a good memory for all the tunes that were singable, those which pleased the lad and those that put him in a rage; and more than once I've known him turn his back on me suddenly and rush off without a word, though he had asked me to sing. For that matter, he is not always civil or kind; but as it is he, I laugh instead of getting angry. I know very well he'll come back, for his memory is not sure, and when he has heard an air that pleases him he comes to me for it, and he is pretty sure to find it in my head."

I remarked to Brulette that as Joseph had such a poor memory he didn't seem to me born to play the bagpipes.

"Oh nonsense!" she said, "it is just there that you have got to turn your opinion wrong side out. You see, my poor Tiennet, that neither you nor I know the *truth of the thing*, as José says. But by dint of living with him and his visions I have come to understand what he either does not know or dares not say. The 'truth of the thing' is that José thinks he can invent his own music; and he does invent it, for sure. He has succeeded in making a flute out of a reed, and he plays upon it; I don't know how, for he won't let me, nor any one else, hear him When he wants to play he goes off, on Sundays and sometimes at night, into lonely places where he can flute as he likes; but when I ask him to play for me he answers that he does not yet know what he wants to know, and that he can't do as I ask until it is worth while. That's why, ever since he invented his instrument, he goes off on Sundays and sometimes, during the week, at night, when his music grips him hard. So you see, Tiennet, that it is all very harmless. But it is time we should have an explanation between us three; for José has now set his mind on spending his next wages—up to this time he has always given them to his mother—in buying a bagpipe; and, as he knows he is a poor hand at farm-labor and yet his heart is set on relieving his mother of hard work, he wants to take up the business of playing the bagpipe because, true enough, it pays well."

"It would be a good idea," said my sister, who was listening to us, "if Joseph really has a talent for it. But, before buying the bagpipe, it is my opinion he ought to know something about using it."

"That's a matter of time and patience," said Brulette, "and there's no hindrance there. Don't you know that for some time past Carnat's son has been learning to play, so as to take his father's place."

"Yes," I answered, "and I see what will come of it. Carnat is old and some one might have a chance for his custom; but his son wants it, and will get it because he is rich and has influence in the neighborhood; while you, José, have neither money to buy your bagpipe nor a master to teach you, nor friends who like your music to push you on."

"That is true," replied Joseph, sadly; "I have nothing but my idea, my reed, and—*her*."

So saying he motioned towards Brulette, who took his hand affectionately as she answered:—

"José, I believe in what you have in your head, but I can't feel certain that you will ever get it out. To will and to do are not the same thing; to dream music and play the flute differ widely. I know what you have in your ears, in your brain, in your heart,—the music of the good God; for I saw it in your eyes when I was a little thing and you took me on your knee and said, in a weird kind of way, 'Listen, and don't make a noise, and try to remember what you hear.' Then I did listen faithfully, and all I heard was the wind talking in the trees, or the brook murmuring along the pebbles; but you, you heard something else, and you were so certain of it that I was, too, for sympathy. Well, my lad, keep the music that is so sweet and dear in your secret heart, but don't try to make yourself a piper by profession; for if you do, one of two things will happen. Either you will never make your bagpipes say what the wind and the brook whisper in your ear, or you will become such a fine and delicate musician that all the petty pipers in the countryside will pick a quarrel with you and prevent you from getting custom. They will wish you ill and do you harm, for that's their way to prevent others from sharing their profits and their fame. There are a dozen here and in the neighborhood who can't agree together, but who will join and support each other in keeping out a new hand. Your mother, who hears them talk on Sundays,—for they are thirsty folk and accustomed to drink late at night after the dances,—is very unhappy to think you want to join such a set of people. They are rough and ill-behaved, and always foremost in quarrels and fights. The habit of being at all festivals and idle resorts makes them drunkards and spendthrifts. In short, they are a tribe unlike any of the people belonging to you, among whom, she thinks, you will go to the bad. As for me, I think they are jealous and revengeful, and would try to crush your spirit, and perhaps your body, too. And so, José, I do ask you to at least put off your plan and lay aside your wishes, and even to give them up altogether, if it is not asking too much of your friendship for me, and for your mother and Tiennet."

As I supported Brulette's arguments, which seemed to me sound, Joseph was in despair; but presently he took courage and said:—

"I thank you for your advice, my friends, which I know is given for my good; but I beg you to leave me my freedom of mind for a short time longer. When I have reached a point I think I shall reach, I will ask you to hear me play the flute, or the bagpipe if it please God to enable me to buy one. Then, if you decide that my music is good for anything it will be worth while for me to make use of my talent and I will face the struggle for love of it. If not, I will go on digging the earth and amusing myself with my reed-pipe on Sundays, without making a living and so offending anybody. Promise me this, and I will have patience."

We made the promise, to quiet him, for he seemed more annoyed by our fears than touched by our sympathy. I looked in his face by the light of the stars, and saw it even more distinctly because the bright water of the fountain was before us like a mirror, which reflected on our faces the whiteness of the sky. I noticed that his eyes had the very color of the water and seemed as usual to be looking at things which the rest of us did not see.

A month later Joseph came to see me at my own house.

"The time has come," he said, with a clear look and a confident voice, "for the two persons whose judgment I trust to hear me play. I want Brulette to come here to-morrow night, because here we can be quiet by ourselves. I know your relations start on a pilgrimage to-morrow on account of that fever your brother had; so that you will be alone in the house, which is far enough in the country for no one to overhear us. I have spoken to Brulette, and she is willing to leave the village after nightfall; I shall wait for her on the lower road, and we can get here without any one seeing us. Brulette relies on you not to tell of it; and her grandfather, who approves of whatever she wishes, consents too, if you will make that promise, which I have given for you."

At the appointed hour I waited in front of my house, having closed all the doors and windows, so that the passers-by (if any there were) should think me in bed or absent. It was now spring; and as it had thundered during the day, the sky was still thick with clouds. Gusts of warm wind brought all the sweet smells of the month of May. I listened to the nightingales answering each other from distance to distance as far as I could hear, and I thought to myself that Joseph would be hard put to it to flute like them. I saw the lights of the houses in the village going out one by one; and about ten minutes after the last disappeared I found the couple I was waiting for close beside me. They had stepped so softly on the young grass and so close to the big bushes at the side of the road that I had neither seen nor heard them. I took them into the house, where the lamp was lit; and when I looked at them—she with her hair so coquettishly dressed, and he, as usual, cold and thoughtful—I could scarcely suppose them to be ardently tender lovers.

While I talked a little with Brulette, to do the honors of the house (which was quite a nice one, and I wanted her to take a fancy to it), Joseph, without a word to me, had set about tuning his flute. He found the damp weather had affected it, and he threw a handful of flax chips on the hearth to warm it. When the chips blazed up they cast a strong light upon his face, which was bent towards the fireplace; and I thought his look so strange that I called Brulette's attention to it in a low voice.

"You may think," I said to her, "that he hides by day and wanders off at night solely to surfeit himself with that flute; but I know that he has in him or about him some secret that he does not tell us."

"Bah!" she exclaimed, laughing; "just because Véret, the sabot-maker, fancies he saw him with a tall, dark man near the Râteau elm!"

"Perhaps Véret dreamed that," I answered; "but as for me, I know what I saw and heard in the forest."

"What did you see?" said José, suddenly, who had heard every word, though we spoke quite low. "What did you hear? You saw him who is my friend, but whom I cannot make known to you; and as for what you heard, you are going now to hear it again if it pleases you to do so."

Thereupon he blew into his flute, his eye on fire and his face blazing as if with fever.

Don't ask me what he played. I don't know if the devil would have understood it; as for me, I didn't, except that it seemed the same air I had heard among the brake, on the bagpipes. At that time I was so frightened that I didn't listen to it all; but now, whether it was that the music was longer, or that Joseph put some of his own into it, he never stopped fluting for a quarter of an hour, setting his fingers very delicately, never losing his breath, and getting such sounds out of his miserable reed that you would have thought, at times, there were three bagpipes going at once. At other times he played so softly that you could hear the cricket indoors and the nightingales without; and when José played low I confess I liked it,— though the whole together was so little like what we were accustomed to that it seemed to me a crazy racket.

"Oh, oh!" I exclaimed, when he had finished; "that's a mad sort of music! Where the devil did you learn that? What is the use of it? Is there any meaning in it?"

He did not answer, and seemed as if he had not heard me. He was looking at Brulette, who was leaning against a chair with her face turned to the wall.

As she did not say a word, José was seized with a rush of anger either against her or against himself, and I saw him make a motion as if to break his flute; but just at that moment the girl looked round, and I was much surprised to see great tears running down her cheeks.

Joseph ran to her and caught her hands.

"Tell me what you feel, my darling!" he cried; "let me know if it is pity for me that makes you cry, or whether it is pleasure."

"I don't know how pleasure in a thing like that could make me cry," she said. "Don't ask me if I feel pain or pleasure; all that I know is that I can't help crying."

"But what were you thinking of while I played?" said Joseph, looking fixedly at her.

"So many things that I can't give account of them," replied Brulette.

"Well, tell me one," he said, in a tone that was impatient and dictatorial.

"I did not think of anything," said Brulette, "but a thousand recollections of old times came into my mind. I seemed not to see you playing, though I heard you clearly enough; you appeared to be no older than when we lived together, and I felt as if you and I were driven by a strong wind, sometimes through the ripe wheat, sometimes into the long grass, at other times upon the running streams; and I saw the fields, the woods, the springs, the flowery meadows, and the birds in the sky among the clouds. I saw, too, in my dream, your mother and my grandfather sitting before the fires, and talking of things I could not understand; and all the while you were in the corner on your knees saying your prayers, and I thought I was asleep in my little bed. Then again I saw the ground covered with snow, and the willows full of larks, and the nights full of falling stars; and we looked at each other, sitting on a hillock, while the sheep made their little noise of nibbling the grass. In short, I dreamed so many things that they are all jumbled up in my head; and if they made me cry, it was not for grief, but because my mind was shaken in a way I can't at all explain to you."

"It is all right," said José. "What I saw and what I dreamed as I played you saw too! Thank you, Brulette. Through you I know now that I am not crazy, and that there is a truth in what we hear within us, as there is in what we see. Yes, yes," he said, taking long strides up and down the room and holding his flute above his head, "it speaks!—that miserable bit of reed! it says what we think; it shows what we see; it tells a tale as if with words; it loves like the heart, it lives, it has a being! And now, José the madman, José the idiot, José the starer, go back to your imbecility; you can afford to do so, for you are as powerful, and as wise, and as happy as others!"

So saying, he sat down and paid no further attention to anything about him.

FIFTH EVENING.

We stared at him, Brulette and I, for he was no longer the José we knew. As for me, there was something in all this which reminded me of the tales they tell among us of the wandering bagpipers, who are supposed to tame wild animals and to lead packs of wolves by night along the roads, just as other people lead their flocks in the meadows. José did not have a natural look as he sat there before me. Instead of being pale and puny, he seemed taller and better in health, as I had seen him in the forest. In short, he looked like a person. His eyes beamed in his head with the glitter of two stars, and any one who had called him the handsomest fellow in the world wouldn't have been mistaken at that particular moment.

It seemed to me that Brulette also was under some spell or witchery, because she had seen so many things in that fluting when I could only see the excitement of it. I sorely wanted to make her admit that José would never get any one but the devil to dance to such music; but she wouldn't listen to me, and asked him to begin again.

He was ready enough to do that, and began with a tune which was like the first, and yet was not quite the same; but I saw that his ideas had not changed, and that he was determined not to give in to our country fashions. Seeing that Brulette listened as if she had a taste for the thing, I made an effort in my mind to see if I couldn't like it too; and I seemed to get accustomed to this new kind of music so quickly that something was stirred inside of me. I too had a vision: I thought I saw Brulette dancing alone by the light of the moon under a hawthorn all in bloom, and shaking her pink apron as if about to fly away. But just then, all of a sudden, a sort of ringing of bells was heard not far off, like that I had heard in the forest, and Joseph stopped fluting, cut short in the very middle of a tune.

I came out of my vision, quite convinced that the bell was not a dream; Joseph himself was interrupted, and stood stock-still, evidently vexed; while Brulette gazed at him, not less astonished than I was.

All my terrors came back to me.

"José," I said, reproachfully, "there is more in this than you choose to confess. You did not learn what you know all by yourself; there's a companion outside who is answering you, whether you will or no. Come, tell him to go away; for I don't want to have him in my house. I invited you, and not him, nor any of his tribe. If he doesn't go, I'll sing him an anthem he won't like."

So saying, I took my father's old gun from over the chimney-piece, knowing it was loaded with three consecrated balls; for the Evil Beast was in the habit of roaming about the Font de Fond, and though I had never seen him, I was always prepared to do so, knowing that my parents feared him very much and that he had frequently molested them.

Joseph began to laugh instead of answering me; then, calling to his dog, he went to open the door. My own dog had followed my family on their pilgrimage, so that I had no way of ascertaining whether they were real people or evil ones who were ringing the bells; for you must know that animals, particularly dogs, are very wise in such matters, and bark in a way that lets human beings know the truth.

It is a fact that Parpluche, Joseph's dog, instead of getting angry, ran at once to the door and sprang out gayly enough; as soon as it was opened but the creature might have been bewitched, and so far as I could see, there was nothing good in the matter.

Joseph went out; the wind, which had grown very high, slammed the door after him. Brulette, who had risen, made as if she would open it to see what was going on; but I stopped her quickly, saying there was certainly some wicked secret under it all, so that she, too, began to be afraid and wished she had never come.

"Don't be frightened, Brulette," said I; "I believe in evil spirits, but I am not afraid of them. They do no harm except to those who seek them, and all they can ever do to real Christians is to frighten them. But that's a fear we can and ought to conquer. Come, say a prayer, and I'll hold the door, and you may be sure no harmful thing can get in."

"But that poor lad," said Brulette; "if he is in danger, ought we not to get him back?"

I made her a sign to be silent, and putting myself close to the door with my loaded gun I listened with all my ears. The wind blew high and the bell could only be heard now and then and seemed to be moving farther off. Brulette was at the farther end of the room, half-laughing, half-trembling, for she was a brave, intrepid sort of girl, who joked about the devil, though she would not have liked to make acquaintance with him.

Presently I heard José coming back and saying, not far from the door,—

"Yes, yes, directly after midsummer. Thank you and the good God! I will do just as you say; you have my word for that."

As he mentioned the good God I felt more confidence, so opening the door a trifle I looked out, and there I saw, by the light that streamed from the house, José, walking beside a villanous-looking man, all black from head to foot, even his face and hands, and behind him two big black dogs who were romping with Joseph's dog. The man answered, with such a loud voice that Brulette heard him and trembled: "Good-bye, little man; we shall meet again. Here, Clairin!"

He had no sooner said that than the bells began to jingle, and I saw a lean little horse come up to him, half-crouching, with eyes like live coals, and a bell which shone bright as gold upon his neck. "Call up your comrades!" said the tall dark man. The little horse galloped away, followed by the two dogs, and his master after shaking hands with José went away too. Joseph came in and shut the door, saying with a scornful air,—

"What were you doing here, Tiennet?"

"And you, José, what have you got there?" I retorted, seeing that he had a parcel wrapped in black oil-cloth under his arm.

"That?" he said, "that is something the good God has sent me at the very hour it was promised. Come, Tiennet; come, Brulette; see the fine present God has made me!"

"The good God doesn't send black angels or make presents to wrong-doers."

"Hush," said Brulette, "let José explain himself."

But she had hardly said the words when a loud commotion, like the galloping of two hundred animals, was heard from the broad grass-ground around the fountain, some sixty feet from the house, from which it was separated by the garden and hemp-field. The bell tinkled, the dogs barked, and the man's rough voice was heard shouting, "Quick, quick! here, here! to me, Clairin! come, come! I miss three! You, Louveteau, you, Satan! off with you, quick!"

For a moment Brulette was so frightened that she ran from Joseph to me, which gave me fine courage, and seizing my gun again I said to Joseph:—

"I don't choose that your people should come racketing round here at night. Brulette has had enough of it and she wants to be taken home. Come now, stop this sorcery or I'll chase your witches."

Joseph stopped me as I was going out.

"Stay here," he said, "and don't meddle with what does not concern you; or maybe you'll regret it later. Keep still, and see what I brought in; you shall know all about it presently."

As the uproar was now dying away in the distance, I did look, all the more because Brulette was crazy to know what was in the parcel; and Joseph, undoing it, showed us a bagpipe, so large, and full, and handsome that it was really a splendid thing, and such as I had never seen before.

It had double bellows, one of which measured five feet from end to end; and the wood of the instrument, which was black cherry, dazzled the eyes with the pewter ornaments, made to shine like silver, which were inlaid at all the joints. The wind-bag was of handsome leather tied with a knot of calico, striped blue and white; indeed, the whole workmanship was done in so clever a way that it only took a very little breath to fill the bag and send out a sound like thunder.

"The die is cast!" said Brulette, to whom Joseph was not listening, so intent was he in taking apart and replacing the various parts of his bagpipe. "You will be a piper, José, in spite of the hindrances you will meet with, and the trouble it will be to your mother."

"I shall be a piper,' he said, "when I know how to play the bagpipe. Before then the wheat will ripen and the leaves will fall. Don't let us trouble ourselves about what will happen, children; but see things as they are, and don't accuse me of dealings with the devil. He who brought me that bagpipe is neither a sorcerer nor a demon. He is a man rather rough at times, for his business requires it, and as he is going to spend the night not far from here I advise you and I beg you, friend Tiennet, not to go where he is. Excuse me for not telling you his name or his business; and also promise me not to say that you have seen him or that he came round this way. It might cause him annoyance as well as the rest of us. Be content to know that he is a man of good sense and good judgment. It is he whom you saw in the underbrush of the forest of Saint-Chartier, playing a bagpipe like this one; for though he is not a piper by trade, he understands it thoroughly, and has played me airs that are much more beautiful than ours. He saw that not having enough money I could not buy such an instrument, and so he was satisfied with a small amount and lent me the rest, promising to buy the instrument and bring it me just about this time, letting me pay for it as I am able. For this thing, you see, costs eight pistoles, nearly one year's wages! Now, as I hadn't a third of it, he said, 'Trust me, give me what you have, and I will trust you in the same way.' That's how the thing happened. I didn't know him a mite and we had no witnesses: he could have cheated me if he wished, and if I had asked your advice you would have dissuaded me from trusting him. But you see now that he is a faithful man, for he said, 'I will come round your way at Christmas and give you an answer.' At Christmas I met him under the Râteau elm, and sure enough he came, and said: 'The thing is not yet finished; but it is being made; between the first and tenth of May I will be here again, and bring it.' This is the eighth. He has come, and just as he turned a little out of his way to look for me in the village he heard the air I was playing, which he was certain no one in these parts knew but me; and as for me, I heard and recognized his bell. That's how it happened, and the devil had nothing to do with it. We said good-evening to each other and promised to meet at midsummer."

"If that is so," I remarked, "why didn't you bring him in here, where he could have rested and been refreshed with a glass of good wine? I would have given him a hearty welcome for keeping his word to you faithfully."

"Oh! as for that," replied Joseph, "he is a man who doesn't always behave like other people. He has his ways, and his own ideas and reasons. Don't ask me more than I ought to tell you."

"Why not? is it because he is hiding from honest people?" asked Brulette. "I think that is worse than being a sorcerer. He must be some one who has done wrong, or he would not be roaming round at night, and you wouldn't be forbidden to speak of him."

"I will tell you all about it to-morrow," said Joseph, smiling at our fears. "To-night, you can think what you please, for I shall tell you nothing more. Come, Brulette, there's the cuckoo striking midnight. I'll take you home and leave my bagpipe hidden away in your charge. For I certainly shall not practise on it in this neighborhood; the time to make myself known has not yet come."

Brulette said good-night to me very prettily, putting her hand into mine. But when I saw that she put her arm into Joseph's to go away, jealousy galloped off with me again, and as they went along the high-road I cut across the hemp-field and posted myself beneath the hedge to see them pass. The weather had cleared a little, but there had been a shower, and Brulette let go of Joseph's arm to pick up her dress, saying, "It is not easy to walk two together; go in front."

If I had been in José's place I should have offered to carry her over the muddy places, or, if I had not dared to take her in my arms, I should have lingered behind her to look at her pretty ankles. But José did nothing of the kind, he concerned himself about nothing but his bagpipe; and as I saw him handling it with care and looking lovingly at it, I said to myself that he hadn't any other love just then.

I returned home, easy in mind in more ways than one, and went to bed, somewhat fatigued both in body and mind.

But it was not half an hour before Monsieur Parpluche, who had been amusing himself with the stranger's dogs, came scratching at the door in search of his master. I rose to let him in, and just then I fancied I heard a noise in my oats, which were coming up green and thick at the back of the house. It seemed to me that they were being cropped and trampled by some four-footed beast who had no business there.

I caught up the first stick that came to hand and ran out, whistling to Parpluche, who did not obey me but made off, looking for his master, after snuffing about the house.

Entering the field, I saw something rolling on its back with its paws in the air, crushing the oats right and left, getting up, jumping about and browsing quite at its ease. For a moment I was afraid to run after it, not knowing what kind of beast it was. I could see nothing clearly but its ears, which were too long for a horse; but the body was too black and stout for a donkey. I approached it gently; it seemed neither wild nor mischievous, and then I knew it was a mule, though I had seldom seen one, for we don't raise them in our part of the country, and the muleteers never pass this way. I was just going to catch him and already had my hand on his mane when he threw up his hindquarters and lashing out a dozen kicks which I had scarcely time to avoid, he leaped like a hare over the ditch and ran away so quickly that in a moment he was out of sight.

Not wishing to have my oats ruined by the return of the beast, I put off going to bed till I could have an easy mind. I returned to the house to get my shoes and waistcoat, and after fastening the doors I went through the fields in the direction the mule had taken. I had little doubt that he belonged to the troop of the dark man, Joseph's friend. Joseph had certainly advised me to see nothing of him, but now that I had touched a living animal I was afraid of nothing. Nobody likes ghosts; but when you know you are dealing with solid things it is another affair; and the moment I realized that the dark man was a man, no matter how strong he was or how much he had daubed himself over, I didn't care for him any more than I did for a weasel.

You must have heard say that I was one of the strongest fellows of these parts in my young days; in fact, such as I am now, I am not yet afraid of any man.

Moreover, I was as nimble as a roach, and I knew that in dangers where the strength of a man was not enough to save him, it would have needed the wings of a bird to overtake me in running. Accordingly, having provided myself with a rope and my own gun (which didn't have consecrated balls, but could carry truer than my father's), I set out on a voyage of discovery.

I had scarcely taken a couple of hundred steps when I saw three more animals of the same kind in my brother-in-law's pasture, where they were behaving themselves just as badly as possible. Like the first brute, they allowed me to approach them, and then immediately galloped off to a farm on the estate of Aulnières, where they met another troop of mules capering about as lively as mice, rearing and kicking in the rising moonlight,—a regular *donkey-chase*, which you know is what they call the dance of the devil's she-asses, when the fairies and the will-o-the-wisps gallop up there among the clouds.

However, there was really no magic here; but only a great robbery of pasture, and abominable mischief done to the grain. The crop was not mine, and I might have said that it was none of my business, but I felt provoked to have run after the troublesome animals for nothing, and you can't see the fine wheat of the good God trampled and destroyed without answer.

I went on into the big wheat-field without meeting a single Christian soul, though the mules seemed to increase in numbers every minute. I meant to catch at least one, which would serve as proof when I complained to the authorities of the damage done to the farm.

I singled out one which seemed to be more docile than the rest, but when I got near him I saw that he wasn't the same game, but the lean little horse with a bell round his neck; which bell, as I learned later, is called in the Bourbonnais districts a *clairin*, and the horse that wears it goes by the same name. Not knowing the habits of these animals, it was by mere good luck that I chanced upon the right way to manage them, which was to get hold of the bell-horse, or *clairin*, and lead him away, being certain to catch a mule or two afterwards if I succeeded.

The little animal, which seemed good-natured and well-trained, let me pet him and lead him away without seeming to care; but as soon as he began to walk, the bell on his neck began to jingle, and great was my surprise to see the crowd of mules, scattered here and there among the wheat, come trooping upon us, and tearing after me like bees after their queen. I saw then that they were trained to follow the *clairin*, and that they knew its ring just as well as good monks know the bell for matins.

SIXTH EVENING.

I did not long debate what I should do with the mischievous horde. I went straight for the manor of Aulnières, thinking that I could easily open the gates of the yard and drive the beasts in; after which I would wake the farmers and they, when informed of the damage done, would do as they saw fit.

I was just nearing the yard when, as it happened, I fancied I saw a man running on the road behind me. I cocked my gun, thinking that if he was the muleteer I should have a bone to pick with him. But it was Joseph, on his way back to Aulnières after escorting Brulette to the village.

"What are you doing here, Tiennet?" he said to me, coming up as fast as he could run. "Didn't I tell you not to leave home to-night? You are in danger of death; Let go that horse and don't meddle with those mules. What can't be helped must be endured for fear of worse evils."

"Thank you, comrade," I answered. "Your fine friends pasture their cavalry in my field and you expect me to say nothing! Very good, very good! go your ways if you are afraid yourself, but as for me, I shall see the thing out, and get justice done by law or might."

As I spoke, having stopped a moment to answer him, we heard a dog bark in the distance, and José, seizing the rope by which I was leading the horse, cried out:—

"Quick, Tiennet! here come the muleteer's dogs! If you don't want to be torn in pieces, let go the horse; see, he hears them and you can't do anything with him now."

Sure enough, the *clairin* pricked his ears to listen; then laying them back, which is a great sign of ill-temper, he began to neigh and rear and kick, which brought all the mules capering round us, so that we had scarcely time to get out of the way before the whole of them rushed by at full speed in the direction of the dogs.

I was not satisfied to yield, however, and as the dogs, having called in their wild troop, showed signs of making straight for us, I took aim with my gun as if to shoot the first of the two that came at me. But Joseph went up to the dog and made him recognize him.

"Ah! Satan," he said to him, "the fault is yours. Why did you chase the hares into the wheat instead of watching your beasts? When your master wakes up you will be whipped if you are not at your post with Louveteau and the *clairin*."

Satan, understanding that he was being reproved for his behavior, obeyed Joseph, who called him towards a large tract of waste land where the mules could feed without doing any damage, and where Joseph, as he told me, intended to watch them until their master returned.

"Nevertheless, José," I said to him, "matters won't blow over as quietly as you think for; and if you will not tell me where the owner of these mules hides himself, I shall stay here and wait for him, and say what I think to his face, and demand reparation for the harm done."

"You don't know muleteers if you think it easy to get the better of them," replied Joseph. "I believe it is the first time any of them have ever passed this way. It is not their usual road; they commonly come down from the Bourbonnais forests through those of Meillant and L'Éspinasse into the Cheurre woods. I happened accidentally to meet them in the forest of Saint-Chartier, where they were halting on their way to Saint-Août; among them was the man who is here now, whose name is Huriel, and who is on his way to the iron works of Ardentes for coal and ore. He has been kind enough to come two hours out of his way to oblige me. And it may be that, having left his companions and the heath country through which the roads frequented by men of his business run, where his mules can pasture without injuring any one, he fancied he was just as free here in our wheat-lands; and though he is altogether wrong, it would be best not to tell him so."

"He will have to know what I think," I answered, "for I see now how the land lays. Ho! ho! muleteers! we know what they are. You remind me of things I have heard my godfather, Gervais the forester, tell of. Muleteers are lawless men, wicked and ignorant, who would kill a man with as little conscience as they would a rabbit. They think they have a right to feed their beasts at the expense of the peasantry, and if any one complains who is not strong enough to resist them, they will come back later or send their comrades to kill the poor man's cattle or burn his house, or worse; they live on plunder, like thieves at a fair."

"As you have heard those things," said Joseph, "you must see that we should be very foolish to draw down some great harm to the farmers and my master and your family in revenge for a little one. I don't defend what has been done, and when Maître Huriel told me he was going to pasture his mules and camp at Nohant, as he does elsewhere at all seasons, I told him about this bit of common and advised him not to let his mules stray into the wheat-fields. He promised he would not; for he is not at all ill-disposed. But his temper is quick, and he wouldn't back down if a whole crowd of people fell upon him. Please go back to your own property, keep clear of these beasts, and don't pick a quarrel with anybody. If you are questioned to-morrow, say you saw nothing; for to swear in a court of law against a muleteer is quite as dangerous as to swear against a lord."

Joseph was right; so I gave in, and took the road towards home; but I was not satisfied, for backing down before a threat is wisdom to old men and bitter wrath to young ones.

As I neared the house, quite resolved not to go to bed, I fancied I saw a light in it. I quickened my steps and finding the door, which I had latched, wide open, I rushed in and saw a man in the chimney-corner lighting his pipe by a blaze he had made. He turned round and looked at me as quietly as if the house were his, and I recognized the charcoal-blackened man whom Joseph called Huriel.

My wrath returned; and closing the door behind me I exclaimed as I went up to him:—

"Well done! I am glad you have walked into the lion's den. I've a couple of words to say to you."

"Three, if you like," he said, squatting on his heels and drawing fire through his pipe, for the tobacco was damp and did not light readily. Then he added, as if scornfully, "There's not even a pair of tongs to pick up the embers."

"No," I retorted, "but there s a good cudgel to flatten you out with."

"And pray why?" he demanded without losing an atom of assurance. "You are angry because I have entered your house without permission. Why were not you at home? I knocked on the door and asked to light my pipe, a thing no one ever refuses. Silence gives consent, so I pulled the latch. Why did not you lock the door if you are afraid of thieves? I looked at the beds and saw the house was empty; I lighted my pipe, and here I am. What have you to say to that?"

So saying, as I tell you, he took up his gun as if to examine the lock, but it was really as much as to say, "If you are armed, so am I; two can play at that game."

I had an idea of aiming at him to make him respect me; but the longer I looked at his blackened face the more I was struck with his frank air and his lively, jovial eye, so that I ceased to be angry and felt only piqued. He was a young man of twenty-five, tall and strong, and if washed and shaved, would have been quite a handsome fellow. I put my gun down beside the wall and went up to him without fear.

"Let us talk," I said, sitting down by him.

"As you will," he answered, laying aside his gun.

"Is it you they call Huriel?"

"And you Étienne Depardieu?"

"How do you know my name?"

"Just as you know mine,—from our little friend Joseph Picot."

"Then they are your mules that I have caught?"

"Caught!" he exclaimed, half-rising in astonishment. Then, laughing, he added: "You are joking! you can't catch my mules."

"Yes, I can," I said, "if I catch and lead the horse."

"Ha! you have learned the trick?" he cried, with a defiant air. "But how about the dogs?"

"I don't fear dogs when I've a gun in my hand."

"Have you killed my dogs?" he shouted, jumping up. His face flamed with anger, which let me know that though he might be jovial by nature he could be terrible at times.

"I might have killed your dogs," I replied, "and I might have led your mules into a farmyard where you would have found a dozen strong fellows to deal with. I did not do it because Joseph told me you were alone, and that it was not fair for a mere piece of mischief to put you in danger of losing your life. I agreed to that reason. But now we are one to one. Your beasts have injured my field and my sister's field, and what's more, you have entered my house in my absence, which is improper and insolent. You will beg pardon for your behavior and pay damages for my oats, or—"

"Or what?" he said, with a sneer.

"Or we will settle the matter according to the laws and customs of Berry, which are, I think, the same as those of the Bourbonnais where fists are lawyers."

"That is to say, the law of the strongest," he replied, turning up his sleeves. "That suits me better than going before the justices, and if you are really alone and don't play traitor—"

"Come outside," I said, "and you shall see that I am alone. You are wrong to insult me in that way, for I might have shot you as I came in. But guns are made to kill wolves and mad dogs. I didn't want to treat you like a beast, and though you have a chance to shoot me at this moment I think it cowardly for men to pepper each other with balls when fists were given to human beings to fight with. As to that, I don't think you are a greater fool than I, and if you have got pluck—"

"My lad," he said, pulling me towards the fire to look at me, "perhaps you are making a mistake. You are younger than I am, and though you look pretty wiry and solid I wouldn't answer for that skin of yours. I would much rather you spoke me fairly about your damages and trusted to my honesty."

"Enough," I said, knocking his hat into the ashes to anger him; "the best bruised of us two will get justice presently."

He quietly picked up his hat and laid it on the table saying,—

"What are the rules in this part of the country?"

"Among young fellows," I replied, "there is no ill-will or treachery. We seize each other round the body, or strike where we can except on the face. He who takes a stick or a stone is thought a scoundrel."

"That is not exactly our way," he said. "But come on, I shan't spare you; if I hit harder than I mean to, surrender; for there's a time, you know, when one can't answer for one's self."

Once outside on the thick sward we off coats (not to spoil them uselessly), and began to wrestle, clasping thighs and lifting one another bodily. I had the advantage of him there, for he was taller than I by a head, and in bending over he gave me a better grip. Besides, he was not angry, and thinking he would soon get the better of me, he didn't put forth his strength. So being, I was able to floor him at the third round, falling on top of him, but there he recovered himself, and before I had time to strike he wound himself round me like a snake and squeezed me so closely that I lost my breath. Nevertheless, I managed to get up first and attack him again. When he saw that he had to do with a free hitter, and caught it well in the stomach and on the shoulders, he gave me as good as I sent, and I must own that his fist was like a sledge-hammer. But I would have died sooner than show I felt it; and each time that he cried out, "Surrender!" I plucked up courage and strength to pay him in his own coin. So for a good quarter of an hour the fight seemed even. Presently, however, I felt I was getting exhausted while he was only warming to the work; for if he had less activity than I, his age and temperament were in his favor. The end of it was that I was down beneath him and fairly beaten and unable to release myself. But for all that I wouldn't cry mercy; and when he saw that I would rather be killed he behaved like a generous fellow.

"Come, enough!" he cried, loosing his grip on my throat; "your will is stronger than your bones, I see that, and I might break them to bits before you would give in. That's right! and as you are a true man let us be friends. I beg your pardon for entering your house; and now let us talk over the damage my mules have done to you. I am as ready to pay you as to fight you; and afterwards, you shall give me a glass of wine so that we may part good friends."

The bargain concluded, I pocketed three crowns which he paid me for myself and my brother-in-law; then I drew the wine and we sat down to table. Three flagons of two pints each disappeared, for we were both thirsty enough after the game we had been playing, and Maître Huriel had a carcass which could hold as much as he liked to put into it. I found him a good fellow, a fine talker, and easy to get on with; and I, not wishing to seem behindhand in words or actions, filled his glass every two minutes and swore friendship till the roof rang.

Apparently, he felt no effects of the fight. I felt them badly enough; but not wishing to show it, I proposed a song, and squeezed one, with some difficulty, from my throat, which was still hot from the grip of his hands. He only laughed.

"Comrade," said he, "neither you nor yours know anything about singing. Your tunes are as flat and your wind as stifled as your ideas and your pleasures. You are a race of snails, always snuffing the same wind and sucking the same bark; for you think the world ends at those blue hills which limit your sky and which are the forests of my native land. I tell you, Tiennet, that's where the world begins, and you would have to walk pretty fast for many a night and day before you got out of those grand woods, to which yours are but a patch of pea-brush. And when you do get out of them you will find mountains and more forests, such as you have never seen, of the tall handsome fir-trees of Auvergne, unknown to your rich plains. But what's the good of telling you about these places that you will never see? You Berry folks are like stones which roll from one rut to another, coming back to the right hand when the cart-wheels have shoved them for a time to the left. You breathe a heavy atmosphere, you love your ease, you have no curiosity; you cherish your money and don't spend it, but also you don't know how to increase it; you have neither nerve nor invention. I don't mean you personally, Tiennet; you know how to fight (in defence of your own property), but you don't know how to acquire property by industry as we muleteers do, travelling from place to place, and taking, by fair means or foul, what isn't given with a good will."

"Oh! I agree to all that," I answered; "but don't you call yours a brigand's trade? Come, friend Huriel, wouldn't it be better to be less rich and more honest? for when it comes to old age will you enjoy your ill-gotten property with a clear conscience?"

"Ill-gotten! Look here, friend Tiennet," he said, laughing, "you who have, I suppose, like all the small proprietors about here, a couple of dozen sheep, two or three goats, and perhaps an old mare that feeds on the common, do you go and offer reparation if, by accident, your beasts bark your neighbor's trees and trample his young wheat? Don't you call in your animals as fast as you can, without saying a word about it; and if your neighbors take the law of you, don't you curse them and the law too? And if you could, without danger, get them off into a corner, wouldn't you make amends to yourself by belaboring their shoulders? I tell you, it is either cowardice or force that makes you respect the law, and it is because we avoid both that you blame us, out of jealousy of the freedom that we have known how to snatch."

"I don't like your queer morality, Huriel; but what has all this got to do with music? Why do you laugh at my song? Do you know a better?"

"I don't pretend to, Tiennet; but I tell you that music, liberty, beautiful wild scenery, lively minds, and, if you choose, the art of making money without getting stupefied,—all belong together like fingers to the hand. I tell you that shouting is not singing; you can bellow like deaf folks in your fields and taverns, but that's not music. Music is on our side of those hills, and not on yours. Your friend Joseph felt this, for his senses are more delicate than yours; in fact, my little Tiennet, I should only lose my time in trying to show you the difference. You are a Berrichon, as a swallow is a swallow; and what you are to-day you will be fifty years hence. Your head will whiten, but your brain will never be a day older."

"Why, do you think me a fool?" I asked, rather mortified.

"Fool? Not at all," he said. "Frank as to heart and shrewd as to interest,—that's what you are and ever will be; but living in body and lively in soul you never can be. And this is why, Tiennet," he added, pointing to the furniture of the room. "See these big-bellied beds where you sleep in feathers up to your eyes. You are spade and pickaxe folk,—toilers in the sun,—but you must have your downy beds to rest in. We forest fellows would soon be ill if we had to bury ourselves alive in sheets and blankets. A log hut, a fern bed,—that's our home and our furniture; even those of us who travel constantly and don't mind paying the inn charges, can't stand a roof over our heads; we sleep in the open air in the depth of winter, on the pack-saddles of our mules, with the snow for a coverlet. Here you have dresses and tables and chairs and fine china, ground glass, good wine, a roasting-jack and soup-pots, and heaven knows what? You think you must have all that to make you happy; you work your jaws like cows that chew the cud; and so, when obliged to get upon your feet and go back to work, you have a pain in your chest two or three times a day. You are heavy, and no gayer at heart than your beasts of burden. On Sundays you sit, with your elbows on the table, eating more than your hunger tells you to, and drinking more than your thirst requires; you think you are amusing yourself by storing up indigestion and sighing after girls who are only bored with you though they don't know why,—your partners in those dragging dances in rooms and barns where you suffocate; turning your holidays and festivals into a burden the more upon your spirits and stomachs. Yes, Tiennet, that's the life you live. To indulge your ease you increase your wants, and in order to live well you don't live at all."

"And how do you live, you muleteers?" I said, rather shaken by his remarks. "I don't speak now of your part of the country, of which I know nothing, but of you, a muleteer, whom I see there before me, drinking hard, with your elbows on the table, not sorry to find a fire to light your pipe and a Christian to talk with. Are you made different from other men? When you have led this hard life you boast of for a score of years, won't you spend your money, which you have amassed by depriving yourself of everything, in procuring a wife, a house, a table, a good bed, good wine, and rest at last?"

"What a lot of questions, Tiennet!" replied my guest. "You argue fairly well for a Berrichon. I'll try to answer you. You see me drink and talk because I am a man and like wine. Company and the pleasures of the table please me even more than they do you, for the very good reason that I don't need them and am not accustomed to them. Always afoot, snatching a mouthful as I can, drinking at the brooks, sleeping under the first oak I come to, of course it is a feast for me to come across a good table and plenty of good wine; but it is a feast, and not a necessity. To me, living alone for weeks at a time, the society of a friend is a holiday; I say more to him in one hour's talk than you would say in a day at a tavern. I enjoy all, and more, than you fellows do, because I abuse nothing. If a pretty girl or a forward woman comes after me in the woods to tell me that she loves me, she knows I have no time to dangle after her like a ninny and wait her pleasure; and I admit that in the matter of love I prefer that which is soon found to that you have to search and wait for. As to the future, Tiennet, I don't know if I shall ever have a home and a family; but if I do, I shall be more grateful to the good God than you are, and I shall enjoy its sweetness more, too. But I swear that my helpmate shall not be one of your buxom, red-faced women, let her be ever so rich. A man who loves liberty and true happiness never marries for money. I shall never love any woman who isn't slender and fair as a young birch,—one of those dainty, lively darlings, who grow in the shady woods and sing better than your nightingales."

"A girl like Brulette," I thought to myself. "Luckily she isn't here, for though she despises all of us, she might take a fancy to this blackamoor, if only by way of oddity."

The muleteer went on talking.

"And so, Tiennet, I don't blame you for following the road that lies before you; but mine goes farther and I like it best. I am glad to know you, and if you ever want me send for me. I can't ask the same of you, for I know that a dweller on the plains makes his will and confesses to the priest before he travels a dozen leagues to see a friend. But with us it isn't so; we fly like the swallows, and can be met almost everywhere. Good-bye. Shake hands. If you get tired of a peasant's life call the black crow from the Bourbonnais to get you out of it; he'll remember that he played the bagpipe on your back without anger, and surrendered to your bravery."

SEVENTH EVENING.

Thereupon Huriel departed to find Joseph, and I went to bed; for if up to that time I had concealed out of pride and forgotten out of curiosity the ache in my bones, I was none the less bruised from head to foot. Maître Huriel walked off gayly enough, apparently without feeling anything, but as for me I was obliged to stay in bed for nearly a week, spitting blood, with my stomach all upset. Joseph came to see me and did not know what to make of it all; for I was shy of telling him the truth, because it appeared that Huriel, in speaking to him of me, hadn't mentioned how we came to an explanation.

Great was the amazement of the neighborhood over the injury done to the wheat-fields of Aulnières, and the mule-tracks along the roads were something to wonder at. When I gave my brother-in-law the money I had earned with my sore bones I told him the whole story secretly, and as he was a good, prudent fellow, no one got wind of it.

Joseph had left his bagpipe at Brulette's and could not make use of it, partly because the haying left him no time, and also because Brulette, fearing Carnat's spite, did her best to put him out of the notion of playing.

Joseph pretended to give in; but we soon saw that he was concocting some other plan and thinking to hire himself out in another parish, where he could slip his collar and do as he pleased.

About midsummer he gave warning to his master to get another man in his place; but it was impossible to get him to say where he was going; and as he always replied, "I don't know," to any question he didn't choose to answer, we began to think he would really let himself be hired in the market-place, like the rest, without caring where he went.

As the Christians' Fair, so-called, is one of the great festivals of the town, Brulette went there to dance, and so did I. We thought we should meet Joseph and find out before the end of the day what master and what region he had chosen. But he did not appear either morning or evening on the market-place. No one saw him in the town. He had left his bagpipe, but he had carried off, the night before, all the articles he usually left in Père Brulet's house.

That evening as we came home,—Brulette and I and all her train of lovers with the other young folks of our parish,—she took my arm, and walking on the grassy side of the road away from the others, she said:—

"Do you know, Tiennet, that I am very anxious about José? His mother, whom I saw just now in town, is full of trouble and can't imagine where he has gone. A long time ago he told her he thought of going away; but now she can't find out where, and the poor woman is miserable."

"And you, Brulette," I said, "it seems to me that you are not very gay, and you haven't danced with the same spirit as usual."

"That's true," she answered; "I have a great regard for the poor lunatic fellow,—partly because I ought to have it, on account of his mother, and then for old acquaintance' sake, and also because I care for his fluting."

"Fluting! does it really have such an effect upon you?"

"There's nothing wrong in its effect, cousin. Why do you find fault with it?"

"I don't; but—"

"Come, say what you mean," she exclaimed, laughing; "for you are always chanting some sort of dirge about it, and I want to say amen to you once for all, so that I may hear the last of it."

"Well then, Brulette," I replied, "we won't say another word about Joseph, but let us talk of ourselves. Why won't you see that I have a great love for you? and can't you tell me that you will return it one of these days?"

"Oh! oh! are you talking seriously, this time?"

"This time and all times. It has always been serious on my part, even when shyness made me pretend to joke about it."

"Then," said Brulette, quickening her step with me that the others might not overhear us, "tell me how and why you love me; I'll answer you afterwards."

I saw she wanted compliments and flattery, but my tongue was not very ready at that kind of thing. I did my best, however, and told her that ever since I came into the world I had never thought of any one but her; for she was the prettiest and sweetest of girls, and had captivated me even before she was twelve years old.

I told nothing that she did not know already; indeed she said so, and owned she had seen it at the time we were catechised. But she added laughing:—

"Now explain why you have not died of grief, for I have always put you down; and tell me also why you are such a fine-grown, healthy fellow, if love, as you declare, has withered you."

"That's not talking seriously, as you promised me," I said.

"Yes, it is," she replied; "I am serious, for I shall never choose any one who can't swear that he has never in his life fancied, or loved, or desired any girl but me."

"Then it is all right, Brulette," I cried. "If that's so, I fear nobody, not even that José of yours, who, I will allow, never looked at a girl in his life, for his eyes can't even see you, or he wouldn't go away and leave you."

"Don't talk of Joseph; we agreed to let him alone," replied Brulette, rather sharply, "and as you boast of such very keen eyes, please confess that in spite of your love for me you have ogled more than one pretty girl. Now, don't tell fibs, for I hate lying. What were you saying so gayly to Sylvia only last year? And it isn't more than a couple of months since you danced two Sundays running, under my very nose, with that big Bonnina. Do you think I am blind, and that nobody comes and tells me things?"

I was rather mortified at first; but then, encouraged by the thought that there was a spice of jealousy in Brulette, I answered, frankly,—

"What I was saying to such girls, cousin, is not proper to repeat to a person I respect. A fellow may play the fool sometimes to amuse himself, and the regret he feels for it afterwards only proves that his heart and soul had nothing to do with it."

Brulette colored; but she answered immediately,—

"Then, can you swear to me, Tiennet, that my character and my face have never been lowered in your esteem by the prettiness or the amiability of any other girl,—never, since you were born?"

"I will swear to it," I said.

"Swear, then," she said; "but give all your mind, and all your religion to what you are going to say. Swear by your father and your mother, by your conscience and the good God, that no girl ever seemed to you as beautiful as I."

I was about to swear, when, I am sure I don't know why, a recollection made my tongue tremble. Perhaps I was very silly to heed it; a shrewder fellow wouldn't have done so, but I couldn't lie at the moment when a certain image came clearly before my mind. And yet, I had totally forgotten it up to that very moment, and should probably never have remembered it at all if it had not been for Brulette's questions and adjurations.

"You are in no hurry to swear," she said, "but I like that best; I shall respect you for the truth and despise you for a lie."

"Well then, Brulette," I answered, "as you want me to tell the exact truth I will do so. In all my life I have seen two girls, two children I might say, between whom I might have wavered as to preference if any one had said to me (for I was a child myself at the time), 'Here are two little darlings who may listen to you in after days; choose which you will have for a wife.' I should doubtless have answered, 'I choose my cousin,' because I knew how amiable you were, and I knew nothing of the other, having only seen her for ten minutes. And yet, when I came to think of it, it is possible I might have felt some regret, not because her beauty was greater than yours, for I don't think that possible, but because she gave me a good kiss on both cheeks, which you never gave me in your life. So I conclude that she is a girl who will some day give her heart generously, whereas your discretion holds me and always has held me in fear and trembling."

"Where is she now?" asked Brulette, who seemed struck by what I said. "What is her name?"

She was much surprised to hear that I knew neither her name nor the place she lived in, and that I called her in my memory "the girl of the woods." I told her the little story of the cart that stuck in the mud, and she asked me a variety of questions which I could not answer, my recollections being much confused and the whole affair being of less interest to me than Brulette supposed. She turned over in her head every word she got out of me, and it almost seemed as if she were questioning herself, with some vexation, to know if she were pretty enough to be so exacting, and whether frankness or coyness was the best way of pleasing the lads.

Perhaps she was tempted for a moment to try coquetry and make me forget the little vision that had come into my head, and which, for more reasons than one, had displeased her; but after a few joking words she answered seriously:—

"No, Tiennet, I won't blame you for having eyes to see a pretty girl when the matter is as innocent and natural as you tell me; but nevertheless it makes me think seriously, I hardly know why, about myself. Cousin, I am a coquette. I feel the fever of it to the very roots of my hair. I don't know that I shall ever be cured of it; but, such as I am, I look upon love and marriage as the end of all my comfort and pleasure. I am eighteen,—old enough to reflect. Well, reflection comes to me like a blow on the stomach; whereas you have been considering how to get yourself a happy home ever since you were fifteen or sixteen, and your simple heart has given you an honest answer. What you need is a wife as simple and honest as yourself, without caprices, or pride, or folly: I should deceive you shamefully if I told you that I am the right kind of girl for you. Whether from caprice or distrust I don't know, but I have no inclination for any of those I can choose from, and I can't say that I ever shall have. The longer I live the more my freedom and my light-heartedness satisfy me. Therefore be my friend, my comrade, my cousin; I will love you just as I love Joseph, and better, if you are faithful to our friendship; but don't think any more about marrying me. I know that your relations would be opposed to it, and so am I, in spite of myself, and with great regret for disappointing you. See, the others are coming after us to break up this long talk. Promise me not to sulk; choose a course; be my brother. If you say yes, we'll build the midsummer bonfire when we get back to the village, and open the dance together gayly."

"Well, Brulette," I answered, sighing, "it shall be as you say. I'll do my best not to love you, except as you wish, and in any case I shall still be your cousin and good friend, as in duty bound."

She took my hand and ran with me to the village market-place, delighted to make her lovers scamper after her; there we found that the old people had already piled up the fagots and straw of the bonfire. Brulette, being the first to arrive, was called to set fire to it, and soon the flames darted higher than the church porch.

We had no music to dance by until Carnat's son, named François, came along with his bagpipe; and he was very willing to play, for he, too, like the rest, was putting his best foot foremost to please Brulette.

So we opened the ball joyously, but after a minute or two everybody cried out that the music tired their legs. François Carnat was new at the business, and though he did his best, we found we couldn't get along. He let us make fun of him, however, and kept on playing,—being, as I suppose, rather glad of the practice, as it was the first time he had played for people to dance.

Nobody liked it, however, and when the young men found that dancing, instead of resting their tired legs, only tired them more, they talked of bidding good-night or spending the evening in the tavern. Brulette and the other girls exclaimed against that, and told us we were unmannerly lads and clodhoppers. This led to an argument, in the midst of which, all of a sudden, a tall, handsome fellow appeared, before it could be seen where he came from.

"Hallo there, children!" he cried, in such a loud tone that it drowned our racket and forced us to listen. "If you want to go on dancing, you shall. Here's a bagpiper who will pipe for you as long as you like, and won't ask anything for his trouble. Give me that," he said to François Carnat, taking hold of his bagpipe, "and listen; it may do you good, for though music is not my business, I know more about it than you."

Then, without waiting for François's consent, he blew out the bag and began to play, amid cries of joy from the girls and with many thanks from the lads.

At his very first words I had recognized the Bourbonnais accent of the muleteer, but I could hardly believe my eyes, so changed was he for the better in looks. Instead of his coal-dusty smock-frock, his old leathern gaiters, his battered hat, and his grimy face, he had a new suit of clothes of fine white woollen stuff streaked with blue, handsome linen, a straw hat with colored ribbons, his beard trimmed, his face washed and as rosy as a peach. In short, he was the handsomest man I ever saw; grand as an oak, well-made in every part of him, clean-limbed and vigorous; with teeth that were bits of ivory, eyes like the blades of a knife, and the affable air and manners of a gentleman. He ogled all the girls, smiled at the beauties, laughed with the plain ones, and was merry, good company with every one, encouraging and inspiriting the dancers with eye and foot and voice (for he did not blow much into his bagpipe, so clever was he in managing his wind), and shouting between the puffs a dozen drolleries and funny sayings, which put everybody in good humor for the evening.

Moreover, instead of doling out exact measure like an ordinary piper, and stopping short when he had earned his two sous for every couple, he went on bagpiping a full quarter of an hour, changing his tunes you couldn't tell how, for they ran into one another without showing the join; in short, it was the best reel music ever heard, and quite unknown in our parts, but so enlivening and danceable that we all seemed to be flying in the air instead of jigging about on the grass.

I think he would have played and we should have danced all night without getting tired, if it had not been that Père Carnat, hearing the music from the wine-shop of La Biaude and wondering much that his son could play so well, came proudly over to listen. But when he saw his own bagpipe in the hands of a stranger, and François dancing away without seeing the harm of yielding his place, he was furious; and pushing the muleteer from behind, he made him jump from the stone on which he was perched into the very middle of the dancers.

Maître Huriel was a good deal surprised, and turning round he saw Carnat, red with anger, ordering him to give up the instrument.

You never knew Carnat the piper? He was getting in years even then, but he was still as sturdy and vicious as an old devil.

The muleteer began by showing fight, but noticing Carnat's white hair, he returned the bagpipe gently, remarking, "You might have spoken with more civility, old fellow; but if you don't like me to take your place I give it up to you,—all the more willingly that I should like to dance myself, if the young people will allow a stranger in their company."

"Yes, yes! come and dance! you have earned it," cried the whole parish, who had turned out to hear the fine music and were charmed with him,—old and young both.

"Then," he said, taking Brulette's hand, for he had looked at her more than at all the rest, "I ask, by way of payment, to be allowed to dance with this pretty girl, even though she be engaged to some one else."

"She is engaged to me, Huriel," said I, "but as we are friends, I yield my rights to you for this dance."

"Thank you," answered he, shaking hands; then he whispered in my ear, "I pretended not to know you; but if you see no harm to yourself so much the better."

"Don't say you are a muleteer and it is all right," I replied.

While the folks were questioning about the stranger, another fuss arose at the musician's stone. Père Carnat refused to play or to allow his son to play. He even scolded François openly for letting an unknown man supplant him; and the more people tried to settle the matter by telling him the stranger had not taken any money, the angrier he got. In fact when Père Maurice Viaud told him he was jealous, and that the stranger could outdo him and all the other neighboring players, he was beside himself with rage.

He rushed into the midst of us and demanded of Huriel whether he had a license to play the bagpipes,—which made every body laugh, and the muleteer most of all. At last, being summoned by the old savage to reply, Huriel said, "I don't know the customs in your part of the country, old man, but I have travelled enough to know the laws, and I know that nowhere in France do artists buy licenses."

"Artists!" exclaimed Carnat, puzzled by a word which, like the rest of us, he had never heard, "What does that mean? Are you talking gibberish?"

"Not at all," replied Huriel. "I will call them musicians if you like; and I assert that I am free to play music wherever I please without paying toll to the king of France."

"Well, well, I know that," answered Carnat, "but what you don't know yourself is that in our part of the country musicians pay a tax to an association of public players, and receive a license after they have been tried and initiated."

"I know that too," said Huriel, "and I also know how much money is paid into your pockets during those trials. I advise you not to try that upon me. However, happily for you, I don't practise the profession, and want nothing in your parts. I play gratis where I please, and no one can prevent that, for the reason that I have got my degree as master-piper, which very likely you have not, big as you talk."

Carnat quieted down a little at these words, and they said something privately to each other that nobody heard, by which they discovered that they belonged to the same corporation, if not to the same company. The two Carnats, having no further right to object, as every one present testified that Huriel had not played for money, departed grumbling and saying spiteful things, which no one answered so as to be sooner rid of them.

As soon as they were gone we called on Marie Guillard, a lass with a carrying voice, and made her sing, so that the stranger might have the pleasure of dancing with us.

He did not dance in our fashion, though he accommodated himself very well to the time and figures. But his style was much the best, and gave such free play to his body that he really looked handsomer and taller than ever. Brulette watched him attentively and when he kissed her, which is the fashion in our parts when each dance begins, she grew quite red and confused, contrary to her usual indifferent and easy way of taking a kiss.

I argued from this that she had rather overdone her contempt for love when talking with me about mine; but I took no notice, and I own that in spite of it all I felt a good deal set up on my own account by the fine manners and talents of the muleteer.

When the dance was over he came up to me with Brulette on his arm, saying,—

"It is your turn now, comrade; and I can't thank you better than by returning the pretty dancer you lent me. She is a beauty like those of my own land, and for her sake I do homage to the Berrichon girls. But why end the evening so early? Is there no other bagpipe in the village besides that of the old cross patch?"

"Yes, there is," said Brulette quickly, letting out the secret she wanted to keep in her eagerness for dancing; then, catching herself up, she added, blushing, "That is to say, there are shepherd's pipes, and herd-boys who can play them after a fashion."

"Pipes indeed!" cried the muleteer; "if you happen to laugh they go down your throat and make you cough! My mouth is too big for that kind of instrument; and yet I want to make you dance, my pretty Brulette; for that is your name, I have heard it," he said, drawing us both aside; "and I know, too, that there's a fine bagpipe in your house, which came from the Bourbonnais, and belongs to a certain Joseph Picot, your friend from childhood, and your companion at the first communion."

"Oh! how did you know that?" cried Brulette, much astonished. "Do you know our Joseph? Perhaps you can tell us where he has gone?"

"Are you anxious about him?" said Huriel, looking narrowly at her.

"So anxious that I will thank you with all my heart if you can give me news of him."

"Well, I'll give you some, my pretty one; but not until you bring me his bagpipe, which he wants me to carry to him at the place where he now is."

"What!" cried Brulette, "is he very far away?"

"So far that he has no idea of coming back."

"Is that true? Won't he come back? has he gone for good and all? That ends my wanting to laugh and dance any more to-night."

"Ho, ho, pretty one!" cried Huriel; "so you are Joseph's sweetheart, are you? He did not tell me that."

"I am nobody's sweetheart," answered Brulette, drawing herself up.

"Nevertheless," said the muleteer, "here is a token which he told me to show you in case you hesitated to trust me with the bagpipe."

"Where is it? what is it?" I exclaimed.

"Look at my ear," said the muleteer, lifting a great lock of his curly black hair and showing us a tiny silver heart hanging to a large earring of fine gold, which pierced his ears after a fashion among the middle classes of those days.

I think that earring began to open Brulette's eyes, for she said to Huriel, "You can't be what you seem to be, but I see plainly that you are not a man to deceive poor folks. Besides, that token is really mine, or rather it is Joseph's, for it is a present his mother made to me on the day of our first communion, and I gave it to him the next day as a remembrance, when he left home to go to service. So, Tiennet," she said, turning to me, "go to my house and fetch the bagpipe, and bring it over there, under the church porch, where it is dark, so that people can't see where it comes from; for Père Carnat is a wicked old man and might do my grandfather some harm if he thought we were mixed up in the matter."

EIGHTH EVENING.

I did as I was told, not pleased, however, at leaving Brulette alone with the muleteer in a place already darkened by the coming night. When I returned, bringing the bagpipe, taken apart and folded up under my blouse, I found them still in the same corner arguing over something with a good deal of vehemence. Seeing me, Brulette said: "Tiennet, I take you to witness that I do not consent to give this man that token which is hung on his earring. He declares he cannot give it back because it belongs to Joseph, but he also says that Joseph does not want it; it is a little thing, to be sure, not worth ten sous, but I don't choose to give it to a stranger. I was scarcely twelve years old when I gave it to José, and people must be suspicious to see any meaning in that; but, as they will have it so, it is only the more reason why I should refuse to give it to another."

It seemed to me that Brulette was taking unnecessary pains to show the muleteer she was not in love with Joseph, and also that Huriel, on his side, was very glad to find her heart was free. However that may be, he did not trouble himself to stop courting her before me.

"My pretty one," he said, "you are too suspicious. I would not show your gifts to any one, even if I had them to boast of; but I admit here, before Tiennet, that you do not encourage me to love you. I can't say that that will stop me; at any rate, you cannot hinder me from remembering you, and I shall value this ten-sous token in my ear above anything I ever coveted. Joseph is my friend, and I know he loves you; but the lad's affection is so quiet he will never think of asking for his token again. So, if it is one year or ten before we meet again, you will see it just where it is; that is, unless the ear is gone."

So saying, he took Brulette's hand and kissed it, and then he set to work to put the bagpipe together and fill it.

"What are you doing?" cried Brulette. "I told you that I had no heart to amuse myself, now that Joseph has left his mother and friends for such a time, and as for you, you'll be in danger of a fight if the other pipers should come this way and find you playing."

"Bah!" said Huriel, "we'll see about that; don't be troubled for me,— you must dance, Brulette, or I shall think you are really in love with an ungrateful fellow who has left you."

Whether it was that Brulette was too proud to let him think that, or that the dancing mania was too strong for her, it is certain that the bagpipe was no sooner fitted and filled and beginning to sound than she held out no longer and let me carry her off for the first reel.

You would hardly believe, friends, what cries of satisfaction and delight filled the marketplace at the resounding noise of that bagpipe and the return of the muleteer, for every one thought him gone. The dancing had flagged and the company were about to disperse when he made his appearance once more on the piper's stone. Instantly such a hubbub arose! no longer four to eight couples were dancing, but sixteen to thirty-two, joining hands, skipping, shouting, laughing, so that the good God himself couldn't have got a word in edgewise. And presently every one in the market-place, old and young, children who couldn't yet use their legs, grandfathers tottering on theirs, old women jigging in the style of their youth, awkward folk who couldn't get the time or the tune,—they all set to spinning; and, indeed, it is a wonder the clock of the parish church didn't spin too. Fancy! the finest music ever heard in our parts and costing nothing! It seemed as if the devil had a finger in it, for the piper never asked to rest, and tired out everybody except himself. "I'm determined to be the last," he cried when they advised him to rest. "The whole parish shall give in before me; I intend to keep it up till sunrise, and you shall all cry me mercy!" So on we went, he piping and we twirling like mad.

Mère Biaude, who kept the tavern, seeing there was profit in it, brought out tables and benches and something to eat and drink; as to the latter article, she couldn't furnish enough for so many stomachs hungry by dancing, so folks living near brought out for their friends and acquaintance the victuals they had laid in for the week. One brought cheese, another a bag of nuts, another the quarter of a kid, or a sucking pig, all of which were roasted and broiled at a fire hastily built in the market-place. It was like a wedding to which every one flocked. The children were not sent to bed, for no one had time to think of them, and they fell asleep, like a heap of lambs, on the piles of lumber which always lay about the market-place, to the wild racket of the dance and the bagpipe, which never stopped except it was to let the piper drink a jorum of the best wine.

The more he drank the gayer he was and the better he played. At last hunger seized the sturdiest, and Huriel was forced to stop for lack of dancers. So, having won his wager to bury us all, he consented to go to supper. Everybody invited him and quarrelled for the honor and pleasure of feasting him; but seeing that Brulette was coming to my table, he accepted my invitation and sat down beside her, boiling over with wit and good humor. He ate fast and well, but instead of getting torpid from digestion he was the first to clink his glass for a song; and although he had blown his pipe like a whirlwind for six hours at a stretch, his voice was as fresh and as true as if he had done nothing. The others tried to hold their own, but even our renowned singers soon gave it up for the pleasure of listening to him; his songs were far beyond theirs, as much for the tunes as the words; indeed, we had great difficulty in catching the chorus, for there was nothing in his throat that wasn't new to our ears, and of a quality, I must own, above our knowledge.

People left their tables to listen to him, and just as day was beginning to dawn through the leaves a crowd of people were standing round him, more bewitched and attentive than at the finest sermon.

At that moment he rose, jumped on his bench, and waved his empty glass to the first ray of sunlight that shone above his head, saying, in a manner that made us all tremble without knowing why or wherefore:—

"Friends, see the torch of the good God! Put out your little candles and bow to the clearest and brightest light that shines on the world. And now," he said, sitting down again and setting his glass bottom up on the table, "we have talked enough and sung enough for one night. What are you about, verger? Go and ring the Angelus, that we may see who signs the cross like a Christian; and that will show which of us have enjoyed ourselves decently, and which have degraded our pleasure like fools. After we have rendered thanks to God I must depart, my friends, thanking you for this fine fête and all your signs of confidence. I owed you a little reparation for some damage I did a few of you lately without intending it. Guess it if you can,—I did not come here to confess it; but I think I have done my best to amuse you; and as pleasure, to my thinking, is worth more than profit, I feel that I am quits with you. Hush!" he added, as they began to question him, "hear the Angelus!"

He knelt down, which led every one to do likewise, and do it, too, with soberness of manner, for the man seemed to have some extraordinary power over his fellows.

When the prayer ended we looked about for him, but he was gone,— and so completely that there were people who rubbed their eyes, fancying that they had dreamed this night of gayety and merriment.

NINTH EVENING.

Brulette was trembling all over, and when I asked her what the matter was and what she was thinking of, she answered, rubbing her cheek with the back of her hand, "That man is pleasant, Tiennet, but he is very bold."

As I was rather more heated than usual, I found courage to say,—

"If the lips of a stranger offend your skin, perhaps those of a friend can remove the stain."

But she pushed me away, saying,—

"He has gone, and it is wisest to forget those who go."

"Even poor José?"

"He! oh, that's different," she answered.

"Why different? You don't answer me. Oh, Brulette, you care for—"

"For whom?" she said, quickly. "What is his name? Out with it, as you know it!"

"It is," I said, laughing, "the black man for whose sake José has given himself over to the devil,—that man who frightened you one night last spring when you were at my house."

"No, no; nonsense! you are joking. Tell me his name, his business, and where he comes from."

"No, I shall not, Brulette. You say we ought to forget the absent, and I would rather you didn't change your mind."

The whole parish was surprised when it was known that the piper had departed before they had thought of discovering who he was. To be sure, a few had questioned him, but he gave them contradictory answers. To one he said he was a Marchois and was named thus and so; to another he gave a different name, and no one could make out the truth. I gave them still another name to throw them off the scent,—not that Huriel the wheat-spoiler need fear any one after Huriel the piper had turned everybody's head, but simply to amuse myself and to tease Brulette. Then, when I was asked where I had known him, I answered, laughing, that I didn't know him at all,—that he had taken it into his head on arriving to accost me as a friend, and that I had answered him in kind by way of a joke.

Brulette, however, sifted me to the bottom, and I was forced to tell her what I knew; and though it was not much, she was sorry she had heard it, for like most country folks, she had a great prejudice against strangers, and muleteers in particular.

I thought this repugnance would soon make her forget Huriel; and if she ever thought of him she never showed it, but continued to lead the gay life she liked so well, declaring that she meant to be as faithful a wife as she was thoughtless a girl, and therefore she should take her time and study her suitors; and to me she kept repeating that she wanted my faithful, quiet friendship, without any thought of marriage.

As my nature never turned to gloominess, I made no complaint; in fact, like Brulette, I had a leaning to liberty, and I used mine like other young fellows, taking pleasure where I found it, without the yoke. But the excitement once over, I always came back to my beautiful cousin for gentle, virtuous, and lively companionship, which I couldn't afford to lose by sulking. She had more sense and wit than all the women and girls of the neighborhood put together. And her home was so pleasant,—always neat and well-managed, never pinched for means, and filled, during the winter evenings and on all the holidays of the year, with the nicest young folks of the parish. The girls liked to follow in my cousin's train, where there was always a rush of young fellows to choose from, and where they could pick up, now and then, a husband of their own. In fact, Brulette took advantage of the respect they all felt for her to make the lads think of the lasses who wanted their attentions; for she was generous with her lovers,—like people rich in other ways who know it is their duty to give away.

Grandfather Brulet loved his young companion, and amused her with his old-fashioned songs and the many fine tales he told her. Sometimes Mariton would drop in for a moment just to talk of her boy. She was a great woman for gossip, still fresh in appearance, and always ready to show the young girls how to make their clothes,—being well dressed herself to please her master Benoit, who thought her handsome face and finery a good advertisement of his house.

It was well-nigh a year that these amusements had been going on without other news of Joseph than by two letters, in which he told his mother he was well in health and was earning his living in the Bourbonnais. He did not give the name of the place, and the two letters were postmarked from different towns. Indeed, the second letter was none so easy to make out, though our curate was very clever at reading writing; but it appeared that Joseph was getting himself educated, and had tried, for the first time, to write himself. At last a third letter came, addressed to Brulette, which Monsieur le curé read off quite fluently, declaring that the sentences were very well turned. This letter stated that Joseph had been ill, and a friend was writing for him; it was nothing more than a spring fever, and his family were not to be uneasy about him. The letter went on to say that he was living with friends who were in the habit of travelling about; that he was then starting with them for the district of Chambérat, from which they would write again if he grew worse in spite of the great care they were taking of him.

"Good gracious!" cried Brulette, when the curate had read her all that was in the letter, "I'm afraid he is going to make himself a muleteer. I dare not tell his mother about either his illness or the trade he is taking up. Poor soul! she has troubles enough without that."

Then, glancing at the letter, she asked what the signature meant. Monsieur le curé, who had paid no attention to it, put on his glasses and soon began to laugh, declaring that he had never seen anything like it, and all he could make out, in place of a name, was the sketch of an ear and an earring with a sort of a heart stuck through it.

"Probably," said he, "it is the emblem of some fraternity. All guilds have their badges, and other people can't understand them."

But Brulette understood well enough; she seemed a little worried and carried off the letter, to examine it, I don't doubt, with a less indifferent eye than she pretended; for she took it into her head to learn to read, and very secretly she did so, by the help of a former lady's-maid in a noble family, who often came to gossip in a sociable house like my cousin's. It didn't take long for such a clever head as Brulette's to learn all she wanted, and one fine day I was amazed to find she could write songs and hymns as prettily turned as anybody's. I could not help asking her if she had learned these fine things above her station so as to correspond with Joseph, or the handsome muleteer.

"As if I cared for a common fellow with earrings!" she cried, laughing. "Do you think I am such an ill-behaved girl as to write to a perfect stranger? But if Joseph comes back educated he will have done a very good thing to get rid of his stupidity; and as for me, I shall not be sorry to be a little less of a goose than I was."

"Brulette, Brulette!" I retorted, "you are setting your thoughts outside your own country and your friends. Take care, harm will come of it! I'm not a bit less uneasy about you here than I am about Joseph down there."

"You can be easy about me, Tiennet; my head is cool, no matter what people say of me. As for our poor boy, I am troubled enough; it will soon be six months since we heard from him, and that fine muleteer who promised to send us news has never once thought of it. Mariton is miserable at Joseph's neglect of her; for she has never known of his illness, and perhaps he is dead without our suspecting it."

I assured her that in that case we should certainly have been informed of the fact, and that no news was always good news in such cases.

"You may say what you like," she replied; "I dreamed, two nights ago, that the muleteer arrived here, bringing his bagpipe and the news that José was dead. Ever since I dreamed that I have been sad at heart, and I am sorry I have let so much time go by without thinking of the poor lad or trying to write to him. But how could I have sent my letter?—for I don't even know where he is."

So saying, Brulette, who was sitting near a window and chanced to look out, gave a loud cry and turned white with fear. I looked out too, and saw Huriel, black with charcoal dust on his face and clothes, just as I saw him the first time. He came towards us, while the children ran out of his way, screaming, "The devil! the devil!" and the dogs yelped at him.

Struck with what Brulette had just said, and wishing to spare her the pain of hearing ill-news suddenly, I ran to meet the muleteer, and my first words were,—

"Is he dead?"

"Who? Joseph?" he replied. "No, thank God. But how did you know he was still ill?"

"Is he in danger?"

"Yes and no. But what I have to say is for Brulette. Is that her house? Take me to her."

"Yes, yes, come!" I cried; and rushing ahead I told my cousin to be comforted, for the news was not nearly so bad as she expected.

She called her grandfather, who was at work in the next room, intending to receive the muleteer in a proper manner; but when she saw him so different from the idea she had kept of him, so unrecognizable in face and clothes, she lost her self-possession and turned away sadly and in much confusion.

Huriel perceived it, for he smiled, and lifting his black hair as if by accident, showed Brulette her token which was still in his ear.

"It is really I," he said, "and no one else. I have come from my own parts expressly to tell you about a friend who, thanks to God, is neither dead nor dying, but of whom I must speak to you at some length. Have you leisure to hear me now?"

"That we have," said Père Brulet. "Sit down, my man, and take something to eat."

"I want nothing," said Huriel, seating himself. "I will wait till your own meal-time. But, first of all, I ought to make myself known to those I am now speaking to."

TENTH EVENING.

"Say on," said my uncle, "we are listening."

Then said the muleteer: "My name is Jean Huriel, muleteer by trade, son of Sebastien Huriel, otherwise called Bastien, the Head-Woodsman, a renowned bagpiper, and considered the best worker in the forests of the Bourbonnais. Those are my names and claims, to which I can bring honorable proof. I know that to win your confidence I ought to present myself in the guise in which I have the right to appear; but men of my calling have a custom—"

"I know your custom, my lad," said Père Brulet, who watched him attentively. "It is good or bad, according as you yourselves are good or bad. I have not lived till now without knowing what the muleteers are; I have travelled outside our own borders, and I know your customs and behavior. They say your fraternity are given to evil deeds,—they are known to abduct girls, attack Christian people, and even kill them in pretended quarrels so as to get their money."

"Well," said Huriel, laughing, "I think that is an exaggerated account of us. The things you speak of are long passed away; you would not hear of such deeds now-a-days. But the fear your people had of us was so great that for years the muleteers did not dare to leave the woods unless in troops and with great precautions. The proof that they have mended their ways and are no longer to be feared is that they no longer fear for themselves; so here I am, alone in the midst of you."

"Yes," said Père Brulet, who was not easy to convince; "but your face is blackened all the same. You have sworn to follow the rule of your fraternity, which is to travel thus disguised through the districts where you are still distrusted, so that if folks see you do an evil deed they can't say afterwards, when they meet your companions, 'That is he,' or, 'That is not he.' You consider yourselves all responsible for one another. This has its good side, for it makes you faithful friends, and each man has the help and good-will of all; but, nevertheless, it leaves the rest of us in doubt as to the character of your morality, and I shall not deny that if a muleteer—no matter how good a fellow he may be nor how much money he may have—comes here to ask for my alliance, I'll cheerfully offer him bite and sup, but I'll not invite him to marry my daughter."

"And I," said the muleteer, his eyes flashing as he boldly looked at Brulette, who pretended to be thinking of something else, "had no such idea in coming here. You are not called upon to refuse me, Père Brulet, for you don't know whether I am married or single. I have said nothing about it."

Brulette dropped her eyes, and I could not tell whether she was pleased or displeased. Then she recovered spirit, and said to the muleteer: "This has nothing to do with the matter—which is José. You have brought news of him; I am distressed at heart about his health. This is my grandfather, who brought him up and takes an interest in him. Please talk of Joseph instead of other things."

Huriel looked steadily at Brulette, seeming to struggle with a momentary vexation and to gather himself together before he spoke; then he said:—

"Joseph is ill,—so ill that I resolved to come and say to the woman who is the cause of it, 'Do you wish to cure him, and are you able to do so?'"

"What are you talking about?" said my uncle, pricking up his ears, which were beginning to be a little hard of hearing. "How can my daughter cure the lad?"

"If I spoke of myself before I spoke of him," continued Huriel, "it was because I have delicate things to say of him which you would scarcely allow a total stranger to mention. Now, if you think me a decent man, allow me to speak my mind freely and tell you all I know."

"Explain everything," said Brulette, eagerly. "Don't be afraid; I shall not care for any idea people take of me."

"I have none but good ideas of you, Brulette," replied the muleteer. "It is not your fault if Joseph loves you; and if you return his love in your secret heart no one can blame you. We may envy Joseph in that case, but not betray him or do anything to trouble you. Let me tell you how things have gone between him and me since the day we first made friends, when I persuaded him to come over to our parts and learn the music he was so crazy about."

"I don't think you did him much good by that advice," observed my uncle. "It is my opinion he could have learned it just as well here, without grieving and distressing his family."

"He told me," replied Huriel, "and I have since found it true, that the other bagpipers would not allow it. Besides, I owed him the truth, because he trusted me at first sight. Music is a wild flower which does not bloom in your parts. It loves our heather; but I can't tell you why. In our woods and dells it lives and thrives and lives again, like the flowers of spring; there it sows and harvests ideas for lands that are barren of them. The best things your pipers give you come from there; but as your players are lazy and niggardly, and you are satisfied to hear the same things over and over again, they only come to us once in their lives, and live on what they learn then for the rest of their days. At this very time they are teaching pupils to strum a corruption of our old music, and they never think of consulting at the fountainhead to find how such airs should be played. So when a well-intentioned young fellow like your José (as I said to him) comes to drink at the spring, he is sure to return so fresh and full that the other players could not stand up against him. That is why José agreed to go over into the Bourbonnais the following midsummer, where he could have enough work in the woods to support him, and lessons from our best master. I must tell you that the finest bagpipers are in Upper Bourbonnais, among the pine forests, over where the Sioule comes down from the Dôme mountains; and that my father, born in the village of Huriel, from which he takes his name, has spent his life among these players, and keeps his wind in good order and his art well-trained. He is a man who does not like to work two years running in the same place, and the older he gets the livelier and more fond of change he is. Last year he was in the forest of Troncay; since then he has been in that of Éspinasse. Just now he is in the woods of Alleu, where Joseph has followed him faithfully, chopping and felling and bagpiping by his side,—for he loves him like a son and boasts that the love is returned. The lad has been as happy as a lover can be when parted from his mistress. But life is not as easy and comfortable with us as with you; and though my father, taught by experience, tried to prevent Joseph (who was in a hurry to succeed) from straining his lungs on our pipes,—which are, as you may have noticed, differently made from yours, and very fatiguing to the chest until you know how to use them,—the poor fellow took a fever and began to spit blood. My father, who understood the disease and knew how to manage it, took away his bagpipe and ordered him to rest; but then, though his bodily health improved, he took sick in another way. He ceased to cough and spit blood, but he fell into a state of depression and weakness which made them fear for his life. So that when I got home from a trip eight days ago I found him so pallid that I scarcely knew him, and so weak on his legs that he could not stand. When I questioned him he burst into tears and said, very sadly: 'Huriel, I know I shall die in the depths of these woods, far from my own country, from my mother and my friends, unloved by her to whom I long to show the art I have learned. This dreadful dulness eats into my mind, impatience withers my heart. I wish your father would give me back my bagpipe and let me die of it. I could draw my last breath in sending from afar to her I love the sweetness my lips can never utter to her, dreaming for a moment that I was at her side. No doubt Père Bastien meant kindly; I know I was killing myself with eagerness. But what do I gain by dying more slowly? I must renounce life any way. On the one hand, I can't chop wood and earn my bread, and must live at your expense; on the other, my chest is too weak to pipe. No, it is all over with me. I shall never be anything; I must die without the joy of remembering a single day of love and happiness.'"

"Don't cry, Brulette," continued the muleteer, taking the hand with which she wiped her tears; "all is not hopeless. Listen to me. Seeing the poor lad's misery, I went after a good doctor, who examined him, and then told us that it was more depression than illness, and he would answer for his cure if Joseph would give up music and wood-cutting for another month. As to that last matter, it was quite convenient, for my father, and I too, thank God, are not badly off, and it is no great merit to us to take care of a friend who can't work. But the doctor was wrong; the same causes remain, and José is no better. He did not want me to let you know his state, but I made him agree to it and I even tried to bring him here with me. I put him carefully on one of my mules, but at the end of a few miles he became so weak I was obliged to take him back to my father, who thereupon said to me: 'Do you go to the lad's people and bring back either his mother or his sweetheart. He is homesick, that's all, and if he sees one or the other of them he will recover health and courage enough to finish his apprenticeship here; or else he must go home with them.' That being said before Joseph, he was much excited. 'My mother!' he cried, like a child; 'my poor mother, make her come quickly!' Then checking himself, he added, 'No, no; I don't want her to see me die; her grief would kill me all the faster.' 'How about Brulette?' I whispered to him. 'Oh! Brulette would not come,' he answered. 'Brulette is good; but she must have chosen a lover by this time who would not let her come and comfort me.' Then I made José swear he would have patience till I returned, and I came off. Père Brulet, decide what ought to be done; and you, Brulette, consult your heart."

"Maître Huriel," said Brulette, rising, "I will go, though I am not Joseph's sweetheart, as you called me, and nothing obliges me to go to him except that his mother fed me with her milk and carried me in her arms. Why do you think the young man is in love with me? Just as true as that my grandfather is sitting there, he never said the first word of it to me."

"Then he did tell me truth!" cried Huriel, as if delighted with what he heard; but catching himself hastily up, he added, "It is none the less true that he may die of it, and all the more because he has no hope; I must therefore plead his cause and explain his feelings."

"Are you deputed to do so?" asked Brulette, haughtily and as if annoyed with the muleteer.

"Deputed or not, I must do it," said Huriel; "I must clear my conscience of it,—for his sake who told me his troubles and asked my help.

This is what he said to me: 'I always longed to give myself up to music, as much because I loved it as for love of my dear Brulette. She considers me as a brother; she has always shown me the greatest kindness and true pity; but for all that she received everybody's attentions except mine, and I can't blame her. The girl loves finery and all that sets her off. She has a right to be coquettish and exacting. My heart aches for it, but if she gives her affections to those who are worth more than I the fault is mine for being worth so little. Such as I am—unable to dig hard, or speak soft, or dance, or jest, or even sing, feeling ashamed of myself and my condition, I deserve that she should think me the lowest of those who aspire to her hand. Well, don't you see that this grief will kill me if it lasts? and I want to find a cure for it. I feel within me something which declares that I can make better music than any one else in our parts; if I could only succeed I should be no longer a mere nothing. I should become even more than others; and as that girl has much taste and a gift for singing, she would understand, out of her own self, what I was worth; moreover, her pride would be flattered at the praises I should receive.'"

"You speak," said Brulette, smiling, "as if I had an understanding with him; whereas he has never said a word of all this to me. His pride has always been up in arms, and I see that it is through pride that he expects to influence me. However, as his illness puts him really in danger of dying, I will, in order to give him courage, do everything that belongs to the sort of friendship I feel for him. I will go to see him with Mariton, provided my grandfather advises and is willing I should do so."

"I don't think it possible that Mariton can go with you," said Père Brulet, "for reasons which I know and you will soon know, my daughter. I can only tell you just now that she cannot leave her master, because of some trouble in his affairs. Besides, if Joseph's illness can really be cured it is better not to worry and upset the poor woman. I will go with you, because I have great confidence that you, who have always managed Joseph for the best, will have influence enough over his mind to bring him back to reason and give him courage. I know what you think of him, and it is what I think too; well, if we find him in a desperate condition we can write to his mother at once to come and close his eyes."

"If you will allow me in your company," said Huriel. "I will guide you as the swallow flies to where Joseph is. I can even take you in a single day if you are not afraid of bad roads."

"We will talk about that at table," replied my uncle. "As for your company, I wish for it and claim it; for you have spoken well, and I know something of the family of honest folks to whom you belong."

"Do you know my father?" cried Huriel. "When he heard us speaking of Brulette he told us, Joseph and me, that his father had had an early friend named Brulet."

"It was I, myself," said my uncle. "I cut wood for a long time, thirty years ago, in the Saint-Amand region with your grandfather, and I knew your father when a boy; he worked with us and played the bagpipes wonderfully well, even then. He was a fine lad, and years can't trouble him much yet. When you named yourself just now I did not wish to interrupt you, and if I twitted you a little about your customs, it was only to draw you out. Now, sit down, and don't spare the food at your service."

During supper Huriel showed as much good sense in his talk and pleasantness in his gravity as he had wit and liveliness on the night of his first appearance at midsummer. Brulette listened attentively and seemed to get accustomed to his blackened face; but when the journey was talked of and the method of making it was mentioned, she grew uneasy about her grandfather, fearing the fatigue and the upsetting of his habits; so, as Huriel could not deny that the journey would be painful to a man of his years, I offered to accompany Brulette in place of my uncle.

"That's the very thing," said Huriel. "If we are only three we can take the cross-cut, and by starting to-morrow morning we can get there to-morrow night. I have a sister, a very steady, good girl, who will take Brulette into her own hut; for I must not conceal from you that where we are now living you will find neither houses nor places to sleep in such as you are accustomed to here."

"It is true," replied my uncle, "that I am too old to sleep on the heather; and though I am not very indulgent to my body, if I happened to fall ill over there, I should be a great trouble to you, my dear children. So, if Tiennet will go, I know him well enough to trust his cousin to him. I shall rely on his not leaving her a foot's length in any circumstances where there may be danger for a young girl; and I rely on you, too, Huriel, not to expose her to any risks on the way."

I was mightily pleased with this plan, which gave me the pleasure of escorting Brulette and the honor of defending her in case of need. We parted early and met again before daylight at the door of the house,— Brulette all ready and holding a little bundle in her hand, Huriel leading his *clairin* and three mules, one of which was saddled with a very soft, clean pad, on which he seated Brulette. Then he himself mounted the horse and I another mule, which seemed much surprised to find me on his back. The other, laden with new hampers, followed of her own accord, while Satan brought up the rear. Nobody was yet afoot in the village; for which I was sorry, for I would have liked to make Brulette's other lovers jealous in return for the rage they had often put me in. But Huriel seemed anxious to get away without being noticed and criticised under Brulette's nose for his blackened face.

We had not gone far before he made me feel that I should not be allowed to manage everything as I liked. We reached the woods of Maritet at noon, which was nearly half-way. There was a little inclosure near by called "La Ronde," where I should have liked to go and get a good breakfast. But Huriel laughed at what he called my love for a knife and fork, and as Brulette, who was determined to think everything amusing, agreed with him, he made us dismount in a narrow ravine, through which ran a tiny river called "La Portefeuille."—so-called because (at that season at least) the water was covered with the green trays of the water-lily and shaded with the leafage of the woods which came to the very banks of the river on either side. Huriel let the animals loose among the reeds, selected a pretty spot covered with wild flowers, opened the hampers, uncorked the flask, and served as good a lunch as we could have had at home,—all so neatly done and with such consideration for Brulette that she could not help showing pleasure. When she saw that before touching the bread to cut it, and before removing the white napkin which wrapped the provisions, he carefully washed his hands, plunging his arms above the elbows in the river, she smiled and said to him, with her gracious little air of command: "While you are about it, could not you also wash your face, so that we might see if you were really the handsome bagpiper of the midsummer dance?"

"No, my pretty one," he replied, "you must get used to the reverse of the coin. I make no claims upon your heart but those of friendship and esteem, though I am only a heathen of a muleteer. Consequently I need not try to please you by my face, and it will not be for your sake that I wash it."

She was mortified, but she would not give up the point.

"You ought not to frighten your friends," she said; "and the fear of you, looking as you now do, takes away my appetite."

"In that case I'll go and eat apart, so as not to upset you."

He did as he said, and sat down upon a little rock which jutted into the water behind the place where we were sitting, and ate his food alone, while I enjoyed the pleasure of serving Brulette.

At first she laughed, thinking she had provoked him, and taking pleasure in it, like all coquettes; but when she got tired of the game and wanted to recall him, and did her best to excite him by words, he held firm, and every time she turned her head toward him he turned his back on her, while answering all her nonsense very cleverly and without the least vexation, which, to her, was perhaps the very worst of the thing. So presently she began to feel sorry, and, after a rather sharp speech which he launched about haughty minxes, and which she fancied was meant for her, two tears rolled from her eyes though she tried hard to keep them back in my presence. Huriel did not see them, and I took very good care not to show her that I did.

When we had eaten all we wanted, Huriel packed up the remainder of the provisions, saying,—

"If you are tired, children, you can take a nap, for the animals want a rest in the heat of the day; that's the time when the flies torment them, and in this copse they can rub and shake themselves as much as they please. Tiennet, I rely on you to keep good guard over our princess. As for me, I am going a little way into the forest, to see how the works of God are going on."

Then with a light step, and no more heed to the heat than if we were in the month of April, instead of the middle of July, he sprang up the slope, and was lost to sight among the tall trees.

ELEVENTH EVENING.

Brulette did her best not to let me see the annoyance she felt at his departure; but having no heart for talk, she pretended to go to sleep on the fine sand of the river-bank, her head upon the panniers which were taken from the mule to rest him, and her face protected from the flies by a white handkerchief. I don't know whether she slept; I spoke to her two or three times without getting any answer, and as she had let me lay my cheek on a corner of her apron, I kept quiet too, but without sleeping at first, for I felt a little agitated by her close neighborhood.

However, weariness soon overtook me, and I lost consciousness for a short time; when I woke I heard voices, and found that the muleteer had returned and was talking with Brulette. I did not dare move the apron that I might hear more distinctly, but I held it tightly in my fingers so that the girl could not have got away even had she wished to.

"I certainly have the right," Huriel was saying, "to ask you what course you mean to pursue with that poor lad. I am his friend more than I can claim to be yours, and I should blame myself for bringing you, if you mean to deceive him."

"Who talks of deceiving him?" cried Brulette. "Why do you criticise my intentions without knowing them?"

"I don't criticise, Brulette; I question you because I like Joseph very much, and I esteem you enough to believe you will deal frankly with him."

"That is my affair, Maître Huriel; you are not the judge of my feelings, and I am not obliged to explain them. I don't ask you, for instance, if you are faithful to your wife."

"My wife!" exclaimed Huriel, as if astonished.

"Why, yes," returned Brulette, "are not you married?"

"Did I say I was?"

"I thought you said so at our house last night, when my grandfather, thinking you came to talk of marriage, made haste to refuse you."

"I said nothing at all, Brulette, except that I was not seeking marriage. Before obtaining the person, one must win the heart, and I have no claim to yours."

"At any rate," said Brulette, "I see you are more reasonable and less bold than you were last year."

"Oh!" returned Huriel, "If I said a few rather warm words to you at the village dance, it was because they popped into my head at the sight of you; but time has passed, and you ought to forget the affront."

"Who said I recollected it?" demanded Brulette. "Have I reproached you?"

"You blame me in your heart; or at any rate you bear the thing in mind, for you are not willing to speak frankly to me about Joseph."

"I thought," said Brulette, whose voice showed signs of impatience, "that I had fully explained myself on that point night before last. But how do the two things affect each other? The more I forget you, the less I should wish to explain to you my feelings for any man, no matter who."

"But the fact is, pretty one," said the muleteer, who seemed not to give in to any of Brulette's little ways, "You spoke about the past last night, and said nothing about the future; and I don't yet know what you mean to say to Joseph to reconcile him with life. Why do you object to tell me frankly?"

"What is it to you, I should like to know? If you are married, or merely pledged, you ought not to be looking into a girl's heart."

"Brulette, you are trying to make me say that I am free to court you, and yet you won't tell me anything about your own position; I am not to know whether you mean some day to favor Joseph, or whether you are pledged to some one else,—perhaps that tall fellow who is lying asleep on your apron."

"You are too inquisitive " exclaimed Brulette, rising and hastily twitching away the apron, which I was forced to let go, pretending to wake at that moment.

"Come, let us start," said Huriel, who seemed not to care for Brulette's ill-humor, but continued to smile with his white teeth and his large eyes,—the only parts of his face which were not in mourning.

We continued our route to the Bourbonnais. The sun was hidden behind a heavy cloud and thunder was rumbling in the distance.

"That storm over there is nothing," said the muleteer, "it is going off to the left. If we don't meet another as we get near the confluence of the Joyeuse, we shall reach our destination without difficulty. But the atmosphere is so heavy we must be prepared for anything."

So saying, he unfolded a mantle, with a woman's hood, new and handsome, which was fastened on his back, and which Brulette admired greatly.

"You won't tell me now," she exclaimed, blushing, "that you are not married,—unless that is a wedding present you have bought on your way."

"Perhaps it is," said Huriel in the same tone, "but if it comes on to rain you can take possession of it; you won't find it too heavy, and your cape is thin."

Just as he predicted, the sky cleared on one side and clouded on the other; and while we were crossing an open heath between Saint-Saturnin and Sidiailles, the weather suddenly grew tempestuous, and we were blown about by a gale of wind. The country itself was wild, and I began to feel anxious in spite of myself. Brulette, too, thought the place very dreary, and remarked that there was not a tree for shelter. Huriel laughed at us.

"Oh! you folks from the wheat-lands!" he cried, "as soon as your feet touch the heather you think you are lost in the wilderness."

He was guiding us in a bee-line, knowing well all the paths and cross-cuts by which a mule could pass to shorten the distance,—leaving Sidiailles on the left, and making straight for the banks of the little river Joyeuse, a poor rivulet that looked harmless enough, but which nevertheless he seemed in a hurry to get over. Just as we had done so, the rain began, and we were forced either to get wet or to stop for shelter at a mill, called the mill of Paulmes. Brulette wanted to go on, and so did the muleteer, who thought we had better not wait till the roads grew worse; but I said that the girl was trusted to my care, and that I could not have her exposed to harm; so Huriel, for once, gave in to my wishes.

We stayed there two hours, and when the weather cleared and we were able to start again the sun was already going down. The Joyeuse was now so swollen that the crossing would have been difficult; happily it was behind us; but the roads had become abominable, and we had still one stream to cross before we entered the Bourbonnais.

We were able to go on as long as daylight lasted; but the night soon grew so dark that Brulette was frightened, without, however, daring to say so; but Huriel, perceiving it from her silence, got off his horse, which he drove before him, for the animal knew the road as well as he did, and taking the bridle of my cousin's mule, led him carefully for several miles, watching that he did not stumble, plunging, himself, into water or sand up to his knees, and laughing whenever Brulette pitied him and entreated him not to expose himself for her. She began to discover now that he was a friend in need, more helpful than her usual lovers, and that he knew how to serve her without making a show of it.

The country grew more and more dreary; it was nothing but little grassy slopes cut into by rivulets bordered with reeds and flowers which smelt good but did not better the hay. The trees were fine, and the muleteer declared the country richer and prettier than ours on account of its pasture and fruit lands. But, for my part, I did not see any prospect of great harvests, and I wished I were at home again,—all the more because I was not assisting Brulette, having enough to do in keeping myself out of the ruts and bogs on the way.

At last the moon shone out, and we reached the woods of La Roche, at the confluence of the Arnon and another river, the name of which I have forgotten.

"Stay there, on that bit of high ground," Huriel said to us; "you can even dismount and stretch your legs. The place is sandy, and the rain has hardly got through the oak-leaves. I am going to see if we can ford the stream."

He went down to the river and came back at once, saying: "The stepping-stones are covered, and we shall have to go up as far as Saint-Pallais to get across. If we had not lost time at the mill we could have crossed before the river rose, and been at our destination by this time. But what is done is done; let us see what to do now. The water is going down. By staying here we can get across in five or six hours, and reach home by daybreak without fatigue or danger, for the plain between the two arms of the Arnon is sure to be dry. Whereas, if we go up to Saint-Pallais, we may stumble about half the night and not get there any sooner."

"Well, then," said Brulette, "let us stay here. The place is dry and the weather is clear; and though the wood is rather wild, I shall not be afraid with you two by me."

"That's a brave girl!" said Huriel. "Come, now let's have supper, as there is nothing better to do. Tiennet, tie the *clairin*, for there are several woods all round us and I can't be sure about wolves. Unsaddle the mules; they won't stray from far the horse; and you, my pretty one, help me make a fire, for the air is damp and I want you to sup comfortably and not take cold."

I felt greatly discouraged and sad at heart, I could hardly tell why. Whether I was mortified at being of no service to Brulette in such a difficult journey, or whether the muleteer seemed to make light of me, certain it is I was already homesick.

"What are you grumbling about?" said Huriel, who seemed all the gayer as we got deeper and deeper into trouble. "Are not you as well off as a monk in his refectory? These rocks make a fine chimney, and here are seats and sideboards. Isn't this the third meal you have had to-day? Don't you think the moon gives a better light than your old pewter lamp? The provisions are not hurt by the rain, for my hampers were tightly covered. This blazing hearth is drying the air all round us; the branches overhead and the moist plants underfoot smell better, it seems to me, than your cheeses and rancid butter. Don't you breathe another breath under these great vaulting branches? Look at them lighted by the flames! They are like hundreds of arms interlaced to shelter us. If now and then a bit of a breeze shakes the damp foliage, see how the diamonds rain down to crown us! What do you find so melancholy in the idea that we are all alone in a place unknown to you? There is everything here that is most comforting; God, in the first place, who is everywhere; next, a charming girl and two good friends ready to stand by each other. Besides, do you think a man ought to live in a hive all his days? I think, on the contrary, that it is his duty to roam; that he will be a hundred times stronger, gayer, healthier in body and mind if he doesn't look after his own comfort too much, for that makes him languid, timid, and subject to diseases. The more you avoid heat and cold the more you will suffer when they catch you. You will see my father, who, like me, has never slept in a bed ten times in his life; he has no rheumatism or lumbago, though he works in his shirtsleeves in the dead of winter. And then, too, is it not glorious to feel you are firmer and more solid than the wind and the thunder? When the storm rages isn't the music splendid? And the mountain torrents which rush down the ravines and go dancing from root to root, carrying along the pebbles and leaving their white foam clinging to the bracken, don't they sing a song as gay as any you can dream of as you fall asleep on some islet they have scooped out around you? Animals are gloomy in bad weather, I admit that; the birds are silent, the foxes run to earth; even my dog finds shelter under the horse's belly; what distinguishes man from beast is that he keeps his heart gay and peaceful through the battles of the air and the whims of the clouds. He alone, who knows how by reasoning to save himself from fear and danger, has the instinct to feel what is so beautiful in the uproar of nature."

Brulette listened eagerly to the muleteer. She followed his eyes and all his gestures and entered into everything he said, without explaining to herself how such novel ideas and words excited her mind and stirred her heart. I felt rather touched by them, too (though I resisted somewhat), for Huriel had such an open, resolute face under all the blacking that he won folks in spite of themselves, just as when we are beaten at rackets by a fine player we admire him though we lose the stakes.

We were in no great hurry to finish our supper, for certainly the place was dry, and when the fire burned down to a bed of hot ashes, the weather had grown so warm and clear that we felt very comfortable and quite ready to listen to the lively talk and fine ideas of the muleteer. He was silent from time to time, listening to the river, which still roared a good deal; and as the mountain brooks were pouring into it with a thousand murmuring voices, there was no likelihood that we could set forth again that night. Huriel, after going down to examine it, advised us to go to sleep. He made a bed for Brulette with the mule-pads, wrapping her well up in all the extra garments he had with him, and talking gayly, but with no gallant speeches, showing her the same interest and tenderness, and no more, that he would have shown to a little child.

Then he stretched himself, without cushion or covering, on the bare ground which was well dried by the fire, invited me to do the same, and was soon as fast asleep as a dormouse—or nearly so.

I was lying quiet, though not asleep, for I did not like that kind of dormitory, when I heard a bell in the distance, as if the *clairin* had got loose and was straying in the forest. I lifted myself a little and saw him still where I had tied him. I knew therefore it was some other *clairin*, which gave notice of the approach or vicinity of other muleteers.

Huriel had instantly risen on his elbow, listening; then he got on his feet and came to me. "I am a sound sleeper," he said, "when I have only my mules to watch; but now that I have a precious princess in charge it is another matter, and I have only been asleep with one eye. Neither have you, Tiennet, and that's all right Speak low and don't move; I don't want to meet my comrades; and as I chose this place for its solitude I think they won't find us out."

He had hardly said the words when a dark form glided through the trees and passed so close to Brulette that a little more and it would have knocked her. It was that of a muleteer, who at once gave a loud cry like a whistle, to which other cries responded from various directions, and in less than a minute half a dozen of these devils, each more hideous to behold than the others, were about us. We had been betrayed by Huriel's dog, who, nosing his friends and companions among the dogs of the muleteers, had gone to find them, and acted as guide to their masters in discovering our retreat.

Huriel tried to conceal his uneasiness; for though I softly told Brulette not to stir, and placed myself before her, it seemed impossible, surrounded as we were, to keep her long from their prying eyes.

I had a confused sense of danger, guessing at more than I really saw, for Huriel had not had time to explain the character of the men who were now with us. He spoke to the first-comer in the half-Auvergnat patois of the Upper Bourbonnais, which he seemed to speak quite as well as the other man, though he was born in the low-country. I could understand only a word here and there, but I made out that the talk was friendly, and that the other was asking him who I was and what he was doing here. I saw that Huriel was anxious to draw him away, and he even said to me, as if to be overheard by the rest, for they could all understand the French language, "Come, Tiennet, let us say good-night to these friends and start on our way."

But instead of leaving us alone to make our preparations for departure, the others, finding the place warm and dry, began to unpack their mules and turned them loose to feed until daybreak.

"I will give a wolf-cry to get them out of sight for a few minutes," whispered Huriel. "Don't move from here, and don't let her move till I return. Meantime saddle the mules so that we can start quickly; for to stay here is the worst thing we can do."

He did as he said, and the muleteers all ran to where the cry sounded. Unhappily I lost patience, and thought I could profit by the confusion to save Brulette. I thought I could make her rise without any one seeing her, for the wrappings made her look like a bale of clothes. She reminded me that Huriel had told us to wait for him; but I was so possessed with anger and fear and jealousy, even suspecting Huriel himself, that I fairly lost my head, and seeing a close copse very near us, I took my cousin firmly by the hand and began to run towards it.

But the moon was bright, and the muleteers so near that we were seen, and a cry arose,—"Hey! hey! a woman!" and all the scoundrels ran after us. I saw at once there was nothing to be done but let myself be killed. So lowering my head like a boar and raising my stick in in the air, I was just about to deliver a blow on the jaws of the first-comer which might have sent his soul to Paradise, when Huriel caught my arm as he came swiftly to my side.

Then he spoke to the others with great vehemence and yet firmness. A sort of dispute arose, of which Brulette and I could not understand a word; and it seemed far from satisfactory, for Huriel was listened to only now and then, and twice one of the miscreants got near enough to Brulette to lay his devilish paw upon her arm as if to lead her away. Indeed, if it had not been for my driving my nails into his buck's skin to make him let go he would have dragged her from my arms by the help of the rest; for there were eight of them, all armed with stout boar-spears, and they seemed used to quarrels and violence.

Huriel, who kept cool and stood firmly between us and the enemy, prevented my delivering the first blow, which, as I saw later, would have ruined us. He merely continued to speak, sometimes in a tone of remonstrance, sometimes with a menacing air, and finally he turned round to me and said in the French language: "Isn't it true, Étienne, that this is your sister, an honest girl, betrothed to me, and now on her way to the Bourbonnais to make acquaintance with my family? These men here, my good friends and comrades in matters of right and justice, are trying to pick a quarrel with me because they don't believe this. They fancy that you and I were talking here with some woman we had just met, and they want to join company. But I tell them, and I swear to God, that before they insult this young woman by so much as a word they will have to kill both you and me, and bear our blood on their souls in sight of God and man."

"Well, what then?" answered one of the wretches, speaking French,— it was the one who first came in my way, and I was thirsting to deliver him a blow in the pit of the stomach with my fist that should fell him to earth. "If you get yourself killed, so much the worse for you! there are plenty of ditches hereabouts to bury fools in. Suppose your friends come to find you; we shall be gone, and the trees and the stones have no tongues to tell what they have seen."

Happily, he was the only real scoundrel in the party. The others rebuked him, and a tall blond fellow, who seemed to have authority, took him by the arm and shoved him away from us, swearing and abusing him in a gibberish that made the whole forest resound.

After that all real danger was over,—the idea of shedding blood having touched the consciences of these rough men. They turned the matter off with a laugh, and joked with Huriel, who answered them in the same tone. Nevertheless, they seemed unwilling to let us go. They wanted to see Brulette's face, which she kept hidden under her hood, wishing, for once in her life, that she was old and ugly.

But all of a sudden she changed her mind, having guessed at the meaning of the words said to Huriel and me in the Auvergne dialect. Stung with anger and pride, she let go my arm, and throwing back her hood she said, with an offended air and plenty of courage: "Dishonorable men! I have the good fortune not to understand what you say, but I see in your faces that you insult me in your hearts. Well, look at me! and if you have ever seen the face of a woman who deserves respect, you may know that you see one now. Shame on your vile behavior! let me go my way without hearing more of you."

Brulette's action, bold as it was, worked marvels. The tall fellow shrugged his shoulders and whistled a moment, while the others consulted together, seeming rather confused; then suddenly he turned his back on us, saying in a loud voice, "There's been talk enough; let us go! You elected me captain of the company, and I will punish any one who annoys Jean Huriel any longer; for he is a good comrade and respected by the whole fraternity."

The party filed off, and Huriel, without saying a word, saddled the mules and made us mount; then, going before but looking round at every step, he led us at a sharp pace to the river. It was still swollen and roaring, but he plunged right in, and when he got to the middle he cried out, "Come, don't be afraid!" and then, as I hesitated to allow Brulette to get wet, he came angrily back to us and struck her mule to make it go on, swearing that it was better to die than be insulted.

"I think so too," answered Brulette in the same tone, and striking the mule herself, she plunged boldly into the current, which foamed higher than the breast of the animal.

TWELFTH EVENING.

There was an instant when the animal seemed to lose footing, but Brulette just then was between us two, and showed a great deal of courage. When we reached the other bank Huriel again lashed the beasts and put them to a gallop, and it was not until we reached open ground in full view of the sky, and were nearing habitations, that he allowed us to draw breath.

"Now," said he, walking his horse between Brulette and me, "I must blame both of you. I am not a child to have led you into danger and left you there. Why did you run from the spot where I told you to wait for me?"

"It is you who blame us, is it?" said Brulette, rather sharply. "I should have thought it was all the other way."

"Say what you have to say," returned Huriel, gravely. "I will speak later. What do you blame me for?"

"I blame you," she answered, "for not having foreseen the dangerous encounter we were likely to make; I blame you, above all, for giving assurances of safety to my grandfather and me, in order to induce me to leave my home and country, where I am loved and respected, and for having brought me through desolate woods where you were scarcely able to save me from the insults of your friends. I don't know what coarse language they used about me, but I understood enough to see that you were forced to answer for my being a decent girl. So, being in your company was enough to make my character doubted! Ah, what a miserable journey! This is the first time in my life I was ever insulted, and I did not think such a thing could happen to me!"

Thereupon, her heart swelling with mortification and anger, she began to cry. Huriel at first said nothing; he seemed very sad. Then he plucked up courage and replied:—

"It is true, Brulette, that you were misjudged. You shall be revenged, I promise you that. But as I could not punish those men at the time without endangering you, I suffer within me such pangs of baffled rage as I cannot describe to you and you could never comprehend."

Tears cut short his words.

"I don't want to be avenged," said Brulette, "and I beg you won't think of it again; I will try to forget it all myself."

"But you will always curse the day when you trusted yourself to me," he said, clenching his fist as though he would fain knock himself down.

"Come, come," I said to them, "you must not quarrel now that the harm and the danger are well over. I admit it was my fault. Huriel enticed the muleteers away in one direction and could have got us away in another. It was I who threw Brulette into the lion's jaws, thinking I could save her quicker."

"There would have been no danger but for that," said Huriel. "Of course, among muleteers, as among all men who lead a half-wild life, there are scoundrels. There was one of the kind in that band; but you saw that they all blamed him. It is also true that many of us are uneducated and make unseemly jokes. But I don't know what you really accuse our fraternity of doing. We may be partners in money and pleasure, as we are in losses and dangers, but we all of us respect women quite as much as other Christian folk do. You saw yourself that virtue was respected for its own sake, because one word from you brought those men at once to their duty."

"Nevertheless," said Brulette, still angry, "you were in a great hurry to get us away; you made us go fast enough to risk being drowned in the river. You know you were not master of those bad men, and you were afraid they might return to their evil wishes."

"It all came from their seeing you run away with Tiennet," said Huriel. "They thought you were doing wrong. If it had not been for your fear and your distrust of me you would never have been seen by my comrades. You may as well confess, both of you, that you had a very bad idea of me."

"I never had a bad idea of you," said Brulette.

"I had," said I, "just then, for a moment; I confess it, for I don't wish to lie."

"It is always better not," returned Huriel, "and I hope you will soon think differently of me."

"I do now," I said. "I saw how firm you were, and how you mastered your anger, and I agree that it was wiser to speak soft in the beginning than to end soft; blows come fast enough. If it were not for you, I should be dead now, and so would you for helping me, which would have been a dreadful thing for Brulette. And now, here we are well out of it, thanks to you; and I think we ought, all three of us, to be the better friends."

"That's good!" cried Huriel, pressing my hand. "That's the Berrichon's best nature; he shows his good sense and his sober judgment. You ought to be a Bourbonnaise, Brulette, you are so hasty and impulsive."

She allowed him to take her hand in his, but she continued thoughtful; and as I feared she might take cold after getting so wet in the river, we entered the first house we came to to change our clothes and refresh ourselves with a little mulled wine. It was now daybreak, and the country-folk seemed very kind and ready to help us.

When we resumed our journey the sun was already warm, and the country, which lay rather high between two rivers, was delightful to the eye and reminded me a little of our own plains. Brulette's vexation was all over; for, in talking with her beside the fire of the good Bourbonnais, I had proved to her that an honest girl was not degraded by the talk of a drunken man, and that no woman was safe if such things were to be considered. The muleteer had left us for a moment, and when he returned to put Brulette into her saddle she could not restrain a cry of amazement. He had washed and shaved and dressed himself properly,—not so handsomely as the first time she had seen him, but looking well enough in face and well enough clothed to do her honor.

However, she uttered neither compliment nor jest; she only looked at him intently when his eyes were not upon her, as if to renew her acquaintance with him. She seemed sorry to have been crabbed with him, and as if she did not know how to make it up; but he talked of other things, explained the Bourbonnais district which we had entered after crossing the river, told me about the manners and customs, and discoursed like a man who was not wanting for sense in any way.

At the end of two hours, without fatigue or further adventure, but still riding up hill, we reached Mesples, the parish adjoining the forest where we were to find Joseph. We passed straight through the village, where Huriel was accosted by many persons who seemed to hold him in much esteem,—not to mention some young girls who eyed with surprise the company he had with him.

We had not, however, reached our destination. We were bound for the depths, or rather I should say the highest part, of the wood; for the forest of the Alleu, which joins that of Chambérat, covers the plateau from which five or six little rivers or brooks come down, forming a wild tract of country surrounded by barren plains, where the view is extensive on all sides, towards other forests and other heaths stretching endlessly away.

We were as yet only in what is called the Lower Bourbonnais, which adjoins the upper part of Berry. Huriel told me that the ground continued to ascend as far as Auvergne. The woods were fine,—chiefly full-grown trees of white oak, which are the finest species. The brooks, which cut into and ravine these woods in every direction, form in many places moist coverts, where alders, willows, and aspen grow; all fine trees, which those of our region can't compare with. I saw also, for the first time, a tree with white stems and beautiful foliage, called the beech, which does not grow with us. It is the king of trees after the oak; for if it is less handsome than the latter, it is certainly quite as lovely. There were but few of them in these forests, and Huriel told me they abounded only in the centre of the Bourbonnais country.

I gazed at all these things with much interest, expecting, however, to see more rare things than there were, and half-believing the trees would have their roots in the air and their heads in the ground, after the manner of those who imagine about distant parts that they have never seen. As for Brulette, whether it was that she had a natural taste for wild scenery, or whether she wanted to console Huriel for the reproaches she had showered on him, it is certain that she admired things out of all reason, and did honor and reverence to the least little wild flower she saw in the path.

We advanced for some time without meeting a living soul, when suddenly Huriel said, pointing to an open and some felled trees: "Here we are, at the clearing; now in a minute more you will see our city and my father's castle."

He laughed as he said it, and we were still looking about us for something like a village, when he added, pointing to some mud huts which were more like the lairs of animals than the abodes of men: "These are our summer palaces, our country-houses. Stay here, and I will call Joseph."

He went off at a gallop, looked into the doorways of all the huts, and came back, evidently uneasy, but hiding it as best he could, to say: "There is no one here, and that is a good sign. Joseph must be better, and has gone to work with my father. Wait for me here; sit down and rest in our cabin; it is the first, right before you; I'll go and see where the patient is."

"No, no," said Brulette; "we will go with you."

"Are you afraid to be alone here? You are quite mistaken. You are now in the domain of the woodsmen, and they are not, like the muleteers, imps of Satan. They are honest country-folk, like those you have at home, and where my father rules you have nothing to fear."

"I am not afraid of your people," replied Brulette, "but it frightens me not to find José. Who knows? perhaps he is dead and buried. The idea has just come into my head and it makes my blood creep."

Huriel turned pale, as if the same thought struck him; but he would not give heed to it. "The good God would never have allowed it," he said. "But get down, leave the mules just here, and come with me."

He took a little path which led to another clearing; but even there we did not find Joseph nor any one else.

"You fancy these woods are deserted," said Huriel; "and yet I see by fresh marks of the axe that the woodsmen have been at work here all the morning. This is the hour when they take a little nap, and they are probably all lying among the bracken, where we should not see them unless we stepped upon them. But listen! there's a sound that delights my heart. My father is playing the bagpipe,—I recognize his method; and that's a sign that José is better, for it is not a sad tune, and my father would be very sad if any misfortune had happened to the lad."

We followed Huriel, and the music was certainly so delightful that Brulette, hurrying as she was to get to Joseph, could not help stopping now and then, as if charmed, to listen. And I myself, without being able to comprehend the thing as she did, felt all five of my natural senses stirred up within me. At every step I fancied I saw differently, heard differently, breathed and walked in a different manner from what I ever did before. The trees seemed finer, so did the earth and sky, and my heart was full of a satisfaction I couldn't give a reason for.

Presently, standing on some rocks, round which a pretty rivulet all full of flowers was murmuring along, we saw Joseph, looking very sad, beside a man who was sitting down and playing a bagpipe to please the poor sick fellow. The dog, Parpluche, was beside them and seemed to be listening too, like an intelligent human being.

As the pair paid no heed to us Brulette held us back, wishing to examine Joseph and judge of his health by his appearance before she spoke to him. He was as white as a sheet and as shrunken as a bit of dead wood, by which we knew that the muleteer had not deceived us; but what was very consoling was the fact that he was nearly a head taller than when he left us; which of course the people about him might not notice, but which, to us, explained his illness as the result of his growth. In spite of his sunken cheeks and white lips, he had grown to be a handsome man; his eyes, notwithstanding his languid manner, were clear, and even bright as running water, his hair fine and parted above his pallid face like that of the blessed Jesus; in short, he was the image of an angel from heaven, which made him as different from other peasants as the almond-flower differs from an almond in its husk. His hands were as white as a woman's, for the reason that he had not worked of late, and the Bourbonnais costume which he had taken to wearing showed off his well-built figure better than the hempen blouses and big sabots of our parts.

Having given our first attention to Joseph we were next compelled to look at Huriel's father, a man I have seldom seen the like of,—one who, without education, had great knowledge and a mind that would not have disgraced the wealthy and famous. He was tall and strong, of fine carriage, like Huriel, but stouter and broader about the shoulders; his head was ponderous and set on like that of a bull. His face was not at all handsome, for his nose was flat, his lips thick, and his eyes round; but for all that, it was one you liked to look at, for it satisfied you with its air of command and of strength and of goodness. His large black eyes glittered like lightning-flashes from his head, and his broad mouth laughed with a glee which would have brought you back from the jaws of death.

At the present moment his head was covered with a blue handkerchief knotted behind, and he wore no other garments than his shirt and breeches, with a big leather apron, which his hands, hardened by toil, matched in color and texture. In fact, his fingers, scarred and crushed by many an accident, for he never spared himself danger, looked like roots of box twisted into knots, and the wonder was that he was able to do any work beyond breaking stones with a pick-axe. Nevertheless he used them as delicately on the chanter of his bagpipe as if they were slender reeds, or tiny bird's claws.

Beside him were the trunks of several large oaks, lately cut down and sawn apart; among them lay his tools,—his axe, shining like a razor, his saw as pliable a reed, and his earthen bottle, the wine of which kept up his strength.

Presently Joseph, who was listening breathlessly to the music, saw his dog Parpluche run towards us; he raised his eyes and beheld us within ten feet of him. From pallid he grew red as fire, but did not stir, thinking probably it was a vision called up by the music which had made him dream.

Brulette ran to him, her arms extended; then he uttered a cry and fell, as if choking, on his knees, which frightened me, for I had no conception of that sort of love, and I thought he had a fit which might kill him. But he recovered himself quickly and began to thank Brulette and me and also Huriel, with such friendly words so readily uttered, that you would never think it was the same José who in the olden time always answered, "I don't know" to everything that was said to him.

Père Bastien, or rather the Head-Woodsman (for such he was always called in these parts), laid aside his bagpipe, and while Brulette and Joseph were talking together, he shook me by the hand and welcomed me as if he had known me from my birth up.

"So this is your friend Tiennet?" he said to his son. "Well, his face suits me, and his body, too, for I warrant I can hardly meet my arms round it, and I have always noticed that the biggest and strongest men are the gentlest. I see it in you, my Huriel, and in myself, too, for I'm always inclined to love my neighbor rather than crush him. So, Tiennet, I give you welcome to our wild woods; you won't find your fine wheaten bread nor the variety of salads you get from your garden, but we will try to regale you with good talk and hearty good-will. I see you have brought that handsome Nohant girl who is half-sister, half-mother to our poor José. That's a good deed done, for he had no heart to get well; now I shall feel easier about him, for I think the medicine is good."

As he said this he looked at José, who was sitting on his heels at Brulette's feet, holding her hand and gazing at her with all his eyes, while he asked questions about his mother, and Père Brulet, and the neighbors, and all the parish. Brulette, observing that the Head-Woodsman was speaking of her, came to him and begged pardon for not having saluted him at first. But he, without more ado, took her round the waist and set her on a high rock, as if to see her all at once, like the figure of a saint or some other precious thing. Then, placing her on the ground again, he kissed her on the forehead, saying to José, who blushed as much as Brulette:—

"You told me true; she is pretty from top to toe. Here, I think, is a bit of nature without a flaw. Body and soul are of the best quality; I can see that in her eye. Tell me, Huriel, for I am so blind about my own children that I can't judge, is she prettier than your sister? I think she is not less so, and if they were both mine I don't know which I should be proudest of. Come, come, Brulette, don't be ashamed of being handsome, and don't be vain of it, either. The workman who made the creatures of this world beautiful did not consult you, and you count for nothing in his work. What he has done for us we can spoil by folly or stupidity; but I see by your appearance that, far from doing that, you respect his gifts in yourself. Yes, yes, you are a beautiful girl, healthy in heart and upright in mind. I know you already, for you have come here to comfort that poor lad, who longed for you as the earth longs for rain. Many another would not have done as you have done, and I respect you for it. Therefore, I ask your friendship for me, who will be to you a father, and for my two children, who will be as brother and sister to you."

Brulette, whose heart was still swelling with the insults of the muleteers in the woods of La Roche, was so gratified by the respect and the compliments of the Head-Woodsman that the tears began to fall, and flinging herself upon his neck she could answer only by kissing him, as though he were her own father.

"The best of all answers," he said, "and I am content with it. Now, my children, my rest hour is over and I must go to work. If you are hungry, here is my wallet with some provisions in it. Huriel will go and find his sister, so that she may keep you company; and, meantime, my Berrichons, you must talk with Joseph, for I imagine you have a deal to say to each other. But don't go far away from the sound of my axe, for you don't know the forest and you might get lost."

Thereupon he set to work among the trees, after hanging his bagpipe to the branches of one that was still standing. Huriel ate some food with us and answered Brulette, who questioned him about his sister.

"My sister Thérence," he said, "is a pretty girl and a good girl, of about your own age. I shall not say, as my father did, that she compares with you; but such as she is she lets people look at her, and her spirit is none of the tamest either. She follows my father to all his stations, so that he may not miss his home; for the life of a woodsman, like that of a muleteer, is very hard and dreary if he has no companionship for his heart."

"Where is she now?" asked Brulette. "Can't we go and find her?"

"I don't know where she is," replied Huriel; "and I rather wonder she did not hear us, for she is seldom far from the lodges. Have you seen her to-day, Joseph?"

"Yes," he answered, "but not since morning. She was feeling ill and complained of head-ache."

"She is not used to complain of anything," said Huriel. "If you will excuse me, Brulette, I will go and fetch her to you as fast as I can."

THIRTEENTH EVENING.

After Huriel left us we walked about and talked to Joseph; but thinking that it was enough for him to have seen me and that he might like to be alone with Brulette, I left them together, without appearing to do so, and went after Père Bastien to watch him at work.

It was a more cheering sight than you can possibly imagine. Never in my life have I seen man's handiwork despatched in so free and jovial a manner. I believe he could, without tiring himself, have done the work of four of the strongest men in his employ; and that, too, while talking and laughing in company, or singing and whistling when alone. He told me that wood-cutters as a general thing lived near the woods where they worked, and that when their houses were within easy distance they went daily to and from their work. Others, living farther off, came by the week, starting from home Monday before daybreak, and returning the following Saturday night. As for those who came down with him from the uplands, they were hired for three months, and their huts were larger and better built and victualled than those of the men who came by the week.

The same plan was followed with the charcoal men, meaning by them not those who buy charcoal to sell, but those who make it on the spot for the benefit of the owners of the woods and forests. There were other men who bought the right to put it in the market, just as there were muleteers who bought and sold charcoal on their own account; but as a general thing, the business of the muleteer was solely that of transporting it.

At the present time this business of the muleteers is going down, and it will probably soon be extinct. The forests are better cleared; there are fewer of those impassable places for horses and wagons where mules alone can make their way. The number of manufactories and ironworks which still use wood-coal is much restricted; in fact, there are but few muleteers now in our part of the country. Only a few remain in the great forests of Cheurre in Berry, together with the woodsmen in the Upper Bourbonnais. But at the time of which I am telling you, when the forests covered one-half of our provinces, all these trades were flourishing and much sought after. So much so that in a forest which was being cleared you might find a whole population of these different trades, each having its customs and its fraternities, and living, as much as possible, on good terms with each other.

Père Bastien told me, and later I saw it for myself, that all men who went to work in the woods grew so accustomed to the roving and hazardous life that they suffered a kind of homesickness if they were obliged to live on the plains. As for him, he loved the woods like a fox or a wolf, though he was the kindest of men and the liveliest companion that you could find anywhere.

For all that, he never laughed, as Huriel did, at my preference for my own region. "All parts of the country are fine," he said, "if they are our own; it is right that every one should feel a particular liking for the region that brought him up. That's a provision of God, without which the barren and dreary places would be neglected and abandoned. I have heard tell of folks who travelled far into lands covered with snow and ice the greater part of the year; and into others where fire came from the mountains and ravaged the land. Nevertheless, people build fine houses on these bedevilled mountains, and hollow caves to live in under the snow. They love, and marry, and dance, and sing, and sleep, and bring up children, just as we do. Never despise any man's home or lodging or family. The mole loves his dark tomb as much as the bird loves its nest in the foliage; and the ant would laugh in your face if you tried to make him believe there were kings who built better palaces than he."

The day was getting on, and still Huriel did not return with his sister Thérence. Père Bastien seemed surprised but not uneasy. I went towards Brulette and José several times, for they were not far off; but as they were always talking and took no notice of my approach, I finally went off by myself, not knowing very well how to while away the time. I was, above all things, the true friend of that dear girl. Ten times a day I felt I was in love with her, and ten times a day I knew I was cured of it; and now I made no pretence of love, and so felt no chagrin. I had never been very jealous of Joseph before the muleteer told us of the great love that was consuming him; and after that time, strange to say, I was not jealous at all. The more compassion Brulette showed for him, the more I seemed to see that she gave it from a sense of friendly duty. And that grieved me instead of pleasing me. Having no hope for myself, I still wanted to keep the presence and companionship of a person who made everything comfortable about her; and I also felt that if any one deserved her, it was the young fellow who had always loved her, and who, no doubt, could never make any one else love him.

I was even surprised that Brulette did not feel it so in her heart, especially when it appeared how José, in spite of his illness, had grown handsome, well-informed, and agreeable in speech. No doubt he owed this change for the better to the companionship of the Head-Woodsman and his son, but he had also set his own will to it, and she ought to have approved of him for that. However, Brulette seemed to take no notice of the change, and I fancied that during the journey she had thought more of the muleteer Huriel than I had known her to do of any other man. That idea began to distress me more and more; for if her fancy turned upon this stranger, two terrible disasters faced me; one was that our poor José would die of grief, the other, that our dear Brulette would leave our part of the country and I should no longer see her, or have her to talk to.

I had got about so far in my reasoning when I saw Huriel returning, bringing with him so beautiful a girl that Brulette could not compare with her. She was tall, slender, broad in the shoulders, and free, like her brother, in all her movements. Her complexion was naturally brown, but living always in the shade of woods she was pale, though not pallid,—a sort of whiteness which was charming to the eye, though it surprised you,—and all the other features of her face were faultless. I was rather shocked by her little straw hat, turned up behind like the stern of a boat; but from it issued a mass of such marvellous black hair that I soon grew reconciled to its oddity. I noticed from the first moment I saw her that, unlike Brulette, she was neither smiling nor gracious. She did not try to make herself prettier than she was, and her whole aspect was of a more decided character, hotter in will and colder in manner.

As I was sitting against a pile of cut wood, neither of them saw me, and when they stopped close by where two paths forked they were speaking to each other as though they were alone.

"I shall not go," said the beautiful Thérence, in a firm voice. "I am going to the lodges to prepare their beds and their supper. That is all that I choose to do at the present time."

"Won't you speak to them? Are you going to show ill-temper?" said Huriel, as if surprised.

"I am not out of temper," answered the young girl. "Besides, if I were, I am not forced to show it."

"You do show it though, if you won't go and welcome that young girl, who must be getting very tired of the company of men, and who will be glad enough to see another girl like herself."

"She can't be very tired of them," replied Thérence, "unless she has a bad heart. However, I am not bound to amuse her. I will serve her and help her; that is all that I consider my duty."

"But she expects you; what am I to tell her?"

"Tell her what you like; I am not obliged to render account of myself to her."

So saying, the daughter of the Head-Woodsman turned into a wood-path and Huriel stood still a moment, thinking, like a man who is trying to guess a riddle.

Then he went on his way; but I remained just where I was, rigid as a stone image. A sort of vision came over me when I first beheld Thérence; I said to myself: "That face is known to me; who is it she is like?"

Then, slowly, as I looked at her and heard her speak, I knew she reminded me of the little girl in the cart that was stuck in the mire,—the little girl who had set me dreaming all one evening, and who may have been the reason why Brulette, thinking me too simple in my tastes, had turned her love away from me. At last, when she passed close by me in going away, I noticed the black mole at the corner of her mouth, and I knew by that that she was indeed the girl of the woods whom I had carried in my arms, and who had kissed me then as readily as she now seemed unwilling even to receive me.

I stayed a long time thinking of many things in connection with this encounter; but finally Père Bastien's bagpipe, sounding a sort of fanfare, warned me that the sun was going down. I had no trouble in finding the path to the lodges, as they call the huts of the woodsmen. That belonging to Huriel was larger and better built than the rest; it consisted of two rooms, one of them being for Thérence. In front of it was a kind of shed roofed with green boughs, which served as a shelter from wind and rain; two boards placed on trestles made a table, laid for the occasion.

Usually the Huriel family lived on bread and cheese, with a little salt meat once a day. This was neither miserliness nor poverty, but simplicity of life and customs; these children of the woods think our need of hot meals and the way we have of keeping our women cooking from morning till night both useless and exacting.

However, expecting the arrival of Joseph's mother or that of Père Brulet, Thérence, wishing to give them what they were accustomed to, had gone the night before to Mesples for provisions. She now lighted a fire in the glade and called her neighbors to assist her. These were the wives of woodsmen, one old and one ugly. There were no other women in the forest, as it is not the custom, nor have these people the means, to take their families into the woods.

The neighboring lodges, six in number, held about a dozen men, who were beginning to assemble on a pile of fagots to sup in each other's company on their frugal bit of lard and rye bread; but the Head-Woodsman, going up to them before he went to his own lodge to put away his tools and his leathern apron, said, in his kind and manly way: "Brothers,

I have a party of strangers with me to-day, whom I shall not condemn to follow our customs. But it shall never be said that roast meat is eaten and the wine of Sancerre served in the lodge of the Head-Woodsman when his friends are not there to partake with him. Come, therefore, that I may make you friendly with my guests; those of you who refuse will give me pain."

No one refused, and we were a company of over twenty,—not all round the table, for these folk don't care for comfort, but seated, some on stones, some on the grass, one lying on his back among the shavings, another perched on the twisted limb of a tree; and all—saving the matter of holy baptism—more like a troop of wild boars than a company of Christian people.

All this time the beautiful Thérence seemed, as she came and went about her duties, not a whit more inclined to take notice of us until her father, who had called to her in vain, caught her as she passed, and leading her up to us against her will, presented her.

"Please excuse her, my friends," he said; "she is a little savage, born and reared in the woods. She is shy and bashful; but she will get over it, and I ask you, Brulette, to help her do so, for she improves on acquaintance."

Thereupon Brulette, who was neither shy nor ill-humored herself, opened both arms and flung them round Thérence's neck; and the latter, not daring to forbid her, yet unable to escape, stood stock-still and threw up her head, looking out of her eyes, which had hitherto been glued to the ground. In this attitude, so near each other, eye to eye and almost cheek to cheek, they made me think of a pair of young bulls, one of which butts his head in play, while the other, distrustful and already conscious of horns, awaits the moment when he can strike him treacherously.

But all of a sudden Thérence seemed conquered by Brulette's soft eyes, and lowering her head she dropped it on the other's shoulder to hide her tears.

"Well, well!" said Père Bastien, teasing and caressing his daughter, "this is what you call skittish! I never should have thought a girl's shyness would bring her to tears. Try to understand these young things if you can! Come, Brulette, you seem the more reasonable of the two; take her away, and don't let go of her till she has talked to you. It is only the first word that costs."

"Very good," answered Brulette. "I will help her, and the first order she gives me I will obey so well that she will forgive me for having frightened her."

As they went off together, Père Bastien said to me: "Just see what women are! The least coquettish of them (and my Thérence is of that kind) cannot come face to face with a rival in beauty without getting scarlet with anger or frozen with fear. The stars live contentedly side by side in the sky, but when two daughters of Mother Eve come together there is always one who is miserable at the comparison that can be made between them."

"I think, father, that you are not doing justice to Thérence in saying that," observed Huriel. "She is neither shy nor envious." Then lowering his voice, "I think I know what grieves her, but it is best to pay no attention."

They brought in the broiled meat, with some fine yellow mushrooms, which I could not make up my mind to taste, though I saw everybody else eat them fearlessly; then came eggs fricasseed with all sorts of strong herbs, buckwheat cakes, and the Chambérat cheeses which are famous everywhere. All the laborers junketed to their heart's content, but in a very different way from ours. Instead of taking their time and chewing each morsel, they swallowed the food whole like famished creatures, a thing that is not considered at all proper with us; in fact, they could not wait to be through eating before they began to sing and dance in the very middle of the feast.

These men, whose blood is not as cool as ours, seemed to me unable to keep still a moment. They would not wait till the dishes were passed round, but carried up their slices of bread to hold the stew, refusing plates, and then returned to their perch in the trees or their bed in the sawdust. Some ate standing, others talking and gesticulating, each telling his own tale and singing his own song. They were like bees buzzing about the hive; it made me giddy, and I felt I was not enjoying the feast at all.

Although the wine was good and the Head-Woodsman did not spare it, no one took more than was good for him; for each man had his work to do and would not let himself be unfitted for the labor of the morrow. So the feast was short, and, although at one time it seemed to me to be getting rather boisterous, still it ended early and peacefully. The Head-Woodsman received many compliments for his hospitality, and it was quite plain that he had a natural control over the whole band, not so much by any method as by the influence of his kind heart and his wise head.

We received many assurances of friendship and offers of service; and I must admit that the people were heartier and readier to oblige than we are in our part of the country. I noticed that Huriel took them up, one after the other, to Brulette, and presented each by name, telling them to regard her as neither more nor less than his sister; whereupon she received so many salutations and civilities that she had never, even in her own village, been so courted. When night came the Head-Woodsman offered to share his cabin with me. Joseph's lodge was next to ours, but it was smaller, and I should have been much cramped. So I followed my host,—all the more willingly because I was charged to watch over Brulette's safety; but I soon saw that she ran no risk, for she shared the bed of the beautiful Thérence, and the muleteer, faithful to his usual habits, had already stretched himself on the ground outside the door, so that neither wolf nor thief could get an entrance.

Casting a glance into the little room where the two girls were to sleep, I saw it contained a bed and a few very decent articles of furniture. Huriel, thanks to his mules, was able to transport his sister's household belongings very easily and without expense. Those of his father gave little trouble, for they consisted solely of a heap of dry fern and a coverlet. Indeed, the Head-Woodsman thought even that too much, and would have preferred to sleep under the stars, like his son.

I was tired enough to do without a bed, and I slept soundly till daylight. I thought Brulette did the same, for I heard no sound behind the plank partition which separated us. When I rose the Woodsman and his son were already up and consulting together.

"We were speaking of you," said the father; "and as we must go to our work, I should like the matter I was talking of to be settled now. I have explained to Brulette that Joseph needs her company for some time yet, and she has promised to stay a week at least; but she could not speak for you, and has asked us to beg you to stay. We hope you will do so, assuring you that it will give us pleasure; you will not be a burden on us; and we beg you to act with us as freely as we would with you if occasion demanded."

This was said with such an air of sincerity and friendship that I could not refuse; and indeed, as it was impossible to abandon Brulette to the company of strangers, I was obliged to give in to her wishes and Joseph's interests, though eight days seemed to me rather long.

"Thank you, my kind Tiennet," said Brulette, coming out of Thérence's room; "and I thank these good people who have given me such a kind reception; but if I stay, it must be on condition that no expense is incurred for us, and that we shall be allowed to provide for ourselves as we intended to do."

"It shall be just as you like," said Huriel; "for if the fear of being a burden on us drives you away, we would rather renounce the pleasure of serving you. But remember one thing; my father and I both earn money, and nothing gives either of us so much pleasure as to oblige our friends and show them hospitality."

It seemed to me that Huriel was rather fond of jingling his money, as if to say, "I am a good match." However, he immediately acted like a man who sets himself aside, for he told us that he was about to start on a journey.

When she heard that Brulette gave a little quiver, which nobody noticed but me, for she recovered instantly and asked, apparently with indifference, where he was going and for how long.

"I am going to work in the woods of La Roche," he replied; "I shall be near enough to come back if you send for me; Tiennet knows the way. I am going now, in the first instance, to the moor round La Croze to get my mules and their trappings. I will stop as I come back and bid you good-bye."

Thereupon he departed, and the Head-Woodsman, enjoining on his daughter to take good care of us, went off to his work in another direction.

So there we were, Brulette and I, in company of the beautiful Thérence, who, though she waited on us as actively as if we were paying her wages, did not seem inclined to be friendly, and answered shortly, yes or no, to all we said to her. This coolness soon annoyed Brulette, who said to me, when we were alone for a moment, "I think, Tiennet, that this girl is displeased with us. She took me into her bed last night as if she were forced to receive a porcupine. She flung herself on the farther edge with her nose to the wall, and except when she asked if I wanted more bedclothes, she would not say a word to me. I was so tired I would gladly have gone to sleep at once; indeed, seeing that she pretended to sleep, to avoid speaking to me, I pretended too; but I could not close my eyes for a long, long time, for I heard her choking down her sobs. If you will consent, we will not trouble her any longer; we can find plenty of empty huts in the forest, and if not, I could arrange with an old woman I saw here yesterday to send her husband to a neighbor and take us in. If it is only a grass bed I shall be content; it costs too much to sleep on a mattress if tears are to pay for it. As for our meals, I suppose that you can go to Mesples and buy all we want, and I'll take charge of the cooking."

"That's all right, Brulette," I answered, "and I'll do as you say. Look for a lodging for yourself, and don't trouble about me. I am not sugar nor salt any more than the muleteer who slept at your door last night. I'll do for you as he did, without fearing that the dew will melt me. However, listen to this: if we quit the Woodsman's lodge and table in this way he will think we are angry, and as he has treated us too well to have given any cause for it himself, he will see at once that his daughter has rebuffed us. Perhaps he will scold her; and that might not be just. You say the girl did all she could, and was even submissive to you. Now, suppose she has some hidden trouble, have we the right to complain of her silence and her sobs? Would it not be better to take no notice, and to leave her free all day to go and meet her lover, if she has one, and spend our own time with José, for whose sake alone we came here? Are not you rather afraid that if we look for a place to live apart in, people may fancy we have some evil motive?"

"You are right, Tiennet," said Brulette. "Well, I'll have patience with that tall sulky girl, and let her come and go as she likes."

FOURTEENTH EVENING.

The beautiful Thérence had prepared everything for our breakfast, and seeing that the sun was getting up she asked Brulette if she had thought of waking Joseph. "It is time," she said, "and he does not like it if I let him sleep too late, because the next night it keeps him wakeful."

"If you are accustomed to wake him, dear," answered Brulette, "please do so now. I don't know what his habits are."

"No," said Thérence, curtly, "it is your business to take care of him now; that is what you have come for. I shall give up and take a rest, and leave you in charge."

"Poor José!" Brulette could not help exclaiming. "I see he has been a great care to you, and that he had better go back with us to his own country."

Thérence turned her back without replying, and I said to Brulette, "Let us both go and call him. I'll bet he will be glad to hear your voice first."

José's lodge joined that of the Head-Woodsman. As soon as he heard Brulette's voice he came running to the door, crying out: "Ah! I feared I was dreaming, Brulette; then it is really true that you are here?"

When he was seated beside us on the logs he told us that for the first time in many months he had slept all night in one gulp: in fact, we could see it on his face, which was ten sous better than it was the night before. Thérence brought him some chicken-broth in a porringer, and he wanted to give it to Brulette, who refused to take it,—all the more because the black eyes of the girl of the woods blazed with anger at José's offer.

Brulette, who was too shrewd to give any ground for the girl's vexation, declined, saying that she did not like broth and it would be a great pity to waste it upon her, adding, "I see, my lad, that you are cared for like a bourgeois, and that these kind people spare nothing for your comfort and recovery."

"Yes," said José, taking Thérence's hand and joining it in his with that of Brulette, "I have been a great expense to my master (he always called the Woodsman by that title, because he had taught him music). Brulette, I must tell you that I have found another angel upon earth beside you. Just as you helped my mind and consoled my heart when I was half an idiot and well-nigh good for nothing, so she has cared for my poor suffering body when I fell ill with fever here. I can never thank her as I ought for all she has done for me; but I can say one thing—there's not a third like you two; and in the day of recompense the good God will grant his choicest crowns to Catherine Brulet, the rose of Berry, and to Thérence Huriel, the sweet-briar of the woods."

It seemed as if Joseph's gentle words poured a balm into the girl's blood, for Thérence no longer refused to sit down and eat with us; and Joseph sat between the two beauties, while I, profiting by the easy ways I had noticed the night before, walked about as I ate, and sat sometimes near one and sometimes near the other.

I did my best to please the woodland lass with my attentions, and I made it a point of honor to show her that we Berrichons were not bears. She answered my civilities very gently, but I could not make her raise her eyes to mine all the time we were talking. She seemed to me to have an odd temper, quick to take offence and full of distrust. And yet, when she was tranquil, there was something so good in her expression and in her voice that it was impossible to take a bad idea of her. But neither in her good moments nor at any other time did I dare ask her if she remembered that I had carried her in my arms and that she had rewarded me with a kiss. I was very sure it was she, for her father, to whom I had already spoken, had not forgotten the circumstance, and declared he had recalled my face without knowing where he had seen it.

During breakfast Brulette, as she told me afterwards, began to have an inkling of a certain matter, and she at once took it into her head to watch and keep quiet so as to get at the bottom of it.

"Now," said she, "do you suppose I am going to sit all day with my arms folded? Without being a hard worker, I don't say my beads from one meal to another, and I beg of you, Thérence, to give me some work by which I can help you."

"I don't want any help," replied Thérence; "and as for you, you don't need any work to occupy you."

"Why not, my dear?"

"Because you have your friend, and as I should be in the way when you talk with him I shall go away if you wish to stay here, or I shall stay here if you wish to go away."

"That won't please either José or me," said Brulette, rather maliciously. "I have no secrets to tell him; all that we had to say to each other we said yesterday. And now the pleasure we take in each other's company will only be increased if you are with us, and we beg you to stay—unless you have some one you prefer to us."

Thérence seemed undecided, and the way she looked at Joseph showed Brulette that her pride suffered from the fear of being in the way. Whereupon Brulette said to Joseph, "Help me to keep her! You want her, don't you? Didn't you say just now that we were your two guardian angels? Don't you want us to work together for your recovery?"

"You are right, Brulette," said Joseph. "Between two such kind hearts I shall get well quickly; and if you both love me I think each will love me better,—just as we do a task better with a good comrade who gives us his strength and doubles ours."

"And you think it is I," said Thérence, "whom your compatriot needs as a companion? Well, so be it! I'll fetch my work and do it here."

She brought some linen cut out for a shirt, and began to sew. Brulette wanted to help her, and when Thérence refused she said to Joseph, "Then bring me your clothes to mend; they must be in need of it by this time."

Thérence let her look through Joseph's whole wardrobe without saying a word; but there was neither a hole to mend nor a button to sew on, so well had they been cared for; and Brulette talked of buying linen the next day at Mesples to make him some new shirts. Then it appeared that those Thérence was making were for Joseph, and that she wanted to finish them, as she had begun them, all by herself. Suspicion grew stronger and stronger in Brulette's mind, and she pretended to insist on sharing the work; even Joseph was obliged to put in a word, for he thought that Brulette would feel dull if she had nothing to do. On that, Thérence flung down her work angrily, saying to Brulette: "Finish them yourself! I won't touch them, again!" and off she went to sulk in the house.

"José," said Brulette, "that girl is neither capricious nor crazy, as I first thought she was. She is in love with you."

Joseph was so overcome that Brulette saw she had said too much. She did not understand that a sick man, ill in body from the action of his mind, fears reflection.

"Why do you tell me so!" he cried; "what new misfortune is to come upon me?"

"Why is it a misfortune?"

"Do you ask me that, Brulette? Do you think I could ever return her feelings?"

"Well," said Brulette, trying to pacify him, "she will get over it."

"I don't know that people ever get over love," he replied; "but if, through ignorance and want of precaution I have done any harm to the daughter of my master, and Huziel's sister, the virgin of the woods, who has prayed to God for me and watched over my life, I am so guilty that I can never forgive myself."

"Did not you ever think that her friendship might change to love?"

"No, Brulette, never."

"That's curious, José."

"Why so? Have not I been accustomed from my youth up to be pitied for my stupidity and helped in my weakness? Did the friendship you have shown me, Brulette, ever make me vain enough to believe that you—" Here Joseph became as red as fire, and did not say another word.

"You are right," said Brulette, who was prudent and judicious just as Thérence was quick and sensitive. "We can easily make mistakes about the feelings which we give and receive. I had a silly idea about the girl, but if you don't share it there can be nothing in it. Thérence is, no doubt, just as I am, ignorant of what they call true love, and waits the time when the good God will put it into her head to live for the man he has chosen for her."

"All the same," said Joseph, "I wish to leave this part of the country and I ought to."

"We came to take you back," I said, "as soon as you feel strong enough to go."

Contrary to my expectation, he rejected the idea vehemently. "No, no," he said, "I have but one power, and that is my force of will to be a great musician; I want to have my mother with me, and live honored and courted in my own country. If I quit these parts now I shall go to the Upper Bourbonnais till I am admitted into the fraternity of bagpipers."

We dared not tell him that we feared he would never have sound lungs.

Brulette talked to him of other things, while I, much occupied with the revelation she had made about Thérence, and indeed anxious about the girl, who had just left her lodge and plunged into the woods, started in the same direction, with no apparent object, but feeling curious and very desirous of meeting her. It was not very long before I heard the sound of choking sighs, which let me know where she was hiding. No longer feeling shy of her when I knew she was in trouble, I went forward and spoke to her resolutely.

"Thérence," I said, observing that she did not weep, and only quivered and choked with repressed anger, "I think my cousin and I are the cause of your annoyance. Our coming displeases you; or rather, Brulette does, for I myself can claim no attention. We were speaking of you this morning, she and I, and I prevented her from leaving your lodge, where she thought she was a burden to you. Now please say frankly if we are, and we will go elsewhere; for though you may have a low opinion of us, we are none the less right-minded towards you and fearful of causing you annoyance."

The proud girl seemed offended by my frankness; she got up from her seat, for I had placed myself near her.

"Your cousin wants to go, does she?" she said, with a threatening air; "she wants to shame me? No, she shall not do it! or else—"

"Or else what?" I asked, determined to make her confess her feelings.

"Or else I will leave the woods, and my father and family, and go and die in the desert."

She spoke feverishly, with so gloomy an eye and so pale a face, that I was frightened.

"Thérence," I said taking her very kindly by the hand and making her sit down again, "either you were born without a sense of justice or you have some reason for hating Brulette. If so, tell me what it is; for it is possible I could clear her of the blame you put upon her."

"No, you can't clear her, for I know her," cried Thérence, no longer controlling herself. "Don't think that I know nothing about her! I have thought enough and questioned Joseph and my brother enough to be able to judge her conduct and to know what an ungrateful heart and deceitful nature hers is. She is a flirt, that's what she is, your compatriot! and all honest girls ought to hate her."

"That's a hard thing to say," I replied, without seeming troubled. "What do you base it on?"

"Doesn't she know," cried Thérence, "that here are three young men in love with her? and she is tricking all of them,—Joseph, who is dying of it; my brother, who is now avoiding her; and you, who are trying to cure yourself. Do you mean to tell me that she does not know all this; or that she has the slightest preference for any one of you? No; she has no preference for any one; she pities Joseph, she esteems my brother, and she does not love you. Your pangs amuse her, and as she has fifty other lovers in her own village, she pretends she lives for all and not for one. Well, I don't care for you, Tiennet, for I don't know you; but as for my brother, who is so often obliged to be away from us, and goes away now to escape her when he might really stay at home; and as for poor Joseph, who is ill and partly crazy for her—Ah! your Brulette is a guilty creature towards both, and ought to blush for not being able to say a tender word to either of them."

Just then Brulette, who overheard her, came forward. Though quite unaccustomed to be spoken of in that way, she was doubtless well-pleased to know the motive of Huriel's absence, and she seated herself by Thérence and took her hand with a serious air which was half pity and half reproach. Thérence was a little pacified, and said, in a gentler tone:—

"Excuse me, Brulette, if I have pained you; but, indeed, I shall not blame myself, if it brings you to better feelings. Come, admit that your conduct is treacherous and your heart hard. I don't know if it is the custom in your country to let men wish for you when you intend only to refuse them; but I, a poor girl of the woods, think such lies criminal, and I cannot comprehend such behavior. Open your eyes, and see the harm you are doing! I don't say that my brother will break down under it, because he is too strong and too courageous a man, and there are too many girls, worth more than you, who love him, among whom he will make his choice one of these days; but have pity upon poor José, Brulette! You don't know him, though you have been brought up with him. You thought him half an imbecile; on the contrary he has a great genius, but his body is feeble and cannot bear up under the grief you persist in causing him. Give him your heart, for he deserves it; it is I who entreat you, and who will curse you if you kill him."

"Do you really mean what you are saying to me, my poor Thérence?" answered Brulette, looking her straight in the eye. "If you want to know what I think, it is that you love Joseph, and that I cause you, in spite of myself, a bitter jealousy, which leads you to impute this wrong-doing to me. Well, look at the matter as it is; I don't want to make José love me; I never thought of doing so, and I am sorry he does. I even long to help you to cure him of it: and if I had known what you have now let me see, I would never have come here, though your brother did tell me it was necessary that I should do so."

"Brulette," said Thérence. "you must think I have no pride if you suppose that I love Joseph in the way you mean, and that I condescend to be jealous of your charms. I have no need to be ashamed before any one of the sort of love I feel for him. If it were as you suppose, I should at least have sufficient pride not to let you think I would dispute him with you. But my friendship for him is so frank that I dare to protect him openly against your wiles. Love him truly, and, far from being jealous, I will love and respect you; I recognize your rights, which are older than mine, and I will help you to take him back into your own country, on condition that you will choose him for your sole lover and husband. Otherwise, you may expect in me an enemy, who will hold you up to condemnation openly. It shall never be said that I loved the poor lad and nursed him in illness only to see a village flirt kill him before my very eyes."

"Very good," said Brulette, who had recovered all her native pride, "I see more plainly than ever that you are in love with him and jealous; and I feel all the more satisfied to go away and leave him to your care. That your attachment to him is honest and faithful I have no doubt; and I have no reasons, such as you have, to be angry or unjust. Still I do wonder why you should want me to remain and to be your friend. Your sincerity gives way there, and I admit that I should like to know the reason why."

"The reason," replied Thérence, "is one you give yourself, when you use shameful words to humiliate me. You have just said that I am lovesick and jealous: that's how you explain the strength and the kindness of my feeling for Joseph! you will, no doubt, put it into his head, and the young man, who owes me respect and gratitude, will think he has the right to despise me, and ridicule me in his heart."

"There you are right, Thérence," said Brulette, whose heart and mind were both too just not to respect the pride of the woodland girl. "I ought to help you to keep your secret, and I will. I don't say that I will help you to the extent of my power over Joseph; your pride would take offence if I did, and I fully understand that you do not want to receive his regard as a favor from me. But I beg you to be just, to reflect, and even to give me some good advice, which I, who am weaker and more humble than you, ask of you to guide my conscience."

"Ask it; I will listen to you," said Thérence, pacified by Brulette's good sense and submission.

"You must first know," said the latter, "that I have never had any love for Joseph; and if it will help you, I will tell you why."

"Tell me; I want to know!" cried Thérence.

"Well, the reason is," continued Brulette, "that he does not love me as I should wish to be loved. I have known Joseph from a baby; he was never amiable to others until he came to live here; he was so wrapped up in himself that I considered him selfish. I am now willing to believe that if he was so it was not in a bad sense; but after the conversation which he and I had together yesterday I am still convinced that I have a rival in his heart that would soon crush me if I were his. This mistress whom he would surely prefer to his wife—don't deceive yourself, Thérence—is music."

"I have sometimes thought that very thing," replied Thérence, after reflecting a moment, and showing by her soothed manner that she would rather struggle with music for Joseph's heart, than with the pretty Brulette. "Joseph," she added, "is often in a state in which I have sometimes seen my father,—when the pleasure of making music is so great that they are not conscious of anything about them; but my father is always so loving and lovable that I am never jealous of his pleasure."

"Well, then, Thérence," said Brulette, "let us hope he will make Joseph like himself and worthy of you."

"Of me? why of me more than of you? God is my witness that I am not thinking of myself when I work and pray for Joseph. My future troubles me very little, Brulette; I don't understand why people should be thinking of themselves in the friendship they give to others."

"Then," said Brulette, "you are a sort of saint, dear Thérence, and I feel I am not worthy of you; for I do think about myself, and a great deal, too, when I dream of love and happiness. Perhaps you do not love Joseph as I fancied you did; but, however that may be, I ask you to tell me how I had better behave to him. I am not at all sure that if I take all hope away from him the blow would kill him; otherwise you would not see me so easy. But he is ill, that's very true; and I owe him great consideration. Here is where my friendship for him has been loyal and sincere; and I have not been as coquettish as you think for. For if it is true that I have, as you say, fifty lovers in my own village, what advantage or amusement would it be to me to follow the humblest of them all into these woods? I think, on the contrary, that I deserve your good-will for having, as it seemed right to do so, sacrificed without regret my lively friends to bring comfort to a poor fellow who asked for my remembrance."

Thérence, understanding at last that she was wrong, threw herself into Brulette's arms, without making any excuses, but showing plainly by tears and kisses that she was heartily sorry.

They were sitting thus together when Huriel, followed by his mules, preceded by his dogs, and mounted on his little horse, appeared at the end of the path where we were. He came to bid us good-bye; but nothing in his air or manner showed the grief of a man who seeks by flight to cure a hopeless love. He seemed, on the contrary, cheerful and content; and Brulette thought that Thérence had put him on the list of her admirers only to give one reason more, good or bad, for her vexation. She even tried to make him tell the real reason for his departure; and when he pretended that it was pressing business, which Thérence denied, urging him to stay, Brulette, rather piqued at his coolness, reproached him with getting tired of his Berrichon guests. He let himself be teased without making any change in his plans; and this finally affronted Brulette, and led her to say,—

"As I may never see you again, Maître Huriel, don't you think you had better return me the little token which you wear in your ear though it does not belong to you?"

"Yes, but it does," he answered. "It belongs to me as much as my ear belongs to my head, for my sister gave it to me."

"Your sister could not have given you what is either Joseph's or mine."

"My sister made her first communion just as you did, Brulette; and when I returned your jewel to José she gave me hers. Ask her if that isn't true."

Thérence colored high, and Huriel laughed in his beard. Brulette thought to herself that the most deceived of the three was Joseph, who was probably wearing Thérence's silver heart round his neck as a souvenir, while the muleteer was wearing the one she had given him. She was resolved not to allow the fraud, so she said to Thérence: "Dearest, I think the token José wears will bring him happiness, and therefore he ought to keep it; but inasmuch as this one belongs to you, I ask you to get it back from your brother, so as to make me a present which will be extremely precious to me as coming from you."

"I will give you anything else you ask of me," replied Thérence, "and with all my heart too; but this thing does not belong to me. What is given is given, and I don't think that Huriel would be willing to give it back."

"I will do so," said Huriel, quickly, "if Brulette requires it. Do you demand it?" he added, turning to her.

"Yes," said Brulette, who could not back down, though she regretted her whim when she saw the hurt look of the muleteer. He at once opened his earring and took off the token, which he gave to Brulette, saying: "Be it as you please. I should be consoled for the loss of my sister's gift if I could think you would neither give it away nor exchange it."

"The proof that I will do neither," said Brulette, fastening it on Thérence's necklace, "is that I give it to her to keep. And as for you, whose ear is now released of its weight, you do not need any token to enable me to recognize you when you come again into our parts."

"That is very handsome of you to say," replied the muleteer; "but as I only did my duty to Joseph, and as you now know all that you need to know to make him happy, I shall not meddle any further in his affairs. I suppose you will take him home with you, and I shall have no further occasion to visit your country Adieu, therefore, my beautiful Brulette; I foretell all the blessings you deserve, and I leave you now with my family, who will serve you while here and conduct you home whenever you may wish to go."

So saying, off he went, singing:—

> "One mule, two mules, three mules,
> On the mountain, don't you see them?
> Hey, the devil! 'tis the band."

But his voice did not sound as steady as he tried to make it; and Brulette, not feeling happy and wishing to escape the searching eyes of Thérence, returned with us both to find Joseph.

FIFTEENTH EVENING.

I shall not give you the history of all the days that we passed in the forest. They differed little from one another. Joseph grew better and better, and Thérence decided that it was wiser not to destroy his hopes, sharing in Brulette's resolution to prevent him from explaining his feelings. This was not difficult to manage, for Joseph had vowed to himself that he would not declare his sentiments till the moment came when he felt worthy of her notice. Brulette must have made herself very seductive indeed to have dragged a word of love out of him. To make doubly sure, she managed to avoid ever being alone with him; and she kept Thérence so cleverly at her side that the woodland nymph began to understand that she was really not deceiving her and sincerely wished that she should manage the health and the mind of the patient in all things.

These three young people did not weary of each other's company. Thérence sewed for Joseph, and Brulette, having made me buy her a white handkerchief, set about scalloping and embroidering it for Thérence, for she was very clever at such work, and it was really marvellous that a country-girl could do such exquisitely fine stitches. She even declared before Joseph and me that she was tired of sewing and taking care of linen, so as to show that she did not work for him, and to force him to thank Thérence, who was doing it so assiduously. But just see how ungrateful men can be when their minds are all upset by a woman! Joseph hardly looked at Thérence's fingers, employed as they were in his service; his eyes were fixed on Brulette's pretty hands, and you would really have thought that every time she drew her needle he counted each stitch as a moment of happiness.

I wondered how love could fill his mind and occupy his whole time, without his ever dreaming of making any use of his hands. As for me, I tried peeling osier and making baskets, or plaiting rye-straw for hats and bonnets, but for all that, at the end of forty-eight hours I was so eaten up with ennui that I was fairly ill. Sunday is a fine thing, for it brings a rest after six days' toil, but seven Sundays in a week is too much for a man who is accustomed to make use of his limbs. I might not have realized this if either of the girls had bestowed any notice on me; indeed, the beautiful Thérence, with her great eyes somewhat sunken in her head and the black mole at the corner of her mouth, could easily have turned my head if she had wanted to; but she was in no humor to think of anything but her one idea. She talked little and laughed less, and if I tried the slightest joking she looked at me with such an astonished air that I lost all courage to make an explanation.

So, after spending three or four days in fluttering with this tranquil trio round the lodges and sitting with them in various places in the woods, and having convinced myself that Brulette was quite as safe in this country as in our own, I looked about me for something to do, and finally asked the Head-Woodsman to allow me to help him. He received my request very kindly, and I began to get much amusement out of his company, when, unfortunately, I told him I did not want to be paid, and was chopping wood only to get rid of the time; on which his kind heart no longer compelled him to excuse my blunders, and he began to let me see that there never was a more exacting man than he in the matter of work. As his trade was not mine and I did not even know how to use his tools, I provoked him by my awkwardness, and I soon saw that he could scarcely restrain himself from calling me a blockhead and imbecile; for his eyes actually started from his head and the sweat rolled down his face.

Not wishing to quarrel with a man who was so kind and agreeable in other ways, I found employment with the sawyers, and they were satisfied with me. But dear me! I soon learned what a dull thing work is when it is nothing but an exercise for the body, and is not joined to the idea of profit for one's self or others.

Brulette said to me on the fourth day, "Tiennet, I see you are very dull, and I don't deny that I am, too; but to-morrow is Sunday, and we must invent some kind of amusement. I know that the foresters meet in a pretty place, where the Head-Woodsman plays for them to dance. Well, let us buy some wine and provisions and give them a better Sunday than usual, and so do honor to our own country among these strangers."

I did as Brulette told me, and the next day we assembled on a pretty bit of grass with all the forest workmen and several girls and women of the neighborhood, whom Thérence invited for a dance. The Head-Woodsman piped for us. His daughter, superb in her Bourbonnais costume, was much complimented, which made no change in her dignified manner. José, quite intoxicated by the charms of Brulette, who had not forgotten to bring a little finery from home, and who bewitched all eyes with her pretty face and her dainty ways, sat looking on at the dancing. I busied myself in regaling the company with refreshments, and as I wished to do things in good style, I had not spared the money. The feast cost me three good silver crowns out of my own pocket, but I never regretted it, for the company were pleased with my hospitality. Everything went well, and they all said that within the memory of man the woodland folk had never been so well entertained. There was even a mendicant friar, who happened to come along, and who, under pretext of begging for his convent, stuffed his stomach as full and drank as much as any woodchopper of them all. This amused me mightily, though it was at my expense, for it was the first time I had seen a Carmelite drink, and I had always heard tell that in the matter of crooking their elbows they were the best men in Christendom.

I was just re-filling his glass, astonished that I didn't intoxicate him, when the dancers fell into confusion and a great uproar arose. I went out of the little arbor which I had made, and where I received the thirsty crowd, to know what had happened; and there I saw a troop of three or perhaps four hundred mules following a *clairin* which had taken it into its head to go through the assembly, and was being pushed, and kicked, and frightened, till it darted right and left among the people; while the mules, who are obstinate beasts, very strong-boned and accustomed to follow the *clairin*, pressed on through the dancers, caring little for blows and kicks, jostling those in their way, and behaving as if they were in a field of thistles. The animals did not go so fast, laden as they were, but what the people had time to get out of their way. No one was hurt, but some of the lads, excited by dancing and provoked at being interrupted, stamped and shouted so vociferously that the scene was most amusing to behold, and the Head-Woodsman stopped piping to hold his sides with laughter.

Presently, knowing the musical call which collects the mules, and which I knew too, having heard it in the forest of Saint-Chartier, Père Bastien sounded it in the usual manner; and when the *clairin* and his followers trotted up and surrounded the cask on which he was seated, he laughed more than ever to see a troup of black beasts dancing round him instead of the late gala company.

Brulette, however, who escaped from the confusion and took refuge with Joseph and me, seemed terrified, and did not take it as a joke.

"What is the matter?" I said to her. "Perhaps it is friend Huriel who has come back for a dance with you."

"No, no!" she answered. "Thérence, who knows her brother's mules, says there is not one of his in the troop; besides, that's not his horse nor his dog. I am afraid of all muleteers except Huriel, and I wish we could get away from here."

As she spoke, we saw some twenty muleteers coming out of the surrounding forest. They presently called off their beasts and stood round to see the dancing. I reassured Brulette; for in full day and in sight of so many people I knew there was nothing to fear. Only I told her not to go away far from me, and then I returned to the arbor, where I saw the muleteers were about to help themselves without ceremony.

As they shouted out, "To drink! something to drink!" like folks in a tavern, I told them civilly that I did not sell my wine, but that if they asked for it politely I should be happy to give them the loving cup.

"Then it is a wedding?" said the tallest of them, whom I recognized by his fair skin as the leader of those we had met so unluckily in the woods of La Roche.

"Wedding or not," I replied, "it is I who give the feast, and with all my heart to those I please; but—"

He did not leave me time to finish before he answered, "We have no rights here,—you are the master; thank you for your good intentions, but you don't know us, and you had better keep your wine for your friends."

He said a few words to the others in their own dialect and led them to a place apart, where they sat down and ate their own suppers very quietly. The Head-Woodsman went to speak with them, and showed much regard for their leader, named Archignat, who was considered an upright man,—as far as a muleteer can be one.

Among those present were several who could play the bagpipe,—not like Père Bastien, who hadn't his equal in the world, and could make the stones dance and the old oaks curtsey if he liked,—but much better than Carnat and his son. So the bagpipe changed hands until it reached those of the muleteer chief Archignat; while the Head-Woodsman, whose heart and body were still young, went to dance with his daughter, of whom he was just as proud—and with as good right, too—as Père Brulet was of his.

But just as he was calling Brulette to come and be his vis-à-vis, a rascally fellow, coming from I don't know where, endeavored to take her hand. Though it was getting dusk, Brulette recognized him as the man who had threatened us in the woods of La Roche, and had even talked of killing her protectors and burying them under a tree that could tell no tales. Fear and horror made her refuse him quickly and press back against me, who, having exhausted all my provisions, was just going to dance with her.

"The girl promised me this dance," I said to the muleteer, seeing he was determined to get her; "find some one else."

"Very good," he said; "but after this set with you, my turn will come."

"No," said Brulette, hastily, "I would rather never dance again."

"That's what we shall see!" he exclaimed, following us to the dance, where he remained standing behind us, and criticising us, I think, in his own language. Every time Brulette passed him he gave vent to language which, from the expression of his bad eyes, I judged to be insolent.

"Wait till I have finished dancing," I said, punching him as I passed; "I'll settle your bill for you in language your back shall understand."

But when the dance was over I could not find him anywhere, he had hidden himself so carefully. Brulette, seeing what a coward he was, got over her fright and danced with the others, who paid her very pretty respect; but just as I ceased for a moment to watch her, the scoundrel came back and took her from the midst of a number of young girls, forcing her into the middle of the dance, and taking advantage of the darkness which hid her resistance, tried to embrace her. At that moment I ran up, not seeing clearly, but thinking I heard Brulette call me. I had no time to do justice on the man myself, for before his blackened face had touched hers the fellow received such a blow on the nape of his neck that his eyes must have bulged like those of a rat pinned in a trap.

Brulette, thinking the help came from me, threw herself into her defender's arms, and was much amazed to find herself in those of Huriel.

I tried to take advantage of the fact that our friend had his arms full, to seize the scoundrel myself; and I would have paid him all I owed him if the company had not interfered between us. As the man now assailed us with words, calling us cowards because we had attacked him two to one, the music stopped; the crowd gathered about the scene of the quarrel, and the Head-Woodsman came up with Archignat,—one forbidding the muleteers, and the other the woodcutters and sawyers, from taking part in the affair until the meaning of it were known.

Malzac—that was our enemy's name (and he had a tongue as venomous as an adder's)—made his statement first, declaring that he had civilly invited the Berrichon girl to dance; that in kissing her he had only used his right and followed the custom of the dance, and that two of the girl's lovers, to wit, Huriel and I, had unfairly attacked him together and foully struck him.

"That is false," I replied. "It is a lasting regret to me that I did not belabor the man who has just addressed you; but the truth is I arrived too late to touch him in any way, fair or foul; for the people round withheld my arm as I was going to strike. I tell you the thing as it happened; but give me a chance, and I will make true, what he has said!"

"As for me," said Huriel, "I took him by the neck as you would a hare, but without striking him, and it is not my fault if his clothes didn't protect his skin. But I owe him a better lesson, and I came here to-night to find an opportunity to give it. Therefore, I demand of Maître Archignat, my chief, and of Maître Bastien, my father, to be heard at once, or directly after this fête is over, and to receive justice if my claim is recognized as good."

On this the mendicant friar came forward and began to preach peace; but he had too much of the good Bourbon wine in his head to manage his tongue, and he couldn't make himself heard in the uproar.

"Silence!" cried the Head-Woodsman, in a voice that would have drowned the thunder of heaven. "Stand back all of you, and let us manage our own affairs; you can listen if you like, but you have no voice in this chapter. Stand here, muleteers, for Malzac and Huriel. And here stand I, and the men of the forest, as sponsors and judges for this youth of Berry. Speak, Tiennet, and bring your charge. What have you against this muleteer? If it be true that he kissed your compatriot in the dance I know that such is the custom in your part of the country as well as in our own. That is not reason enough even to think of striking a man. Tell us the cause of your anger against him; that is where we must begin."

I did not need urging, and although such an assemblage of muleteers and foresters caused me some embarrassment, I managed to oil my tongue sufficiently to tell, in a proper manner, the story of what happened in the woods of La Roche; and I claimed the testimony of chief Archignat himself, to whom I did justice, even more perhaps than he deserved; but I saw very well that I must not throw any blame on him if I wished to have him favorable to me; and in this way I proved to him that Berrichons are not greater fools than other people, nor any easier to put in the wrong.

The company, who had already formed a good opinion of Brulette and me, blamed Malzac's conduct; but the Head-Woodsman again commanded silence, and addressing Maître Archignat, demanded to know if there were anything false in my statement.

The tall red-haired chief was a shrewd and prudent man. His face was as white as a sheet, and no matter what annoyance he felt, he never seemed to have a drop more or a drop less of blood in his body. His parti-colored eyes were soft and not deceitful in expression; but his mouth, partly hidden by his red beard, smiled every now and then with a silly air which concealed a fund of intelligent malevolence. He did not like Huriel, though he behaved as if he did, and he was generally considered an honest man. In reality, he was the greatest pillager of them all, and his conscience set the interests of his fraternity above every other consideration. They had chosen him chief on account of his cool-bloodedness, which enabled him to act by stratagem and thus save the band from quarrels and legal proceedings, in which indeed he was considered as clever as a lawyer's clerk.

He made no answer to the Head-Woodsman's question,—whether from caution or stupidity it was impossible to say; for the more his attention was roused, the more he looked like a man who was half-asleep and did not hear what was said to him. He merely made a sign to Huriel as if to ask if the testimony he was going to give would agree with his own. But Huriel who, without being sly, was as cautious as he, answered: "Master, you are appealed to as witness by this young man. If it please you to corroborate him, I am not needed to corroborate you; and if you think fit to blame him, the customs of our fraternity forbid me to contradict you. No one here has anything to do with our affairs. If Malzac has been to blame I know beforehand that you will blame him. My affair is a totally different matter. In the dispute we had together before you in the woods of La Roche, the cause of which I am not obliged to reveal, Malzac told me three times that I lied, and he threatened me personally. I don't know if you heard him, but I declare it on my oath; and as I was then insulted and dishonored I now claim the right of battle according to the rules of our order."

Archignat consulted the other muleteers in a low voice, and it appeared that they all sustained Huriel, for they formed a ring, and the chief uttered one word only, "Go!" on which Malzac and Huriel advanced and faced each other.

I tried to put myself forward, declaring it was for me to revenge my cousin, and that my complaint was of more importance than that of Huriel; but Archignat shoved me aside, saying: "If Huriel is beaten, you can come forward; but if Malzac goes down you must be satisfied with what you have seen done."

"The women will retire!" cried the Head-Woodsman, "they are out of place here."

He was pale as he said it, but he did not flinch from the danger his son was about to meet.

"They can retire if they choose," said Thérence, who was pale, too, but quite as firm as he. "I must remain for my brother; he may need me to stanch his blood."

Brulette, more dead than alive, implored Huriel and me not to go on with the quarrel; but it was too late to listen to her. I gave her to Joseph's care, and he took her to a distance, while I laid aside my jacket to be ready to revenge Huriel if he fell.

I had no idea what sort of fight it would be, and I watched it carefully, so as not to be taken unawares when my turn should come. They had lighted two pine torches and had measured, by pacing, the space to which the combatants should be confined. Each was furnished with a holly stick, short and knotted, and the Head-Woodsman assisted Archignat in making these preparations with a calmness which was not in his heart and which it grieved me to see.

Malzac, who was short and thin, was not as strong as Huriel, but he was quicker in his movements and knew better how to fight; for Huriel, though skilful with the stick, was so kindly in temper that he had seldom had occasion to use it. All this passed through my mind during the few moments in which they were feeling each other's strength; and I confess my heart thumped within me, as much from fear for Huriel as from anger against his enemy.

For two or three minutes, which seemed to me hours by the clock, not a blow reached its aim, each being well parried on either side; presently, however, we began to hear that the sticks no longer struck wood, and the muffled sound they made falling on flesh gave me a cold sweat. In our part of the country we never fight under rules except with fists, and I own that my feelings were not hardened enough to stand the idea of split heads and broken jaws. I felt disgust, anger, and pity for the whole thing, and yet I watched with open mouth and eyes to lose nothing of it; for the wind blew the flame of the torches, and sometimes nothing more than a hazy light surrounded the combatants. Suddenly, however, one of the two gave a moan like that of a tree cut in two by a blast of wind, and rolled in the dust.

Which was it? I could not see, for the dazzles were in my eyes, but I heard Thérence exclaim,—

"Thank God, my brother has won!"

I began to see again. Huriel was standing erect, waiting, like a fair fighter, to see if his adversary rose, but not approaching him, for fear of some treachery, of which he knew the man capable.

But Malzac did not rise, and Archignat, forbidding the others to move, called him three times. No answer being given he advanced towards him, saying,—

"Malzac, it is I, don't touch me."

Malzac appeared to have no desire to do so,—he lay as still as a stone; and the chief stooping over him, touched him, looked at him, and then called two of the muleteers by name and said to them:—

"The game is up with him; do what there is to do."

They immediately took him by the feet and head and disappeared at full speed in the forest, followed by the other muleteers, who prevented all who did not belong to their fraternity from making any inquiry as to the result of the affair. Maître Archignat was the last to go, after saying a word to the Head-Woodsman, who replied,—

"That's enough; adieu."

Thérence had fastened on her brother, and was wiping the perspiration from his face with a handkerchief, asking him if he was wounded, and trying to detain him and examine him. But he, too, whispered in her ear, and she at once replied,—

"Yes, yes—adieu!"

Huriel then took Archignat's arm, and the pair disappeared in the darkness; for, as they went, they knocked over the torches, and I felt for a moment as if I were in the act of waking out of an ugly dream, full of lights and noises, into the silence and thick darkness of the night.

SIXTEENTH EVENING.

However, I began to see clearly, little by little, and my feet, whose soles had seemed pegged to the ground, followed the Head-Woodsman in the direction of the lodges. I was much surprised to find that there was no one there but his daughter, Brulette, Joseph, and three or four old men who had been at the fight. All the others, it appeared, had run away when they saw the sticks produced, to avoid giving witness in a court of justice if the matter ended fatally. These woodland people never betray each other, and to escape being summoned and harassed by the law, they manage so as to see nothing and have nothing to say. The Head-Woodsman spoke to the old men in their own language, and I saw them go back to the place where the fight occurred, without understanding what they intended to do there. Meantime I followed Joseph and the women, and we reached the lodges without saying a word to each other.

As for me, I had been so shaken in mind that I did not want to talk. When we entered the lodge and sat down we were all as white as if we were afraid. The Head-Woodsman, who soon joined us, sat down too, evidently in deep thought, with his eyes fixed to the earth. Brulette, who had compelled herself not to ask questions, was crying in a corner; Joseph, as if worn out with fatigue, had thrown himself at full length on a pile of dried ferns; Thérence alone came and went, and prepared the beds for the night; but her teeth were set, and when she tried to speak she stammered.

After a while the Head-Woodsman rose and looking round upon us said: "Well, my children, after all, what is it? A lesson has been given, and justly given, to a bad man, known everywhere for his evil conduct,—a man who abandoned his wife and let her die of grief and poverty. Malzac has long disgraced the fraternity of muleteers, and if he were to die no one would regret him. Must we make ourselves unhappy because Huriel gave him a few hard blows in honest battle? Why do you cry, Brulette? Have you such a soft heart that you are shedding tears for the beaten man? Do you not think that my son was right to defend your honor and his own? He had told me all that happened in the woods of La Roche, and I knew that out of prudent regard for your safety he refrained from punishing that man at the time. He even hoped that Tiennet would have said nothing about it to-night, so that the cause might never be known. But I, who never approve of concealing the truth, allowed Tiennet to say what he liked. I am well-pleased that he was prevented from entering a fight which is most dangerous for those who do not understand the passes. I am also well-pleased that victory was with my son; for as between an honest man and a bad man, my heart would have gone with the honest man even if he were not blood of my blood and flesh of my flesh. And so let us thank God, who judged the right, and ask him to be ever with us, in this and in all things."

The Head-Woodsman knelt down and offered the evening prayer; which comforted and tranquillized every one of us. Then we separated in hearty friendship to seek some rest.

It was not long before I heard the Head-Woodsman, whose little chamber I shared, snoring loudly, in spite of the anxiety he had undergone. But in his daughter's room Brulette was still crying, unable to recover herself, and evidently ill. I heard her talking to Thérence, and so, not from curiosity but out of pity for her trouble, I put my ear to the partition to hear what I could.

"Come, come," Thérence was saying, in decided tones, "stop crying and you will go to sleep. Tears won't do any good, and, as I told you, I must go; if you wake my father, who does not know he is wounded, he will want to go too, and that may compromise him in this bad business; whereas for me, I risk nothing."

"You terrify me, Thérence; how can you go alone among those muleteers? They frighten me badly enough, but you must let me go with you; I ought to, for I was the cause of the fight. Let us call Tiennet—"

"No, no! neither you nor him! The muleteers won't regret Malzac if he should die,—quite the reverse; but if he had been injured by any one not belonging to their own body, especially a stranger, your friend Tiennet would be in the greatest danger. Let him sleep; it is enough that he tried to meddle in the affair to make it important that he should keep quiet now. As for you, Brulette, you would be very ill-received; you have not, as I have, a family interest to take you there. No one among them would attempt to injure me; they all know me, and they are not afraid to let me into their secrets."

"But do you think you will still find them in the forest? Did not your father say they were going to the uplands, and would not spend the night in this neighborhood?"

"They must wait long enough to dress the wounds. But if I do not find them I shall be all the more easy; for it will prove that my brother is not seriously hurt, and that he could start with them at once."

"Did you see his wound? tell me, dear Thérence, don't hide anything from me."

"I did not see it,—no one saw it; he said he was not hurt, and did not even think of himself. But see, Brulette,—only don't cry out,—here is the handkerchief with which, as I thought, I wiped the perspiration from his face. When I got back here I found it was saturated with blood; and I had to gather all my courage to hide my feelings from my father, who is very anxious, and from Joseph, who is really ill."

Then came silence, as if Brulette, taking or gazing at the handkerchief, was choking. Presently Thérence said: "Give it back to me; I must wash it in the first brook I come to."

"Ah, no!" said Brulette, "let me keep it; I'll hide it safely."

"No, my dear," replied Thérence; "if the authorities get wind of the battle they will come and rummage every place here,—they will even search our persons. They have grown very annoying of late; they want us to give up our old customs, which are dying out of themselves, without their meddling in the matter."

"Alas!" said Brulette, "isn't it to be wished that the custom of these dangerous fights should be given up?"

"Yes, but that depends on many things which the officers of the law cannot or will not do. For instance, they ought to do justice, and that they never do except to those who have the means to pay for it. Is it different in your parts? You don't know? well, I will bet it is the same thing there. Only, the Berrichon blood is sluggish, and your people are patient under the wrongs done them, and so they don't expose themselves to worse. Here it is not so. A man who lives in the forest could not live at all if he did not defend himself against bad men as he would against wolves and other dangerous beasts. Surely you don't blame my brother for having demanded justice of his own people for an insult and a threat he was made to endure before you? Perhaps you are slightly to blame in the matter; think of that, Brulette, before you blame him. If you had not shown such anger and fear at the insults of that muleteer he might have overlooked those to himself, for there never was a gentler man than Huriel or one more ready to forgive; but you held yourself insulted, Huriel promised you reparation, and he kept his word. I am not reproaching you, nor him either; I might have been just as sensitive as you, and as for him, he only did his duty."

"No, no!" said Brulette, beginning to cry again; "He ought not to have exposed himself for me, and I was very wrong to show such pride. I shall never forgive myself if any harm, no matter what, comes to him; and you and your father, who have been so good to me, can never forgive me either."

"Don't fret about that," replied Thérence. "Whatever happens is God's will, and you will never be blamed by us. I know you now, Brulette; I know that you deserve respect. Come, dry your eyes and go to sleep. I hope I shall bring you back good news, and I am certain my brother will be consoled and half-cured if you will let me tell him how sorry you are for his wound."

"I think," said Brulette, "that he will think more of your regard, for there is no woman in the world he could ever love like his own good and brave sister. And, Thérence, that is why I am sorry I made you ask him for that token, and if he had a fancy to have it back, I dare say you would give it to him."

"That's right, Brulette," cried Thérence; "I kiss you for those words. Sleep in peace, I am off."

"I shall not sleep," replied Brulette; "I shall pray to God to help you till I see you safe back again."

I heard Thérence softly leave the lodge, and a minute later I also went out. I could not bring my conscience to allow a beautiful girl to expose herself all alone to the dangers of the night; nor could I, out of fear for myself, withhold what power I had to give her assistance. The people she was going to seek did not seem to me such gentle and good Christians as she made them out to be, and besides, perhaps they were not the only ones in the wood that night. Our dance had attracted beggars, and we know that folks who ask charity don't always show it to others when occasion offers. Moreover,—and I am sure I don't know why,—the red and shining face of the Carmelite friar, who had paid such attention to my wine, kept coming into my head. He struck me as not lowering his eyes very much when he passed near the girls, and I hadn't noticed what became of him in the general hullaballoo.

But Thérence had declared to Brulette that she did not want my company in her search for the muleteers; so, not wishing to displease her, I determined not to let her see me, and to follow her only within hearing, in case she had occasion to cry for help. Accordingly, I let her get about a minute in advance, not more, though I would have liked to stay and tranquillize Brulette by telling her my plan. I was, however, afraid to delay and so lose the trail of the woodland beauty.

I saw her cross the open and enter a copse which sloped toward the bed of a brook, not far from the lodges. I entered after her, by the same path, and as there were numerous turns, I soon lost sight of her; but I heard the sound of her light step, which every now and then broke a dead branch, or rolled a pebble. She seemed to be walking rapidly, and I did the same, to prevent her getting too far in advance of me. Two or three times I thought I was so near her that I slackened my pace in order that she might not see me. We came thus to one of the roads which lead through the woods; but the shadow of the tall trees was so dense that I, looking from right to left, was unable to see anything that indicated which way she had gone.

I listened, ear to earth, and I heard in the path, which continued across the road, the same breaking of branches which had already guided me. I hastened forward till I reached another road which led down to the brook; there I began to fear I had lost trace of her, for the brook was wide and the bank muddy, and I saw no sign of footsteps. There is nothing so deceiving as the paths of a wood. In some places the trees stand so that one fancies there must be a path; or perhaps wild animals going to water have beaten out a track; and then all of a sudden we find ourselves tangled in underbrush, or sinking in such a bog that it is useless trying to go further.

However, I persisted, because I still heard the noise before me, and it was so distinct that finally I began to run, tearing my clothes in the brambles, and plunging deeper and deeper into the thicket, when suddenly a savage growl let me know that the creature I was pursuing was a boar, which was beginning to be annoyed by my company, and wished to show that he had had enough of it. Having no weapon but a stick, and not knowing how to deal with that kind of beast, I turned round and retraced my steps, rather uneasy lest the boar should take it into his head to accompany me. Fortunately, he did not think of it, and I returned as far as the first road, where by mere chance I took the direction which led to the entrance of the woods of Chambérat, where we had held the fête.

Though baffled, I did not choose to renounce my search; for Thérence might meet some wild beast, as I had, and I didn't believe she knew any language that that kind of enemy would listen to. I already knew enough of the forest not to get lost for any length of time, and I soon reached the place where we had danced. It took me a few moments to be certain that it was the same open, for I expected to find my arbor, with the utensils which I had not had time to carry away; but the place where I left it was as smooth as if it had never been there. Nevertheless, searching carefully, I found the holes where I had driven in the stakes, and the place where the feet of the dancers had worn off the turf.

I wanted to find the spot where the muleteers had disappeared leading Huriel and carrying Malzac, but try as I would, I had been so confused in mind just then that I could not recall it. So I was forced to advance haphazard, and I marched in that way all night,—weary enough, as you may suppose, stopping often to listen, and hearing nothing but the owls hooting in the branches, or some poor hare who was more afraid of me than I of him.

Though the Chambérat wood was really at that time joined to those of Alleu, I did not know it, having only entered it once since coming to that part of the country. I soon got lost; which did not trouble me, however, because I knew that neither wood was extensive enough to reach to Rome. Besides, the Head-Woodsman had already taught me to take my bearings, not by the stars, which are not always to be seen in a forest, but by the bend of the leading branches, which, in our midland provinces, are lashed by north-westerly winds and lean permanently toward the east.

The night was very clear, and so warm that if I had not been goaded by worry of mind and fatigued in body, I should have enjoyed the walk. It was not moonlight, but the stars shone in a cloudless sky, and I saw my way quite plainly even under the foliage. I was much improved in courage since the time when I was so frightened in the little forest of Saint-Chartier; for, although I knew I was going wrong, I felt as easy as if on our own roads, and when I saw that the animals ran away from me, I had no anxiety at all. I began to see how it was that these covered glades, these brooks murmuring in the ravines, the soft herbage, the sandy paths, and the trees of splendid growth and lofty pride made this region dear to those who belonged to it. There were certain large wild-flowers the name of which I did not know, something like a foxglove, white with yellow spots, the perfume of which was so keen and delicious that I could almost have fancied myself in a garden.

Keeping steadily toward the west, I struck the heath and skirted the edge of it, listening and looking about me. But I saw no signs of human beings, and about daybreak I began to return toward the lodges without finding Thérence or anybody else. I had had enough of it, and seeing that I could not make myself useful, I tried a short cut through the woods, where, in a very wild place, beneath a large oak, I saw something which seemed to me a person. Day was beginning to light up the bushes, and I walked noiselessly forward till I recognized the brown garment of the Carmelite friar. The poor man, whom in my heart I had suspected, was virtuously and devoutly on his knees, saying his prayers without thought of evil.

I coughed as I approached, to let him know I was there and not to frighten him; but there was no need of that, for the monk was a worthy soul who feared none but God,—neither devil nor man. He raised his head and looked at me without surprise; then burying his face in his cowl he went on muttering his orisons, and I could see nothing but the end of his beard, which jerked up and down as he spoke, like that of a goat munching salt.

When he seemed to have finished, I bade him good-morning, hoping to get some news out of him, but he made me a sign to hold my tongue; then he rose, picked up his wallet, looked carefully at the place where he had been kneeling, and with his bare feet poked up the grass and levelled the sand he had disturbed; after which he led me to a little distance, and said in a muffled voice:—

"Inasmuch as you know all about it, I am not sorry to talk to you before I go on my way."

Finding he was inclined to talk, I took care not to question him, which might have made him mistrustful; but just as he was opening his mouth to speak, Huriel appeared, and seemed so surprised and even annoyed to see me that I was greatly embarrassed, as if I had in some way done wrong.

I must also remark that Huriel would probably have frightened me if I had met him alone in the gloom of the morning. He was more daubed with black than I had ever seen him, and a cloth bound round his head hid his hair and his forehead, so that all one saw of his face was his big eyes, which seemed sunken and as if they had lost their usual fire. In fact, he looked like his own spirit rather than his own body, and he glided gently upon the heather as if he feared to awaken even the crickets and the gnats which were asleep in it.

The monk was the first to speak; not as a man who accosts another, but as one who continues a conversation after a break in it.

"As he is here," he said, pointing to me, "it is best to give him some useful instructions, and I was on the point of telling him—"

"As you have told him everything—" began Huriel, cutting him short with a reproachful look.

Here I, in turn, interrupted Huriel to tell him I knew nothing as yet, and that he was free to conceal what he was just going to say.

"That's all right in you," replied Huriel, "not to seek to know more than you need; but if this is the way, Brother Nicolas, that you keep a secret of such importance, I am sorry I ever trusted you."

"Fear nothing," said the Carmelite. "I thought the young man was compromised with you."

"He is not compromised at all, thank God!" said Huriel; "one is enough!"

"So much the better for him if he only sinned by intention," replied the monk. "He is your friend, and you have nothing to fear. But as for me,

I should be glad if he would tell no one that I passed the night in these woods."

"What harm could that do you?" asked Huriel. "A muleteer met with an accident; you succored him, and thanks to you, he will soon be well. Who can blame you for that charity?"

"True, true," said the monk. "Keep the phial and use the stuff twice a day. Wash the wound carefully in running water as often as you can do so; don't let the hair stick in the wound, and keep it covered from dust; that is all that is necessary. If you have any fever get yourself well bled by the first friar you meet."

"Thank you," said Huriel, "but I have lost enough blood as it is, and I think we can never have too much. May you be rewarded, my brother, for your kind help, which I did not greatly need, but for which I am none the less grateful. And now permit us to say good-bye, for it is daylight and your prayers have detained you here too long."

"No doubt," answered the monk, "but will you let me depart without a word of confession? I have cured your flesh,—that was the first thing to be done; but is your conscience in any better state? Do you think you have no need of absolution, which is to the soul what that balsam is to the body?"

"I have great need of it, my father," said Huriel, "but you would do wrong to give it to me; I am not worthy to receive it until I have done penance. As to my confession, you do not need to hear it, for you saw me commit a mortal sin. Pray God for me; that is what I ask of you, and see that many masses are said for the soul of—those who let anger get the better of them."

I thought at first he was joking; but I knew better when I saw the money he gave to the friar, and heard the sad tone of his last words.

"Be sure you shall receive according to your generosity," said the friar putting the money in his wallet. Then he added, in a tone in which there was nothing hypocritical: "Maître Huriel, we are all sinners and there is but one just judge. He alone, who has never sinned, has the right to condemn or to absolve the faults of men. Commit yourself to him, and be sure that whatever there is to your credit he will in his mercy place to your account. As for the judges of earth, very foolish and very cowardly would he be who would send you before them, for they are weak or hardened creatures. Repent, for you have cause to, but do not betray yourself; and when you feel that grace is calling you to a confession of repentance go to some good priest, though he may only be a poor barefooted Carmelite like Brother Nicolas. And you, my son," added the good man, who felt in a preaching mood and wanted to sprinkle me too with his holy water, "learn to moderate your appetites and conquer your passions. Avoid occasions for sin; flee from quarrels and bloody encounters—"

"That will do, that will do, Brother Nicolas," interrupted Huriel. "You are preaching to a believer, you need not call a man with pure hands to repentance. Farewell. Go, I tell you; it is high time."

The monk departed, after shaking hands with us kindly and with a great air of frankness. When he had got to a distance Huriel, taking me by the arm, led me back to the tree where I had found the monk in prayer.

"Tiennet," he said, "I have no distrust of you, and if I compelled the good friar to hold his tongue it was only to make him cautious. However, there is no danger from him. He is own uncle to our chief Archignat, and he is, moreover, a safe man, always on good terms with the muleteers, who often help him to carry the provisions he collects from one place to another. But though I am not afraid of you or of him, it does not follow that I should tell you what you have no need to know, unless you make it a test of my friendship."

"You shall do as you like," I answered. "If it is useful for you that I should know the results of your fight with Malzac, tell me, even though I may deeply regret to hear them; if not, I would just as soon not know what has become of him."

"What has become of him!" echoed Huriel, whose voice was choked by some great distress. He stopped me when we reached the first branches which the oak stretched toward us, as if he feared to tread upon a spot where I saw no trace of what I was beginning to guess. Then he added, casting a look black with gloom before him, and speaking as if something were forcing him to betray himself: "Tiennet, do you remember the threatening words that man said to us in the woods of La Roche?—'There is no lack of ditches in the forest to bury fools in, and the stones and the trees have no tongues to tell what they see.'"

"Yes," I answered, feeling a cold sweat creeping over my whole body. "It seems that evil words tempt fate, and bring disaster to those who say them."

SEVENTEENTH EVENING.

Huriel crossed himself and sighed. I did as he did, and then turning from the accursed tree we went our way.

I wished, as the friar did, to say a few comforting words to him, for I saw that his mind was troubled; but, besides being a poor hand at moralizing, I felt guilty myself after a fashion. I knew, for instance, that if I had not related aloud the affair that happened in the woods of La Roche, Huriel might not have remembered his promise to Brulette to avenge her; and that if I had not been in such a hurry to be the first to defend her in presence of the muleteers and the foresters, Huriel would not have been so eager to get that honor before me in her eyes.

Worried by these thoughts, I could not help telling them to Huriel and blaming myself to him, just as Brulette had blamed herself to Thérence.

"My dear friend Tiennet," replied the muleteer, "you are a good fellow with a good heart. Don't trouble your conscience for a thing which God, in the day of judgment, will not lay at your door, perhaps not at mine. Brother Nicolas is right, God is the only judge who renders just judgment, for he alone knows things as they are. He needs no witnesses and makes no inquiry into the truth. He reads all hearts; he knows that mine has never sworn nor sought the death of a man, even at the moment when I took that stick to punish the evil-doer. Those weapons are bad, but they are the only ones which our customs allow us to use in such cases, and I am not responsible for their use. Certainly a fight with fists alone would be far better,—such as you and I had that night in your field, all about my mules and your oats. But let me tell you that a muleteer is bound to be as brave and jealous for his honor as any of the great lords who bear the sword. If I had swallowed Malzac's insults without demanding reparation I should deserve to be expelled from our fraternity. It is true that I did not demand it coolly, as I ought to have done. I had met Malzac alone that morning, in that same wood of La Roche, where I was quietly at work without thinking of him. He again annoyed me with foolish language, declaring that Brulette was nothing better than a dried-wood picker, which means, with us, a ghost that walks by night,—a superstition which often helps girls of bad lives to escape recognition, for good people are afraid of these ghosts. So, among muleteers, who are not as credulous, the term is very insulting. Nevertheless, I bore with him as long as possible, until at last, driven to extremities, I threatened him in order to drive him away. He replied that I was a coward, capable of attacking him in a lonely place, but that I dared not challenge him to open fight with sticks before witnesses; that everybody knew I had never had occasion to show my courage, for when I was in company of others I always agreed with what they said so as not to be obliged to measure swords with them. Then he left me, saying there was a dance in the woods of Chambérat, and that Brulette gave a supper to the company; for which she had ample means, as she was the mistress of a rich tradesman in her own country; and, for his part, he should go and amuse himself by courting the girl, in defiance of me if I had courage to go and see him do it. You know, Tiennet, that I intended never to see Brulette again, and that for reasons which I will tell you later."

"I know them," said I; "and I see that your sister met you to-night; for here, hanging to your ear below the bandage, is a token which proves something I had strongly suspected."

"If it is that I love Brulette and value her token," replied Huriel, "you know all that I know myself; but you cannot know more, for I am not even sure of her friendship, and as for anything else—but that's neither here nor there. I want to tell you the ill-luck that brought me back here. I did not wish Brulette to see me, neither did I mean to speak to her, because I saw the misery Joseph endured on my account. But I knew Joseph had not the strength to protect her, and that Malzac was shrewd and tricky enough to escape you. So I came at the beginning of the dance, and kept out of sight under the trees, meaning to depart without being seen, if Malzac did not make his appearance. You know the rest until the moment when we took the sticks. At that moment I was angry, I confess it, but it couldn't have been otherwise unless I were a saint in Paradise. And yet my only thought was to give a lesson to my enemy, and to stop him from saying, especially while Brulette was here, that because I was gentle and patient I was timid as a hare. You saw that my father, sick of such talk, did not object to my proving myself a man; but there! ill-luck surely pursues me, when in my first fight and almost at my first blow—ah! Tiennet, there is no use saying I was driven into it, or that I feel within me kind and humane; that is no consolation for having a fatal hand. A man is a man, no matter how foul-mouthed and ill-behaved he be. There was little or no good in that one, but he might have mended, and I have sent him to his account before he had come to repentance. Tiennet, I am sick of a muleteer's life; I agree with Brulette that it is not easy for a God-fearing man to be one of them and maintain his own conscience and the respect of others. I am obliged to stay in the craft for some time longer, owing to engagements which I have made; but you may rely upon it, I shall give up the business as soon as possible, and find another that is quiet and decent."

"That is what you want me to tell Brulette, isn't it?" I said.

"No," replied Huriel, with much decision, "not unless Joseph gets over his love and his illness so entirely as to give her up. I love Joseph as much as you all love him; besides, he told me his secret, and asked my advice and support; I will not deceive him, nor undermine him."

"But Brulette does not want him as a lover or a husband, and perhaps he had better know it as soon as possible. I'll take upon myself to reason with him, if the others dare not, for there is somebody in your house who could make Joseph happy, and he never could be happy with Brulette. The longer he waits and the more he flatters himself she will love him, the harder the blow will seem; instead of which, if he opens his eyes to the true attachment he might find elsewhere—"

"Never mind that," said Huriel, frowning slightly, which made him look like a man who was suffering from a great hole in his head, which in fact there was under the bloody handkerchief. "All things are in God's hand, and in our family nobody is in a hurry to make his own happiness at the expense of others. As for me, I must go, for I could make no lying answer to those who might ask me where Malzac is and why no one sees him any more. Listen, however, to another thing about Joseph and Brulette. It is better not to tell them the evil I have done. Except the muleteers, and my father and sister, the monk and you, no one knows that when that man fell he never rose again. I had only time to say to Thérence, 'He is dead, I must leave these parts.' Maître Archignat said the same thing to my father; but the other foresters know nothing, and wish not to know anything. The monk himself would have seen only part of it if he had not followed us with remedies for the wound. The muleteers were inclined to send him back at once, but the chief answered for him, and I, though I might be risking my neck, could not endure that the man should be buried like a dog, without Christian prayer. The future is in God's hands. You understand, of course, that a man involved as I am in a bad business cannot, at least for a long time, think of courting a girl as much sought after and respected as Brulette. But I do ask you, for my sake, not to tell her the extent of the trouble I am in. I am willing she should forget me, but not that she should hate or fear me."

"She has no right to do either," I replied, "since it was for love of her—"

"Ah!" exclaimed Huriel, sighing and passing his hand before his eyes, "it is a love that costs me dear!"

"Come, come," I said, "courage! she shall know nothing; you may rely upon my word; and all that I can do, if occasion offers to make her see your merits, shall be done faithfully."

"Gently, gently, Tiennet," returned Huriel, "I don't ask you to take my side as I take Joseph's. You don t know me as well, neither do you owe me the same friendship; I know what it is to push another into the place we would like to occupy. You care for Brulette yourself; and among three lovers, as we are, two must be just and reasonable when the third is preferred. But, whatever happens, I hope we shall all three remain brothers and friends."

"Take me out of the list of suitors," I said, smiling without the least vexation. "I have always been the least ardent of Brulette's lovers, and now I am as calm as if I had never dreamed of loving her. I know what is in the secret heart of the girl; she has made a good choice, and I am satisfied. Adieu, my Huriel; may the good God help you, and give you hope, and so enable you to forget the troubles of this bad night."

We clasped each other for good-bye, and I inquired where he was going.

"To the mountains of the Forez," he replied. "Write to me at the village of Huriel, which is my birth-place and where we have relations. They will send me your letters."

"But can you travel so far with that wound in your head? Isn't it dangerous?"

"Oh no!" he said, "it is nothing. I wish *the other's* head had been as hard as mine!"

When I was alone I began to think over with amazement all that must have happened that night in the forest without my hearing or detecting the slightest thing. I was still more surprised when, passing once more, in broad daylight, the spot where the dance had taken place, I saw that since midnight persons had returned to mow the grass and dig over the ground to remove all trace of what had happened. In short, from one direction persons had come twice to make things safe at this particular point; from the other, Thérence had contrived to communicate with her brother; and, besides all this, a burial had been performed, without the faintest appearance or the lightest sound having warned me of what was taking place, although the night was clear and I had gone from end to end of the silent woods looking and listening with the utmost attention. It turned my mind to the difference between the habits, and indeed the characters, of these woodland people and the laborers of the open country. On the plains, good and evil are too clearly seen not to make the inhabitants from their youth up submit to the laws and behave with prudence. But in the forests, where the eyes of their fellows can be escaped, men invoke no justice but that of God or the devil, according as they are well or ill intentioned.

When I reached the lodges the sun was up; the Head-Woodsman had gone to his work; Joseph was still asleep; Thérence and Brulette were talking together under the shed. They asked me why I had got up so early, and I noticed that Thérence was uneasy lest I had seen or heard something. I behaved as if I knew nothing, and had not gone further than the adjoining wood.

Joseph soon joined us, and I remarked that he looked much better than when we arrived.

"Yet I have hardly slept all night," he replied; "I was restless till nearly day-break; but I think the reason was that the fever which has weakened me so much left me last evening, for I feel stronger and more vigorous than I have been for a long time."

Thérence, who understood fevers, felt his pulse, and then her face, which looked very tired and depressed, brightened suddenly.

"See!" she cried; "the good God sends us at least one happiness; here is our patient on the road to recovery! The fever has gone, and his blood is already recovering strength."

"If you want to know what I have felt this night," said Joseph, "you must promise not to call it a dream; but here it is—In the first place, however, tell me if Huriel got off without a wound, and if the other did not get more than he wanted. Have you had any news from the forest of Chambérat?"

"Yes, yes," replied Thérence, hastily. "They have both gone to the upper country. Say what you were going to say."

"I don't know if you will comprehend it, you two," resumed Joseph, addressing the girls, "but Tiennet will. When I saw Huriel fight so resolutely my knees gave way under me, and, feeling weaker than any woman, I came near losing consciousness; but at the very moment when my body was giving way my heart grew hot within me, and my eyes never ceased to look at the fight. When Huriel struck the fellow down and remained standing himself, I could have shouted 'Victory!' like a drunken man, if I had not restrained myself; I would have rushed if I could to embrace him. But the impulse was soon gone, and when I got back here I felt as though I had received and given every blow, and as if all the bones in my body were broken."

"Don't think any more about it," said Thérence; "it was a horrid thing to see and recollect. I dare say it gave you bad dreams last night."

"I did not dream at all," said Joseph; "I lay thinking, and little by little I felt my mind awakened and my body healed, as if the time had come to take up my bed and walk, like the paralytic of the Gospels. I saw Huriel before me, shining with light; he blamed my illness, and declared it was a cowardice of the mind. He seemed to say: 'I am a man, you are a child; you shake with fever while my blood is fire. You are good for nothing, but I am good in all ways, for others and for myself. Come, listen to this music.' And I heard an air muttering like a storm, which raised me in my bed as the wind lifts the fallen leaves. Ah, Brulette, I think I have done with being ill and cowardly; I can go now to my own country and kiss my mother, and make my plans to start,—for start I must, upon a journey; I must see and learn, and make myself what I should be."

"You wish to travel?" said Thérence, her face, so lately lighted like a star with pleasure, growing white and cloudy as an autumn moon. "You think to find a better teacher than my father, and better friends than people here? Go and see your mother, that is right, if you are strong enough to go,—unless, indeed, you are deceiving us and longing to die in distant parts—"

Grief and displeasure choked her voice. Joseph, who watched her, suddenly changed both his language and his manner.

"Never mind what I have been dreaming this morning, Thérence," he said; "I shall never find a better master or better friends. You asked me to tell my dreams, and I did tell them, that is all. When I am cured I shall ask advice of all three of you, and of your father also. Till then pay no attention to what comes into my head; let us be happy for the time that we are together."

Thérence was pacified; but Brulette and I, who knew how dogged and obstinate Joseph could be under his gentle manner, and remembered how he had left us without allowing us a chance to remonstrate or persuade him, felt sure that his mind was already fully made up, and that no one could change it.

During the next two days I once more felt dreadfully dull; and so did Brulette, though she amused herself by finishing the embroidery she wanted to give Thérence, and spent some hours in the woods with Père Bastien, partly to leave Joseph to the care of Thérence, and partly to talk of Huriel and comfort the worthy man for the danger and distress the fight had caused him. The Head-Woodsman, touched by the friendship which she showed him, told her the truth about Malzac, and, far from her blaming Huriel, as the latter had feared, it only drew her closer to him through the gratitude which she now felt she owed him.

On the sixth day we began to talk of separating. Joseph was getting better hourly; he worked a little, and did his best in every way to recover his strength. He had decided to go with us and spend a few days at home, saying that he should return almost immediately to the woods of Alleu,— which Brulette and I doubted, and so did Thérence, who was almost as uneasy about his health as she had been about his illness. I don't know if it was she who persuaded her father to accompany us half-way, or whether the notion came into Père Bastien's own mind; at any rate, he made us the offer, which Brulette instantly accepted. Joseph was only half pleased at this, though he tried not to show it.

The little trip naturally diverted the Head-Woodsman's thoughts from his anxieties, and while making his preparations the evening before our departure he recovered much of his natural fine spirits. The muleteers had left the neighborhood without hindrance, and nothing had been said about Malzac, who had neither relations nor friends to inquire for him. A year or two might go by before the authorities troubled themselves to know what had become of him, and indeed, they might never do so; for in those days there was no great policing in France, and a man might disappear without any notice being taken of it. Moreover, the Head-Woodsman and his family would leave those parts at the end of the chopping season, and as father and son never stayed six months in the same place, the law would be very clever indeed to know where to catch them.

For these reasons the Head-Woodsman, who had feared only the first results of the affair, finding that no one got wind of the secret, grew easy in mind and so restored our courage.

On the morning of the eighth day he put us all into a little cart he had borrowed, together with a horse, from a friend of his in the forest, and taking the reins he drove us by the longest but safest road to Saint-Sevère, where we were to part from him and his daughter.

Brulette inwardly regretted returning by a new way, where she could not revisit any of the scenes she had passed through with Huriel. As for me, I was glad to travel and to see Saint-Pallais in Bourbonnais and Préveranges, two little villages on the heights, also Saint-Prejet and Pérassay, other villages lower down along the banks of the Indre; moreover, as we followed that river from its source and I remembered that it ran through our village I no longer felt myself a stranger in a strange land. When we reached Saint-Sevère, I felt at home, for it is only six leagues from our place, and I had already been there two or three times. While the rest were bidding each other farewell, I went to hire a conveyance to take us to Nohant, but I could only find one for the next day as early as I wanted it.

When I returned and reported the fact, Joseph seemed annoyed. "What do we want with a conveyance?" he said. "Can't we start in the fresh of the morning on foot and get home in the cool of the evening? Brulette has walked that distance often enough to dance at some assembly, and I feel able to do as much as she."

Thérence remarked that so long a walk might bring back his fever, and that only made him more obstinate; but Brulette, seeing Thérence's vexation, cut the matter short by saying she was too tired, and she would prefer to pass the night at the inn and start in a carriage the next morning.

"Well, then," said the Head-Woodsman, "Thérence and I will do the same. Our horse shall rest here for the night, and we will part from you at daybreak to-morrow morning. But instead of eating our meal in this inn which is full of flies, I propose that we take the dinner into some shady place or to the bank of the river, and sit there and talk till it is time to go to bed."

So said, so done. I engaged two bedrooms, one for the girls, the other for us men, and wishing to entertain Père Bastien (who I had noticed was a good eater) according to my own ideas, I filled a big basket with the best the inn could afford in patés, white bread, wine, and wine-brandy, and carried it outside the village. It was lucky that the present fashion of drinking coffee and beer did not exist in those days, for I shouldn't have spared the cost, and my pockets would have been emptied.

Saint-Sevère is a fine neighborhood, cut into by ravines that are well watered and refreshing to the eye. We chose a spot of rising ground, where the air was so exhilarating that not a crust nor a drop remained after the feast. Presently Père Bastien, feeling lively, picked up his bagpipe, which never left him, and said to Joseph:—

"My lad, we never know who is to live or who to die; we are parting, you say, for three or four days; in my opinion, you are thinking of a much longer absence; and it may be in God's mind that we shall never meet again. This is what all persons who part at the crossways ought to say and feel to each other. I hope that you leave us satisfied with me and with my children; I am satisfied with you and with your friends here; but I do not forget that the prime object of all was to teach you music, and I regret that your two months' illness put a stop to it. I don't say that I could have made you a learned musician; I know there are such in the cities, both ladies and gentlemen, who play instruments that we know nothing about, and read off written airs just as others read words in a book. Except chanting, which I learned in my youth, I know very little of such music, and I have taught you all I know, namely, the keys, notes, and time measures. If you desire to know more you must go to the great cities, where the violinists will teach you both minuet and quadrille music; but I don't know what good that would be to you unless you want to leave your own parts and renounce the position of peasant."

"God forbid!" replied Joseph, looking at Brulette.

"Therefore," continued the Head-Woodsman, "you will have to look elsewhere for instruction on the bagpipe or the hurdy-gurdy. If you choose to come back to me, I will help you; but if you think you can do better in the Upper country, you must go there. What I should wish to do would be to guide you slowly till your lungs grew so strong that you could use them without effort, and your fingers no longer failed you. As for the idea within us, that can't be taught; you have your own, and I know it to be of good quality. I gave you, however, what was in my own head, and whatever you can remember of it you may use as you like. But as your wish seems to be to compose, you can't do better than travel about, and so compare your ideas and stock of knowledge with that of others. You had better go as far up as Auvergne and the Forez, and see how grand and beautiful the world is beyond our valleys, and how the heart swells when we stand on the heights of a real mountain, and behold the waters, whose voice is louder than the voice of man, rolling downward to nourish the trees the verdure of which never dies. Don't go into the lowlands of those other regions. You will find there what you have left in your own country, and that isn't what you want. Now is the time to give you a bit of information which you should never forget; listen carefully to what I say to you."

EIGHTEENTH EVENING.

Père Bastien, observing that Joseph listened with great attention, continued as follows:—

"Music has two modes which the learned, as I have heard tell, call major and minor, but which I call the clear mode and the troubled mode; or, if you like it better, the blue-sky mode and the gray-sky mode, or, still otherwise, the mode of strength and joy, and the mode of dreaminess and gloom. You may search till morning and you will find no end to the contrasts between the two modes; but you will never find a third, for all things on this earth are light or darkness, rest or action. Now listen to me, Joseph! The plains sing in the major, and the mountains in the minor mode. If you had stayed in your own country your ideas would belong to the clear and tranquil mode; in returning there now, you ought to see the use that a soul like yours could make of that mode; for the one mode is neither less nor more than the other. But while you lived at home, feeling yourself a thorough musician, you fretted at not hearing the minor sound in your ears. The fiddlers and the singing-girls of your parts only acquire it; for song is like the wind which blows everywhere and carries the seeds of plants from one horizon to another. But inasmuch as nature has not made your people dreamy and passionate, they make a poor use of the minor mode, and corrupt it by that use. That is why you thought your bagpipes were always false. Now, if you want to understand the minor, go seek it in wild and desolate places, and learn that many a tear must be shed before you can duly use a mode which was given to man to utter his griefs, or, at any rate, to sigh his love."

Joseph understood Père Bastien so well that he asked him to play the last air he had composed, so as to give us a specimen of the sad gray mode which he called the minor.

"There, there!" cried the old man; "so you overheard the air I have been trying for the last week to put to certain words. I thought I was singing to myself; but, as you were listening, here it is, such as I expect to leave it."

Lifting his bagpipe he removed the chanter, on which he softly played an air which, though it was not melancholy, brought memories of the past and a sense of longing after many things to the consciousness of those who listened.

Joseph was evidently not at ease, and Brulette, who listened without stirring, seemed to waken from a dream when it ended.

"And the words," said Thérence, "are they sad too, father?"

"The words," said he, "are, like the air, rather confused and demand reflection. They tell the story of how three lovers courted a girl."

Whereupon he sang a song, now very popular in our parts, though the words have been a good deal altered; but this is how the Père Bastien sang them:—

Three woodsmen there were,
In springtime, on the grass
(Listen to the nightingale);
Three woodsmen were there,
Speaking each with the lass.

The youngest he said,
He who held the flower
(Listen to the nightingale),
The youngest then said he
I love thee, but I cower.

The oldest cried out,
He who held the tool
(Listen to the nightingale),
The oldest cried aloud,
When I love I rule.

The third sang to her,
Bearing the almond spray
(Listen to the nightingale),
The third sang in her ear,
I love thee and I pray.

Friend shall never be
You who bear the flower
(Listen to the nightingale),
Friend shall never be
A coward, or I cower.

Master will I none,
You who hold the tool
(Listen to the nightingale),
No master thou of mine,
Love obeys no rule.

Lover thou shalt be
Who bear the almond spray
(Listen to the nightingale),

My lover shalt thou be,
Gifts are for those who pray.

I liked the air when joined to the words better than the first time I heard it; and I was so pleased that I asked to hear it again; but Père Bastien, who had no vanity about his compositions, declared it was not worth while, and went on playing other airs, sometimes in the major, sometimes in the minor, and even employing both modes in the same song, teaching Joseph, as he did so, how to pass from one to the other and then back again.

The stars were casting their light long before we wanted to retire; even the townspeople assembled in numbers at the foot of the ravine to listen, with much satisfaction to their ears. Some said: "That's one of the Bourbonnais bagpipers, and what is more, he is a master; he knows the art, and not one of us can hold a candle to him."

On our way back to the inn Père Bastien continued to instruct Joseph, and the latter, never weary of such talk, lagged a little behind us to listen and question him. So I walked in front with Thérence, who, useful and energetic as ever, helped me to carry the baskets. Brulette walked alone between the pairs, dreaming of I don't know what,—as she had taken to doing of late; and Thérence sometimes turned round as if to look at her, but really to see if Joseph were following.

"Look at him well, Thérence," I said to her, at a moment when she seemed in great anxiety, "for your father said truly, 'When we part for a day it may be for life.'"

"Yes," she replied, "but on the other hand, when we think we are parting for life it may be for only a day."

"You remind me," said I, "that when I first saw you you floated away like a dream and I never expected to see you again."

"I know what you mean," she exclaimed. "My father reminded me of it yesterday, in speaking of you. Father really loves you, Tiennet, and has great respect for you."

"I am glad and honored, Thérence; but I don't know what I have done to deserve it, for there is nothing in me that is different from the common run of men."

"My father is never mistaken in his judgment, and what he says, I believe; why should that make you sigh, Tiennet?"

"Did I sigh, Thérence? I didn't mean to."

"No, of course you did not," she replied; "but that is no reason why you should hide your feelings from me. You love Brulette and are afraid—"

"I love Brulette very much, that is true, but without any love-sighing, and without any regrets or worries about what she thinks of me. I have no love in my heart, because it would do me no good to have any."

"Ah, you are very lucky, Tiennet!" she cried, "to be able to govern your feelings by your mind in that way."

"I should be better worth something, Thérence, if, like you, I governed them by my heart. Yes, yes, I know you; I have watched you, and I know the true secret of your conduct. I have seen how, for the last eight days, you have set aside your own feelings to cure Joseph, and how you secretly do everything for his good without letting him see so much as your little finger in it. You want him to be happy, and you said true when you told Brulette and me that if we can do good to those we love there is no need to be thinking of our own happiness. That's what you do and what you are; and though jealousy may sometimes get the better of you, you recover directly. It is marvellous to see how strong and generous you are; it is saintly. You must allow that if either of us two is to respect the other, it is I you, not you me. I am a rather sensible fellow, and that is all; you are a girl with a great heart, and a stern hand upon yourself."

"Thanks for the good you think of me," replied Thérence, "but perhaps I don't deserve it, my lad. You want me to be in love with Joseph, and I am not. As God is my judge, I have never thought of being his wife, and the attachment I feel to him is rather that of a sister or a mother."

"Oh! as for that, I am not sure that you don't deceive yourself, Thérence. Your disposition is impulsive."

"That is just why I do not deceive myself. I love my father and brother deeply and almost madly. If I had children I should defend them like a wolf and brood over them like a hen; but the thing they call love, such, for instance, as my brother feels for Brulette,—the desire to please, and a nameless sort of feeling which makes him suffer when alone, and not be able to think of her without pain,—all that I do not feel at all, and I cannot imagine it. Joseph may leave us forever if it will do him good, and I shall thank God, and only grieve if it turns out that he is the worse for it."

Thérence's way of looking at the matter gave me a good deal to think of. I could not understand it very well, for she now seemed to me above all others and above me. I walked a little way beside her without saying a word, not knowing whither my mind was going; for I was seized with such a feeling of ardent friendship that I longed with all my heart to embrace her, with all respect and thinking no harm, till suddenly a glance at her, so young and beautiful, filled me with shame and fear. When we reached the inn I asked her, apropos of what I forget, to tell me exactly what her father had said of me.

"He said," she replied, "that you were a man of the strongest good sense he had ever known."

"You might as well call me a good-natured fool at once, don't you think so?" I said, laughing, but rather mortified.

"Not at all!" cried Thérence; "here are my father's very words: 'He who sees clearest into the things of this world is he who acts with the highest justice.' Now it is true that great good sense leads to great kindness of heart, and I do not think that my father is mistaken."

"In that case, Thérence," I cried, rather agitated at the bottom of my heart, "have a little regard for me."

"I have a great deal," she said, shaking the hand which I held out to her; but it was said with an air of good-fellowship which killed all vaporing, and I slept upon her speech with no more imagination than justly belonged to it.

The next day came the parting. Brulette cried when she kissed Père Bastien, and made him promise that he would come and visit us and bring Thérence; then the two dear girls embraced each other with such pledges of affection that they really seemed unable to part. Joseph offered his thanks to his late master for all the benefits he had received from him, and when he came to part with Thérence he tried to say the same to her; but she looked at him with a perfect frankness which disconcerted him, and pressing each other's hands, they said only, "Good-bye, and take care of yourself."

Not feeling at the moment too shy, I asked Thérence to allow me to kiss her, thinking to set a good example to Joseph; but he took no notice, and got hastily into the carriage to cut short these parting civilities. He seemed dissatisfied with himself and others. Brulette took the last seat in the conveyance, and, so long as she could see our Bourbonnais friends, she kept her eyes upon them, while Thérence, standing at the inn-door, seemed to be thinking rather than grieving.

We did the rest of the journey somewhat sadly. Joseph said not a word. Perhaps he hoped that Brulette might take some notice of him; but according as Joseph grew stronger, Brulette had recovered her freedom of thinking about other people, and being full of her friendship for Huriel's father and sister, she talked to me about them, regretting to part with them and singing their praises, as if she had really left her heart behind and regretted even the country we were quitting.

"It is strange," she said to me, "how, as we get nearer home, the trees seem to me so small, the grass so yellow, and the river sluggish. Before I ever left the plains I fancied I could not endure three days in the woods, and now I believe I could pass my life there like Thérence, if I had my old father with me."

"I can't say as much, cousin," said I. "Though, if I were forced to do so, I don't suppose I should die of it. But the trees may be as tall, the grass as green, and the streams as sparkling as they please; I prefer a nettle in my own land to an oak in foreign parts. My heart jumps with joy at each familiar rock and bush, as if I had been absent two or three years, and when I catch sight of the church clock I mean, for sure, to take off my hat to it."

"And you, José?" said Brulette, noticing the annoyed look of our companion for the first time. "You, who have been absent more than a year, are not you glad to get home again?"

"Excuse me, Brulette, I don't know what you are talking about. My head is full of that song the Head-Woodsman sang last night, and in the middle of it there is a little refrain which I can't remember."

"Bah!" cried Brulette, "it is where the song says, 'Listen to the nightingale.'"

So saying, she sang the tune quite correctly, which roused Joseph so much that he jumped with joy in the cart, clapping his hands.

"Ah, Brulette!" he cried, "how lucky you are to remember like that! Again! sing it again! 'Listen to the nightingale.'"

"I would rather sing the whole song," she answered; and thereupon she sang it straight through without missing a word, which delighted Joseph so much that he pressed her hands, saying, with a courage I didn't think him capable of, that only a musician could be worthy of her.

"Well, certainly," said Brulette, thinking of Huriel, "if I had a lover I should wish him to be both a good singer and a good bagpiper."

"It is rare to be both," returned Joseph. "A bagpipe ruins the voice, and except the Head-Woodsman—"

"And his son," said Brulette, heedlessly.

I nudged her elbow, and she began to talk of something else, but Joseph, who was eaten up with jealousy, persisted in harking back to the song.

"I believe," he said, "that when Père Bastien composed those words he was thinking of three fellows of our acquaintance; for I remember a talk we had with him after supper the day of your arrival in the forest."

"I don't remember it," said Brulette, blushing.

"But I do," returned Joseph. "We were speaking of a girl's love, and Huriel said it couldn't be won by tossing up for it. Tiennet declared, laughing, that softness and submission were of no use, and to be loved we must needs be feared, instead of being too kind and good. Huriel argued against Tiennet, and I listened without saying a word. Am not I the one who 'bears the flower,—the youngest of the three, who loves and cowers'? Repeat the last verse, Brulette, as you know it so well—about 'gifts for those who ask.'"

"Since you know it as well as I do," said Brulette, rather nettled, "keep it to sing to the first girl you make love to. If Père Bastien likes to turn the talk he hears into songs, it is not for me to draw conclusions. Besides, I know nothing about it. But my feet are tingling with cold, and while the horse walks up this hill, I shall take a run to warm them."

Not waiting till I could stop the horse, she jumped on to the road and walked off in front of us as light as a little milkmaid.

I wanted to get down too, but Joseph caught me by the arm and, always pursuing his own ideas, "Don't you think," said he, "that we despise those who show their desires as much as those who do not show them at all?"

"If you mean me—"

"I mean no one. I was only thinking of the talk we had over there, which Père Bastien turned into a song against your speech and my silence. It seems that Huriel will win his suit with the girl."

"What girl?" I said, out of patience, for Joseph had never taken me into his confidence before, and I was none too pleased to have him give it out of vexation.

"What girl?" he cried in a tone of angry sarcasm, "the girl of the song."

"Then what suit is Huriel to win? does the girl live at a distance? is that where Huriel has gone?"

Joseph thought a moment and then continued: "It is true enough, what he said, that between mastership and silence, there is prayer. That comes round to your first remark, that in order to attract we must not love too well. He who loves too well is the timid, silent one; not a word can he tear from his throat, and he is thought a fool because he is dumb with desire and false shame."

"No doubt of that," I said. "I have gone through it myself many a time. But it also happened to me sometimes to speak out so badly that I had better have held my tongue; I might have fancied myself beloved a little longer."

Poor Joseph bit his lips and said no more. I was sorry I had vexed him, and yet I could not prevent myself from resenting his jealousy of Huriel, knowing as I did how the latter had done his best for him against his own interests. I took, at this very time, such a disgust for jealousy that since then I have never felt a twinge of it, and I don't think I could now without good reason.

I was, however, just going to speak kindly to him, when we noticed that Brulette, who was still ahead of us, had stopped on the wayside to speak to a monk, who looked short and fat, like the one I had seen in the woods of Chambérat. I whipped up the horse, and soon convinced myself that it was really Brother Nicolas. He had asked Brulette if he were far from our village, and, as he was still three miles distant and said he was very tired, she had offered to give him a lift in our conveyance.

We made room for him and for a large covered basket which he was carrying, and which he deposited with much precaution on his knees. None of us dreamed of asking what it contained, except perhaps myself, who am naturally rather curious; but I feared to be indiscreet, for I knew the mendicant friars gathered up all sorts of things from pious shopkeepers, which they sold again for the benefit of their monastery. Everything came handy for this traffic, even women's trumpery, which, however, some of them did not venture to dispose of openly.

I drove at a trot, and presently we caught sight of the church clock and the old elms on the market-place, then of all the houses of the village, both big and little,—which did not afford me as much pleasure as I had expected, for the meeting with Brother Nicolas had brought to mind certain painful things about which I was still uneasy. I saw, however, that he was on his guard as well as I, for he said not a word before Brulette and Joseph showing that we had met elsewhere than at the dance, or that he and I knew more of what had happened than the rest.

He was a very pleasant man, with a jovial nature that might have amused me under other circumstances, but I was in a hurry to reach home and get him alone by himself, so as to ask if he had any news of the affair. As we entered the village Joseph jumped off, and notwithstanding that Brulette begged him to come and rest at her grandfather's, he took the road to Saint-Chartier, saying that he would pay his respects to Père Brulet after he had seen and embraced his mother.

I fancied that the friar rather urged it on him as a duty, as if to get rid of him; and then, instead of accepting my proposal that he should dine and sup at my house, Brother Nicolas declared that he could stop only an hour at Père Brulet's, with whom he had business.

"You will be very welcome," said Brulette; "but do you know my grandfather? I have never seen you at the house."

"I do not know either him or your village," answered the monk, "but I am charged with an errand to him, which I can deliver only at his house."

"I returned to my first notion, namely, that he had ribbons and laces in his basket, and that, having heard from the neighbors that Brulette was the smartest girl in these parts, he wanted to show her his merchandise without exposing himself to gossip, which, in those days, spared neither good monks nor wicked ones."

I thought this idea was in Brulette's head too, for when she got down first at the door, she held out both arms for the basket, saying, "Don't be afraid; I guess what is in it." But the friar refused to give it up, saying it was valuable and he feared it might get broken.

"I see, Brother," I said to him in a low voice, detaining him a moment, "that you are very busy. I don't want to hinder you, but I should like you to tell me quickly if there is any news from over there."

"None that I know of," he said in the same tone; "but no news is good news." Then shaking me by the hand in a friendly way, he entered the house after Brulette, who was already hanging to her grandfather's neck.

I thought old Brulet, who was generally polite, owed me a hearty welcome and some thanks for the care I had taken of his granddaughter; but instead of keeping me even a moment, he seemed more interested in the arrival of the friar; for, taking him at once by the hand, he led him into an inner room, begging me to excuse him and saying he had matters of importance to discuss and wished to be alone with his granddaughter.

NINETEENTH EVENING.

I am not easily affronted, but I was so now at being thus received; and I went off home to put up the cart and to inquire after my family. After that, the day being too far gone to go to work, I sauntered about the village to see if everything was in its old place, and found no change, except that one of the trees felled on the common before the cobbler's door had been chopped up into sabots, and that Père Godard had trimmed up his poplar and put new flags on his path. I certainly supposed that my journey into the Bourbonnais had made a stir, and I expected to be assailed with questions which I might find it hard to answer; but the folks in our region are very indifferent, and I seemed, for the first time, to realize how dull they were,— being obliged to tell a good many that I had just returned from a trip. They did not even know I had been away.

Towards evening, as I was loitering home, I met the friar on his way to La Chatre, and he told me that Père Brulet wanted me to sup with him.

What was my astonishment on entering the house to see Père Brulet on one side of the table, and his granddaughter on the other, gazing at the monk's basket which lay open before them, and in it a big baby about a year old, sitting on a pillow and trying to eat some blackheart cherries, the juice of which had daubed and stained his face!

Brulette seemed to me thoughtful and rather sad; but when she saw my amazement she couldn't help laughing; after which she wiped her eyes, for she seemed to me to have been shedding tears of grief or vexation rather than of gayety.

"Come," she said at last, "shut the door tight and listen to us. Here is grandfather who wants to tell you all about the fine present the monk has brought us."

"You must know, nephew," said Père Brulet, who never smiled at pleasant things any more than he frowned at disagreeable ones, "that this is an orphan child; and we have agreed with the monk to take care of him for the price of his board. We know nothing about the child, neither his father, his mother, his country, nor anything else. He is called Charlot, and that is all we do know. The pay is good, and the friar gave us the preference because he met Brulette in the Bourbonnais, and hearing where she lived and how well-behaved she was, and, moreover, that she was not rich and had time at her disposal, he thought he could give her a pleasure and do her a service by putting the little fellow under her charge and letting her earn the money."

Though the matter was tolerably surprising, I was not much astonished at first hearing of it, and only asked if the monk was formerly known to Père Brulet, and whether he could trust him as to the future payment.

"I had never seen him," replied the old man, "but I knew that he had been in this neighborhood several times, and he is known to persons in whom I have confidence, and who informed me, two or three days ago, of the matter he was to come about. Besides, a year's board is paid in advance, and when the money doesn't come it will be soon enough to worry."

"Very good, uncle; you know your own affairs; but I should not have expected to see my cousin, who loves her freedom, tied down to the care of a little monkey who is nothing to her, and who, be it said without offence, is not at all nice in his appearance."

"That is just what annoys me," said Brulette, "and I was saying so to my grandfather as you came in. And," she added, rubbing the muzzle of the little animal with her handkerchief, "no wiping will make his mouth any better; I wish I could have begun my apprenticeship with a child that was prettier to kiss. This one looks surly, and won't even smile; he cares only for things to eat."

"Bah!" said Père Brulet, "he is not uglier than all children of his age, and it is your business to make him nice. He is tired with his journey, and doesn't know where he is, nor what we mean to do with him."

Père Brulet went out to look for his knife, which he had left at a neighbor's, and I began to get more and more surprised when alone with Brulette. She seemed annoyed at times, and even distressed.

"What worries me is that I don't know how to take care of a child," she said. "I could not bear to let a poor creature that can't help itself suffer; but I am so unhandy; I am sorry now that I never was inclined to look after the little ones."

"It is a fact," I said, "that you don't seem born for the business, and I can't understand why your grandfather who I never thought was eager after money, should put such a care upon you for the sake of a few crowns."

"You talk like a rich man," she said. "Remember that I have no dower, and that a fear of poverty has always deterred me from marrying."

"That's a very bad reason, Brulette. You have been and still will be sought after by men who are richer than you, and who love your sweet eyes and your pretty chatter."

"My sweet eyes will fade, and my pretty chatter won't be worth much when the beauty has gone. I don't wish to be reproached at the end of a few years with having lost my dower of charms and brought nothing more solid into the household."

"Is it that you are really thinking of marrying—since we left the Bourbonnais?" I asked. "This is the first time I ever heard you talk of money."

"I am not thinking of it any more than I have always thought," returned Brulette, but in a less confident tone than usual, "I never said I meant to live unmarried."

"I see how it is!" I cried, laughing, "you are thinking of it, and you needn't try to hide it from me, for I have given up all hopes of my own. I see plainly enough that in taking care of this little wretch, who has money and no mother, you are laying up a store, like the squirrels. If not, your grandfather, whom you have always ruled as if he were your grandson, would not have forced you to take such a boy to nurse."

Brulette lifted the child from the table, and as she carried him to her grandfather's bed she gave him a rather sad look.

"Poor Charlot!" she said, "I'll do my best for you; you are much to be pitied for having come into the world, and it is my belief that nobody wanted you."

But her gayety soon returned; she even had some hearty laughs at supper in feeding Charlot, who had the appetite of a little wolf, and answered all her attentions by trying to scratch her face.

Toward eight o'clock Joseph came in and was very well received by Père Brulet; but I observed that Brulette, who had just been putting Charlot to bed, closed the curtains quickly as if to hide him, and seemed disturbed all the time that Joseph remained. I observed also that not a word was said to him of this singular event, either by the old man or by Brulette, and I therefore thought it my duty to hold my tongue. Joseph was cross, and said as little as possible in answer to my uncle's questions. Brulette asked him if he had found his mother in good health, and if she had been surprised and pleased to see him. Then, as he said "yes" to everything, she asked if he had not tired himself too much by walking to Saint-Chartier and back in one evening.

"I did not wish to let the day go by without paying my respects to your grandfather," he said; "and now, as I really am tired, I shall go and spend the night with Tiennet, if I don't inconvenience him."

I answered that it would give me pleasure, and took him to my house where, after we were in bed, he said: "Tiennet, I am really on the point of departure. I came here only to get away from the woods of Alleu, for I was sick of them."

"That's the worst of you, Joseph; you were there with friends who took the place of those you left here in the same way—"

"Well, it is what I choose to do," he said, rather shortly; then in a milder tone he added: "Tiennet, Tiennet, there are some things one can tell, and others which force us to keep silence. You hurt me to-day in telling me I could never please Brulette."

"Joseph, I never said anything of the kind, for the reason that I don't know if you really care for her."

"You do know it," he replied; "and you blame me for not having opened my heart to you. But how could I? I am not one of those who tell their secrets willingly. It is my misfortune; I believe I have really no other illness than one sole idea, always stretching toward the same end, and always beaten back when it rises to my lips. Listen to me now, while I do feel able to talk; for God knows how soon I may fall mute again. I love; and I see plainly I am not loved. So many years have passed in this way (for I loved Brulette when we were little children) that I have grown accustomed to the pain. I have never flattered myself that I could please her; I have lived in the belief that she would never care for me. Lately, however, I saw by her coming to the Bourbonnais that I was something to her, and it gave me strength and the will not to die. But I soon perceived that she met some one over there who suited her better than I."

"I know nothing about it," I replied; "but if it were so, that some one you speak of gave you no ground for complaint or reproach."

"That is true," said Joseph; "and my anger is unjust,—all the more because Huriel, knowing Brulette to be an honest girl, and not being able to marry her so long as he remains in the fraternity of muleteers, has himself done what he could to separate from her. I can still hope to return to Brulette hereafter, more worthy of her than I have been; but I cannot bear to stay here now, for I am still nothing better than I was in the past. There is something in the manner and language of every one who speaks to me that seems to mean: 'You are sick, you are thin, you are ugly, you are feeble, you know nothing new and nothing good that can interest us in you.' Yes, Tiennet, what I tell you is exactly so; my mother seemed frightened by my face when she saw me, and she cried so when she kissed me that the pain of seeing her was greater than the joy. This evening, too, Brulette looked annoyed when I came in, and her grandfather, good and kind as he always is to me, seemed uneasy lest I should stay too long. Now don't tell me that I imagined all that. Like all those who speak little, I see much. My time has not yet come; I must go, and the sooner the better."

"I think you ought to take at least a few days' rest," I said; "for I fancy you mean to go to a great distance, and I do not think it friendly in you to give us unnecessary anxiety."

"You need not be anxious, Tiennet. I have all the strength I want, and I shall not be ill again. I have learned one thing; and that is that frail bodies, to which God has given slender physical powers, are provided with a force of will which carries them farther than the vigorous health of others. I was not exaggerating when I told you over there that I became, as it were, a new man on seeing Huriel fight so boldly; and that I was wide awake in the night when I heard his voice saying to me, 'Come, cheer up! I am a man, and as long as you are not one you will count for nothing.' I want therefore to shake myself free of my poor nature, and return here some day as good to look at and better to hear than all Brulette's other lovers."

"But," I said, "suppose she makes her choice before you return? She is going on nineteen, and for a girl as much courted as she is it is time to decide."

"She will decide only between Huriel and me," answered Joseph, in a confident tone. "There is no one but him and myself who are capable of teaching her to love. Excuse me, Tiennet; I know, or at least I believe, that you dreamed of it."

"Yes," I replied, "but I don't dream of it any longer."

"Well for you!" said Joseph; "for you could never have been happy with her. She has tastes and ideas which don't belong to the ground she has grown in; she needs another wind to rock her; the one that blows here is not pure enough and it might wither her. She feels all this, though she may not know how to say it; and I tell you that unless Huriel is treacherous, I shall find her still free, a year or two hence."

So saying, Joseph, as if wearied out by letting himself talk so much, dropped his head on his pillow and went to sleep. For the last hour I had been struggling to keep awake, for I was tired out myself. I slept soundly, and when at daybreak I called him he did not answer. I looked about, and he was gone without awaking any one.

Brulette went the next day to see Mariton, to break the news to her, and find out what had passed between her and her son. She would not let me accompany her, and told me on her return that she could not get Mariton to say much, because her master Benoît was ill and even in some danger from congestion of the brain. I concluded, therefore, that the woman, being obliged to nurse her master, had not had time to talk with her son as much as he would have liked, and consequently he had become jealous, as his nature led him to be at such times.

"That is very likely," said Brulette, "for the wiser Joseph gets through ambition the more exacting he becomes. I think I liked him better when he was simple and submissive as he used to be."

When I related to Brulette all that he had said to me the night before, she replied: "If he really has so high an ambition, we should only hamper him by showing an anxiety he does not wish for. Leave him in God's care! If I were the flirt you declared I was in former times, I should be proud to be the cause of his endeavoring to improve his mind and his career; but I am not; and my feeling is chiefly regret that he does nothing for his mother or himself."

"But isn't he right when he says that you can only choose between Huriel and him?"

"There is time enough to think about that," she said, laughing with her lips, though her face was not cheerful, "especially as the only two lovers Joseph allows me are running away as fast as their legs can go."

During the next week the arrival of the child which the monk had brought was the subject of village gossip and the torment of the inquisitive. So many tales were founded upon it that Charlot came near being the son of a prince, and every one wanted to borrow money of Père Brulet, or sell goods to him, convinced that the stipend which induced his granddaughter to take up a duty so contrary to her tastes must at least be a princely revenue. The jealousy of some and the discontent of others made the old man enemies, which he had never had in his life, and he was much astonished by it; for, simple, pious soul that he was, it had never occurred to him that the matter might give occasion for gossip. Brulette, however, only laughed and persuaded him to pay no attention to it.

Days and weeks went by and we heard nothing of Joseph, or of Huriel, or of the Woodsman and his daughter. Brulette wrote to Thérence and I to Huriel, but we got no answers. Brulette was troubled and even annoyed; so much so that she told me she did not mean to think anything more of those foreigners, who did not even remember her, and made no return for the friendship she had offered them. So she began once more to dress herself smartly and appear at the dances; for the gallants complained of her gloomy looks and the headaches she talked of ever since her trip to the Bourbonnais. The journey had been rather criticised; people even said she had some secret love over there, either for Joseph or for some one else;

and they expected her to be more amiable than ever, before they would forgive her for going off without a word to any one.

Brulette was too proud to give in to cajoling them, but she dearly loved pleasure, and being drawn in that direction, she gave Charlot in charge of her neighbor, Mère Lamouche, and took her amusement as before.

One evening, as I was coming back with her from the pilgrimage of Vaudevant, which is a great festival, we heard Charlot howling, far as we were from the house.

"That dreadful child," said Brulette, "is never out of mischief. I am sure I don't know who can ever manage him."

"Are you sure," I said, "the Mère Lamouche takes as good care of him as she promised you?"

"Of course she does. She has nothing else to do, and I pay her enough to satisfy her."

Charlot continued to yell, and the house looked as though it were locked up and there was no one in it. Brulette ran and knocked loudly on the door, but no one answered except Charlot, who screamed louder than ever, either from fright, or loneliness, or anger.

I was obliged to climb to the thatch of the roof and clamber down through the trap-door of the loft. I opened the door for Brulette and then we saw Charlot all alone, rolling in the ashes, where by great good luck there was no fire, and purple as a beet from screaming.

"Heavens!" cried Brulette, "is that the way to care for the poor little wretch? Well, whoso takes a child gets a master. I ought to have known it, and either not taken this one, or given up my own enjoyments."

So saying, she carried Charlot to her own home, half in pity and half impatiently, and having washed, fed, and consoled him as best she could, she put him to sleep, and sat down to reflect, with her head in her hands. I tried to show her that it would be easy enough, by sacrificing the money she was gaining, to employ some kindly, careful woman to take charge of the boy.

"No," she exclaimed, "I must look after him, because I am responsible for him, and you see what looking after him means. If I think I can let up for one day it is just that very day that I ought not to have done so. Yes, that's it, I ought not," she said, crying. "It would be wrong; and I should be sorry for it all my life."

"On the other hand, you would do wrong if the child were to be the gainer by it. He is not happy with you, and he might be elsewhere."

"Why, isn't he happy with me? I hope he is, except on the days when I am absent; and so I say I will not absent myself again."

"I tell you he is no better off when you are here."

"What do you mean?" cried Brulette, striking her hands with vexation; "where have you heard that? Did you ever see me ill-treat the child, or even threaten him? Can I help it if he is an unpleasant child with a sulky disposition? If he were my own I could not do better for him."

"Oh! I know you are not unkind to him and never let him want for anything, because you are a dear, sweet Christian; but you can't love him, for that doesn't depend upon yourself. He feels this without knowing it, and that keeps him from loving and caressing others. Animals know when people like them or dislike them; why shouldn't little human beings do the same?"

TWENTIETH EVENING.

Brulette colored, pouted, began to cry, and said nothing; but the next day I met her leading her beasts to pasture with Charlot in her arms. She sat down in the middle of the field with the child on the skirt of her gown, and said to me:—

"You were right, Tiennet. Your reproaches made me reflect, and I have made up my mind what to do. I can't promise to love this Charlot much, but I'll behave as if I did, and perhaps God will reward me some day by giving me children of my own more lovable than this one."

"Ah, my darling!" I cried. "I don't know what makes you say that. I never blamed you; I have nothing to reproach you with except the obstinacy with which you now resolve to bring up the little wretch yourself. Come, let me write to that friar, or let me go and find him and make him put the child in another family. I know where the convent is, and I would rather make another long journey than see you condemned to this sort of thing."

"No, Tiennet," replied Brulette. "We must not even think of changing what was agreed upon. My grandfather promised for me, and I was bound to consent. If I could tell you—but I can't! One thing I want you to know; it is that money counts for nothing in the bargain, and that my grandfather and I will never accept a penny for a duty we are bound to perform."

"Now you do surprise me. Whose child is it? It must belong to some of your relatives,—consequently, mine."

"Possibly," she replied. "Some of our family live away from here. But consider that I have told you nothing, for I cannot and ought not to do so. Let people believe that the little monkey is a stranger to us, and that we are paid for the care of him. Otherwise, evil tongues might accuse those who don't deserve it."

"The devil!" said I. "If you haven't set me on thorns! I can't think—"

"That's just it," she said, "you are not to think; I forbid it,—though I am quite sure you never could find out."

"Very good! but do you really mean to wean yourself from all amusements, just as that child is weaned of the breast? The devil take your grandfather's promise!"

"My grandfather did right, and if I had gone against him I should have been a heartless girl. I repeat, I don't choose to do things by halves, even if I die of it."

Brulette was resolute. From that day such a change came over her that she was scarcely recognizable. She never left the house except to pasture her sheep and her goats with Charlot beside her; and when she had put him to bed for the night she would take her work and sit near him. She went to none of the dances, and bought no more finery, having no longer any occasion for it. This dull life made her serious and even sad, for she soon found herself neglected. There is no girl so pretty but what she is forced to be amiable with everybody if she wants to have followers; and Brulette, who now showed no desire to please, was called sullen, all the more because she had once been so much the reverse. In my opinion she had only changed for the better, for, having never played the coquette, only my lady the princess with me, she seemed to my mind more gentle in manner, more sensible and interesting in her behavior; but others didn't think so. In the past she had allowed her lovers just so much hope as now made each of them feel affronted by her neglect, as if he considered he had a right to her; and although her coquetry had always been very harmless she was punished for it as if it were a wrong done to others; which proves, as I think, that men have as much, if not more, vanity than women, and consider that no one ever does enough to please or pacify the conceit they have of themselves.

There is one thing certain at least, and that is that many persons are very unjust,—even young men who seem such good fellows and such willing slaves as long as they are in love. Many of Brulette's old admirers now turned against her, and more than once I had words with them in defending my cousin from the blame they put upon her. Unfortunately, they were encouraged by the gossips and the selfish folk who were jealous of Père Brulet's supposed bit of luck; until finally Brulette was obliged to refuse to see these maliciously inquisitive people, and even the false friends who came and repeated to her what they had heard others say.

This is how it was that in less than one year the queen of the village, the Rose of Nohant, was condemned by evil minds and abandoned by fools. They told dark stories about her, and I shuddered lest she should hear them; indeed, I myself was often harassed and puzzled how to answer them. The worst lie of all was one Père Brulet ought to have expected, namely, that Charlot was neither some poor foundling nor the son of a prince, brought up secretly, but really Brulette's own child. In vain I pointed out that the girl had always lived openly under the eyes of everybody; and having never encouraged any particular lover she could not have committed a fault so difficult to hide. They answered that such and such a one had boldly concealed her condition till the very last day, and had reappeared, sometimes the day after, as composed and lively as if nothing had happened, and had even hidden the consequences until she was married to the author, or the dupe, of her sin. Unfortunately, this had happened more than once in our village. In these little country places, where the houses are surrounded by gardens, and separated from each other by hemp and lucern fields, some of them of great extent, it is not easy to see and hear from one to another at all hours of the night, and, indeed, things are done at any time which the good God alone takes account of.

One of the worst tongues against Brulette was that of Mère Lamouche, ever since Brulette had found her out and taken the boy away from her. She had so long been the willing servant and slave of the girl that she knew she could look for no further gain from her, and in revenge she invented and told anything that people wanted her to say. She related, to whoever listened, how Brulette had sacrificed her honor to that "puny fellow, José," and that she was so ashamed of it that she had forced him to leave the place. José had submitted, on condition that she would marry no one else; and he was now in foreign parts trying to earn enough money to marry her. The child, said the woman, had been taken into the Bourbonnais country by men with blackened faces who called themselves muleteers, and whose acquaintance Joseph had made under pretence of buying his bagpipe; but there had never been any other bagpipe in the case than that squalling Charlot. About a year after his birth Brulette had gone to see her lover and the baby, in company with me and a muleteer who was as ugly as the devil. There we made acquaintance with a mendicant friar, who offered to bring the baby back for us, and with whom we concocted the story of its being a rich foundling; which was altogether false, for this child had brought not one penny of profit to Père Brulet.

When Mère Lamouche invented this tale, in which, you see, lies were mixed up with facts, her word was believed by everybody, and Joseph's short and almost secret visit assisted the belief. So, with much laughter and derision, Brulette was nicknamed "Josette."

In spite of my wrath at these outrageous stories, Brulette took so little pains to make herself agreeable, and showed by her care for the child such contempt for the gossips, that I began to get bewildered myself. Was it absolutely impossible that I had been a dupe? Once upon a time I had certainly been jealous of Joseph. However virtuous and discreet a girl might be, however shy the lad, it had often happened that love and ignorance got the better of them, and some young couples had never known the meaning of evil until they had committed it. If she had once done wrong, Brulette, a clever girl, was none the less capable of hiding her misfortune, being too proud to confess it, yet too right-minded to deceive others. Was it not by her orders that Joseph wished to make himself a worthy husband and father? It was certainly a wise and patient scheme. Was I deceived in thinking she had a fancy for Huriel? I might have been; but even if she had felt it, in spite of herself, she had not yielded to her feelings, and so had done no wrong to Joseph. In short, was it conscientious duty, or strength of friendship, which made her go to the relief of the poor sick man? In either case she was right to do so. If she were a mother, she was a good mother, though her natural inclinations were not that way. All women can have children, but all women are not fond of children for all that, and Brulette ought therefore to have the more credit for taking back her own in spite of her love for company, and the questions she thus raised as to the truth.

All things considered, I did not see, even in what I might suppose the worst of my cousin's conduct, anything that lowered my friendship for her. Only I felt she had been so contradictory in her statements that I no longer knew how to rely on them. If she loved Joseph then she had certainly been artful; but if she did not love him, she had been too lively in spirits and forgetful of what had happened, for a person who was resolved to do her duty.

If she had not been so ill-treated by the community, I might have lessened my visits, for these doubts certainly lowered my confidence in her; but on the contrary, I controlled myself and went to the house every day, taking pains not to show her the least distrust. For all this, I was continually surprised at the difficulty with which she broke herself in, as it were, to the duties of a mother. In spite of the weight of care I believed she had on her mind, there were times when all her beauty and youth came back to her. She wore neither silk nor laces, that is true, but her hair was silky, her stockings well-fitting, and her pretty little feet were itching for a dance wherever she saw a bit of greensward or heard the sound of the bagpipes. Sometimes at home, when the thought of a Bourbonnais reel came over her, she would put Charlot on her grandfather's knee and make me dance it with her, singing and laughing and carrying herself jauntily, as if all the parish were there to see her; but a minute later, if Charlot cried or wanted to go to bed, or to be carried, or to be fed when he wasn't hungry, or given drink that he didn't want, she would take him in her arms with tears in her eyes, like a dog who is being chained up, and then, with a sigh, she would croon him a tune or pamper him with a bit of cake.

Seeing how she regretted her gay life, I offered her my sister's services in taking care of the little one, while she went to the fêtes at Saint-Chartier. I must tell you that in those days there lived in the old castle (of which nothing is now left but the shell) an old maiden lady, who was very good-natured and gave balls to all the country round. Tradesmen and noblemen, peasants and artisans, as many as liked, went there. You saw gentlemen and ladies going along the abominable roads in mid-winter, mounted on horses and donkeys, and wearing silk stockings, silver shoe-buckles, and powdered wigs as white as the snow on the trees along the road. Nothing deterred the company, rich or poor, for they amused them hugely and were well entertained from midday till six at night.

The lady of Saint-Chartier, who had noticed Brulette dancing in the market-place the year before, and was always anxious to have pretty girls at her daylight balls, invited her, and by my advice, she went once. I thought it was good advice, for she seemed to be getting depressed and to make no effort to raise her spirits. She was always so sweet to look at, and so ready with the right thing to say, that I never thought it possible people wouldn't receive her kindly, especially when she dressed so well and looked so handsome.

When she entered on my arm, whisperings went round, but no one dared to do more. She danced first with me, and as she had that sort of charm that everybody yields to, others came and asked her, possibly intending to show her some freedom, but not daring to risk it. All went well till a party of rich folks came into the room where we were; for the peasantry, I should tell you, had their ballroom apart and did not mix with the rich till nearly the end, when the ladies, deserted by their partners, would come and mingle with the country girls, who attracted people of all kinds by their lively chatter and their healthy looks.

Brulette was at first stared at as the handsomest article of the show, and the silk stockings paid such attention to the woollen stockings that no one could get near her. Then, in the spirit of contradiction, all those who had been tearing her to pieces for the last six months became frantically jealous all at once, and more in love than they had ever been. So then it was a struggle who should invite her first; in fact, they were almost ready to fight for the kiss that opened the dance.

The ladies and the young ladies were provoked; and our class of women complained to the lads for not keeping up their ill-will; but they might as well have talked to the winds; one glance of a pretty girl has more sweetness than the tongue of an ugly one has venom.

"Well, Brulette," I said, on our way home, "Wasn't I right to tell you to shake off your low spirits? You see the game is never lost if you know how to play it boldly."

"Thank you, cousin," she replied; "you are my best friend; indeed, I think, you are the only true and faithful friend I have ever had. I am glad to have got the better of my enemies, and now, I think I shall never be dull at home again."

"The devil! how fast you change! Yesterday it was all sulks, and to-day it is all merriment! You'll take your place as queen of the village."

"No," she said, "you don't understand me. This is the last ball I mean to go to so long as I keep Charlot; for, if you want me to tell you the truth, I haven't enjoyed myself one bit. I put a good face on it to please you, and I am glad, now it is over, to have done it; but all the while I was thinking of that poor baby. I fancied him crying and howling, no matter how kind your sister might be to him; he is so awkward in making known his wants, and so annoying to others.'

Brulette's words set my teeth on edge. I had forgotten the little wretch when I saw her laughing and dancing. The love she no longer concealed for him brought to my mind what seemed to be her past lies, and I began to think she must be an utter deceiver, who had now grown tired of restraining herself.

"Then you love him as your own flesh and blood?" I cried, not thinking much of the words I used.

"My own flesh and blood?" she repeated, as if surprised. "Well, yes, perhaps we love all children that way when we think of what we owe them. I never pretended, as some girls do when they are craving to get married, that my instincts were those of a brooding hen. Perhaps my head was too giddy to deserve a family in my young days. I know girls who can't sleep for thinking about it before they are sixteen. But I have got to be twenty, without feeling that I am rather late. If it is wrong, it is not my fault. I am as God made me, and I have gone along as he pushed me. To tell the truth, a baby is a hard task-master, unreasonable as a crazy husband and obstinate as a hungry animal. I like justice and good sense, and I should much prefer quieter and more sensible company. Also I like cleanliness; you have often laughed at me for worrying about a speck of dust on the dresser and letting a fly in the milk turn my stomach. Now a baby is always getting into the dirt, no matter how you may try to prevent it. And then I am fond of thinking, and dreaming, and recollecting things; but a baby won't let you think of anything but his wants, and gets angry if you pay no attention to him. But all that is neither here nor there, Tiennet, when God takes the matter in hand. He invented a sort of miracle which takes place inside of us when need be; and now I know a thing which I never believed until it happened to me, and that is that a child, no matter how ugly and ill-tempered it is, may be bitten by a wolf or trampled by a goat, but never by a woman, and that he will end by managing her—unless she is made of another wood than the rest of us."

As she said this we were entering my house, where Charlot was playing with my sister's children. "Well, I'm glad you have come," said my sister to Brulette; "you certainty have the most ill-tempered child that ever lived. He has beaten mine, and bitten them, and provoked them, and one needs forty cartloads of patience and pity to get along with him."

Brulette laughed, and going up to Charlot, who never gave her any welcome, she said, as she watched him playing after his fashion, and as if he could understand what she said: "I knew very well you could not make these kind people love you. There is no one but me, you poor little screech-owl, who can put up with your claws and your beak."

Though Charlot was only eighteen months old it seemed as if he really understood what Brulette was saying; for he got up, after looking at her for a moment with a thoughtful air, and jumped upon her and seized her hand and devoured it with kisses.

"Hey!" cried my sister, "then he really has his good moments, after all?"

"My dear," said Brulette, "I am just as much astounded as you are. This is the first time I have ever known him behave so." Then, kissing Charlot on his heavy eyelids she began to cry with joy and tenderness.

I can't tell why I was overcome by the action, as if there were something marvellous in it. But, in good truth, if the child was not hers, Brulette at that moment was transformed before my eyes. This girl, so proud-spirited that she wouldn't have shrunk before the king six months ago, and who that very morning had had all the lads of the neighborhood, rich and poor, at her knee, had gathered such pity and Christianity into her heart that she thought herself rewarded for all her trouble by the first kisses of an odious little slobberer, who had no pleasant ways and indeed seemed half-idiotic.

The tears were in my eyes, thinking of what those kisses cost her, and taking Charlot on my shoulder, I carried him back with her to her own door.

Twenty times I had it on my tongue to ask her the truth; for if she had done wrong as to Charlot, I was ready to forgive her the sin, but if, on the contrary, she was bearing the burden of other people's guilt, I desired to kiss her feet as the sweetest and most patient winner of Paradise.

But I dared not ask her any questions, and when I told my doubts to my sister, who was no fool, she replied: "If you dare not question her it is because in the depths of your heart you know her to be innocent. Besides," she added, "such a fine girl would have manufactured a better-looking boy. He is no more like her than a potato is like a rose."

TWENTY-FIRST EVENING.

The winter passed and the spring came, but Brulette never went back to her amusements. She did not even regret them, having seen that she could still be mistress of all hearts if she chose; but she said that so many men and women had betrayed her friendship that now she should care for quality only, not quantity. The poor child did not then know all the wrong that had been done to her. Everybody had vilified her, but no one had yet dared to insult her. When they looked at her they saw virtue written on her face; but when her back was turned they revenged themselves in words, for the respect which they could not help feeling, and they yelped at her heels like a cowardly dog that dares not spring at your face.

Père Brulet was getting old; he grew deafer, and lived so much in himself, like all aged people, that he paid no attention to the talk of the town. Father and daughter were therefore less troubled than people hoped to make them, and my own father, who was of a wise and Christian spirit (as were the rest of my family), advised me, and also set me the example, not to worry them about it, saying that the truth would come to light some day and the wicked tongues be punished.

Time, which is a grand sweeper, began, before long, to get rid of the vile dust. Brulette, who disdained revenge, would take none but that of receiving very coldly the advances that were made to her. It happened, as it usually does, that she found friends among those who had never been her lovers, and these friends, having no interest of their own, protected her in a way that she was not aware of. I am not speaking of Mariton, who was like a mother to her, and who, in her inn bar-room, came very near flinging the jugs at the heads of the drinkers when they ventured to sing out "Josette;" but I mean persons whom no one could accuse of blindly supporting her, and who shamed her detractors.

Thus it was that Brulette had brought herself down, at first with difficulty, then, little by little, contentedly, to a quieter life than in the past. She was visited by sensible persons, and came often to our house, bringing Charlot, whose swollen face had improved during the preceding winter, while his temper had grown much more amiable. The child was really not so ugly as he was coarse, and after Brulette had tamed him by the winsome force of her gentleness and affection we saw that his big black eyes were not without intelligence, and that when his broad mouth was willing to smile it was really more funny than hideous. He had passed through a drooling illness, during which Brulette, formerly so easily disgusted, had nursed him and wiped him and tended him carefully, till he was now the healthiest little fellow, and the nicest and the cleanest in the village. His jaws were still too heavy and his nose too short for beauty, but inasmuch as health is the chief thing with the little beggars, every one took notice of his size, his strength, and his determined air.

But the thing that made Brulette proudest of her handiwork was that Charlot became every day prettier in speech and more generous in heart. When she first had him he swore in a way to daunt a regiment; but she had made him forget all that, and had taught him a number of nice little prayers, and all sorts of amusing and quaint sayings, which he employed in his own way to the entertainment of everybody. He was not born affectionate and would never kiss any one willingly, but for his darling, as he called Brulette, he showed such a violent attachment that if he had done anything naughty,—such as cutting up his pinafore to make cravats, or sticking his sabots into the soup-pot, he would forestall all reproaches and cling to her neck with such strength that she hadn't the heart to scold him.

In May of that year we were invited to the wedding of a cousin at Chassin, who sent over a cart the night before to fetch us, with a message to Brulette that if she did not come and bring Charlot, it would throw a gloom over the marriage day.

Chassin is a pretty place on the river Gourdon, about six miles distant from our village. The country reminded me slightly of the Bourbonnais. Brulette, who was a small eater, soon left the noise of the feast, and went to walk outside and amuse Charlot. "Indeed," she said to me, "I should like to take him into some quiet, shady place; for this is his sleeping-time, and the noise of the party keeps him awake, and I am afraid he will be very cross this evening."

As it was very hot, I offered to take her into a little wood, formerly kept as a warren, which adjoins the old castle, and being chokeful of briers and ditches, is a very sheltered and retired spot. "Very good," she said, "the little one can sleep on my petticoat, and you can go back and enjoy yourself."

When we got there I begged her to let me stay.

"I am not so devoted to weddings as I once was," I said to her. "I shall amuse myself as well, if not better, talking with you. A party is very tiresome if you are not among your own people and don't know what to do."

"Very well," she replied, "but I see plainly, my poor cousin, that I am a weight upon your hands; and yet you take it with such patience and good-will that I don't know how I shall ever do without it. However, that time must come, for you are now of an age to settle, and the wife you choose may cast an evil eye upon me, as so many do, and might never be brought to believe that I deserve your friendship and hers."

"It is too soon to worry yourself about that," I replied, settling the fat Charlot on my blouse, which I laid on the grass while she sat down beside him to keep off the flies. "I am not thinking of marriage, and if I were, I swear my wife should keep on good terms with you or I would be on bad terms with her. She would have a crooked heart indeed if she could not see that my regard for you is the most honorable of all friendships, and if she couldn't comprehend that having followed you through all your joys and all your troubles, I am so accustomed to your companionship that you and I are one. But how about you, cousin? are you thinking of marriage, or have you sworn off on that subject?"

"Oh! as for me, yes, I think so, Tiennet, if it suits the will of God. I am all but of age, and I think I have waited so long for the wish to marry that now I have let the time go by."

"Perhaps it is only just beginning, dear. The love of amusement has gone, and the love of children has come, and I see how you are settling down to a quiet home life; but nevertheless you are still in your spring-time, like the earth whose flowers are just blooming. You know I don't flatter you, and so you may believe me when I tell you that you have never been so pretty, though you have grown rather pale—like Thérence, the girl of the woods. You have even caught a sad little look like hers, which goes very well with your plain caps and that gray gown. The fact is, I believe your inside being has changed and you are going to be a sister of charity—if you are not in love."

"Don't talk about that, my dear friend," cried Brulette. "I might have turned either to love or piety a year ago. I felt, as you say, changed within. But now, here I am, tied to the cares of life without finding either the sweetness of love or the strength of faith. It seems to me that I am tied to a yoke and can only push forward by my head, without knowing what sort of cart I am dragging behind me. You see that I am not very sad under it and that I don't mean to die of it; and yet, I own that I regret something in my life—not what has been, but what might have been."

"Come, Brulette," I said, sitting down by her and taking her hand, "perhaps the time has come for confidence. You can tell me everything without fear of my feeling grief or jealousy. I am cured of wishing for anything that you can't give me. But give me one thing, for it is my due,— give me your confidence about your troubles."

Brulette became scarlet and made an effort to speak, but could not say a word. It almost seemed as if I were forcing her to confess to her own soul, and she had foreborne so long that now she did not know how to do it.

She raised her beautiful eyes and looked at the country before us, for we were sitting at the edge of the wood, on a grassy terrace overlooking a pretty valley broken up into rolling ground green with cultivation. At our feet flowed the little river, and beyond, the ground rose rapidly under a fine wood of full-grown oaks, less extensive but boasting as large trees as any we had seen in the forest of Alleu. I saw in Brulette's eyes the thoughts she was thinking, and taking her hand, which she had withdrawn from mine to press her heart as if it pained her, I said, in a tone that was neither jest nor mischief,—

"Tell me, is it Huriel or Joseph?"

"It is not Joseph!" she replied, hastily.

"Then it is Huriel; but are you free to follow your inclinations?"

"How can I have any inclinations," she answered, blushing more and more, "for a person who has doubtless never thought of me?"

"That is no reason."

"Yes it is, I tell you."

"No, I swear it isn't. I had plenty of inclination for you."

"But you got over it."

"And you are trying hard to get over yours; that shows you are still ill of it. But Joseph?"

"Well, what of Joseph?"

"You were never bound to him?"

"You know that well enough!"

"But—Charlot?"

"Charlot?"

As my eyes turned to the child, hers turned too; then they fell back on me, so puzzled, so clear with innocence, that I was ashamed of my suspicions as though I had offered her an insult.

"Oh, nothing," I replied, hastily. "I said 'Charlot' because I thought he was waking up."

At that moment a sound of bagpipes reached us from the other side of the river among the oaks, and Brulette trembled like a leaf in the wind.

"There!" said I, "the bride's dance is beginning, and I do believe they are sending the music to fetch you."

"No, no," said Brulette, who had grown very pale, "neither the air nor the instrument belong to this region. Tiennet, Tiennet, either I am crazy— or he who is down there—"

"Do you see him?" I cried, running to the edge of the terrace and looking with all my eyes; "can it be Père Bastien?"

"I see no one," she said, having followed me, "but it was not Père Bastien—neither was it Joseph—it was—"

"Huriel, perhaps! that seems to me less certain than the river that parts us. But let us go at any rate; we may find a ford, and if he is there we shall certainly catch him, the gay muleteer, and find out what he is thinking about."

"No, Tiennet, I can't leave Charlot."

"The devil take that child! Then wait for me here; I am going alone."

"No, no, no! Tiennet," cried Brulette, holding me with both hands; "it is dangerous to go down that steep place."

"Whether I break my neck or not, I am going to put you out of your misery."

"What misery?" she exclaimed, still holding me, but recovering from her first agitation by an effort of pride. "What does it matter to me whether Huriel or some one else is in the wood? Do you suppose I want you to run after a man who, knowing I was close by, wanted to pass on?"

"If that is what you think," said a soft voice behind us, "I think we had better go away."

We turned round at the first word, and there was Thérence, the beautiful Thérence, before our eyes.

At the sight Brulette, who had fretted so much at being forgotten by her, lost all her nerve and fell into Thérence's arms with a great burst of tears.

"Well, well!" said Thérence, kissing her with the energy of a daughter of the woods. "Did you think I had forgotten our friendship? Why do you judge hardly of people who have never passed a day without thinking of you?"

"Tell her quickly if your brother is here, Thérence," I cried, "for—" Brulette, turning quickly, put her hand on my lips, and I caught myself up, adding, with a laugh, "for I am dying to see him."

"My brother is over there," said Thérence, "but he does not know you are so near. Listen, he is going farther off; you can hardly hear his music now."

She looked at Brulette, who had grown pale again, and added, laughing: "He is too far off to call him; but he will soon turn and come round by the ruined castle. There, if you don't disdain him, Brulette, and will not prevent me, I shall give him a surprise he does not expect; for he did not think of seeing you till to-night. We were on our way to your village to pay you a visit, and it is a great happiness to me to have met you here and saved a delay in our meeting. Let us go under the trees, for if he sees you from where he is, he is capable of drowning himself in that river in trying to get to you, not knowing the fords."

We turned back and sat down near Charlot, Thérence asking, with that grand, simple manner of hers, whether he was mine. "Not unless I have been married a long time," I answered, "which is not so."

"True," she said, looking closely at the child, "he is already a little man; but you might have been married before you came to us."

Then she added, laughing, that she knew little about the growth of babies, never seeing any in the woods where she always lived, and where few parents ever reared their children. "You will find me as much of a savage as ever," she continued, "but a good deal less irritable, and I hope my dear Brulette will have no cause to complain of my ill-temper."

"I do think," said Brulette, "that you seem gayer, and better in health,—and so much handsomer that it dazzles my eyes to look at you."

The same thought had struck my mind on seeing Thérence. She had laid in a stock of health and fresh clear color in her cheeks which made her another woman. If her eyes were still too deep sunken, the black brows no longer lowered over them and hid their fire; and though her smile was still proud, there was a charming gayety in it at times, which made her teeth gleam like dewdrops on a flower. The pallor of fever had left her face, which the May sun had rather burned during her journey, though it had made the roses bloom; and there was something, I scarcely know what, so youthful, so strong, so valiant in her face, that my heart jumped with an idea that came to me, heaven knows how, as I looked to see if the velvety black mark at the corner of her mouth was still in the same place.

"Friends," she said, wiping her beautiful hair, which curled naturally and which the heat had glued to her forehead, "as we have a little time to talk before my brother joins us, I want to tell you my story, without any false shame or pretences; for several other stories hang upon it. Only, before I begin, tell me, Brulette, if Tiennet, whom you used to think so much of, is, as I think he is, still the same, so that I can take up the conversation where we left it—a year ago come next harvest."

"Yes, dear Thérence, that you may," answered my cousin, pleased at her friend's tone.

"Well, then, Tiennet," continued Thérence, with a valiant sincerity all her own, which made the difference between her and the reserved and timid Brulette, "I reveal nothing you did not know in telling you that before your visit to us last year I attached myself to a poor fellow, sick and sad in mind and body, very much as a mother is attached to her child. I did not then know he loved another girl, and he, seeing my regard for him, which I did not hide, had not the courage to tell me it was not returned. Why Joseph—for I can name him, and you see, dear friends, that I don't change color in doing so—why Joseph, whom I had so often entreated to tell me the causes of his grief, should have sworn to me it was nothing more than a longing for his mother and his own country, I do not know. He must have thought me base, and he did me great injustice; for, had he told me the truth, I myself would have gone to fetch Brulette without a murmur, and without making the great mistake of forming a low opinion of her which I did, and which I now confess, and ask her to pardon."

"You did that long ago, Thérence, and there is nothing to pardon where friendship is."

"Yes, dear," replied Thérence, "but the wrong which you forget, I remember, and I would have given the world to repair it by taking good care of Joseph, and showing him friendship and good-nature after you left us. Remember, friends, that I had never said or done a false thing; so that in my childhood, my father, who is a good judge, used to call me Thérence the Sincere. When I last saw you, on the banks of your own Indre, half-way to your village, I spoke privately with Joseph for a moment, begging him to return to us and promising there should be no change in my interest and care for his health and well-being. Why, then, did he disbelieve me in his heart; and why, promising with his lips to return (a lie of which I was not the dupe),—why did he contemptuously leave me forever, as though I were a shameless girl who would torment him with love-sick folly?"

"Do you mean to say," I interrupted, "that Joseph, who stayed only twenty-four hours with us, did not return to your woods,—if only to tell you his plans and say good-bye? Since he left us that day we have heard nothing of him."

"If you have had no news of him," replied Thérence, "I have some to give you. He did return—by night, like a thief who fears the sunshine. He went to his own lodge and took his clothes and his bagpipe, and went away without crossing the threshold of my father's hut, or so much as glancing our way. I was awake and saw it all. I watched every action, and when he disappeared in the woods, I felt I was as rigid as death. My father warmed me in the rays of the good God and his own great heart. He took me away to the open moor, and talked to me all one day, and all the next night, till I was able to pray and sleep. You know my father a little, dear friends, but you cannot know how he loves his children, how he comforts them, how he finds just the right thing to say to make them like himself, who is an angel from heaven hidden under the bark of an old oak! My father cured me. If it were not for him, I should despise Joseph; as it is, I have only ceased to love him."

Ending thus, Thérence again wiped her fine forehead, wet with perspiration, drew a long breath, kissed Brulette, and held out to me, laughing, her large and well-shaped white hand, and shook mine with the frankness of a young man.

TWENTY-SECOND EVENING.

I saw that Brulette was inclined to blame Joseph very severely, and I thought I ought to defend him a little. "I don't approve of his conduct so far as it shows ingratitude to you, Thérence," I said, "but inasmuch as you are now able to judge him quite fairly, won't you admit that at the bottom of his heart there was a sense of respect for you and a fear of deceiving you? All the world is not like you, my beautiful girl of the woods, and I think that very few persons have a pure enough heart and courage enough to go straight to the point and tell things just as they are. You have an amount of strength and virtue in you of which Joseph, and many others in his place, would be wholly incapable."

"I don't understand you," said Thérence.

"I do," said Brulette; "Joseph feared, perhaps, to put himself in the way of being charmed by your beauty, and of loving you for that, without giving you his whole heart as you deserved."

"Oh!" cried Thérence, scarlet with wounded pride, "that is just what I complain of. Say it boldly. Joseph feared to entice me into wrong-doing. He took no account of my good sense or my honor. Well, his respect would have consoled me; his fear is humiliating. Never mind, Brulette, I forgive him, because I no longer suffer, and I feel myself above him; but nothing can ever take out of my heart the sense that Joseph was ungrateful to me, and took a low view of his duty. I would ask you to let us say no more about it, if I were not obliged to tell you the rest; but I must speak, otherwise you will not know what to think of my brother's conduct."

"Ah, Thérence!" said Brulette, "I long to know what were the consequences of that misfortune which troubled us all so much over there."

"My brother did not do as we expected," replied Thérence. "Instead of hiding his unfortunate secret in distant places, he retraced his steps at the end of a week, and went to find the Carmelite friar in his convent, which is over by Montluçon. 'Brother Nicolas,' he said to him, 'I can't live with such a weight on my heart. You told me to confess myself to God, but there is such a thing as justice on this earth; it may not be practised, but it is none the less a law from heaven. I must confess before men, and bear the blame and the penalty I deserve.' 'One moment, my son,' answered the friar; 'men invented the penalty of death, which God disapproves, and they might kill you deliberately for having killed another unintentionally.' 'That is not possible,' said my brother; 'I never intended to kill him, and I can prove it.' 'To prove it you must call witnesses,' said the monk, 'and that will compromise your comrades and your chief, who is my nephew, and no more a murderer than you in his heart; you will expose them all to be harassed by the law, and you will see them forced to betray the oaths of your fraternity. Come, stay here in my convent, and wait for me. I will undertake to settle the matter, provided you won't ask me too closely how I have done it.'

"Thereupon the friar went to consult his abbé, who sent him to the bishop, whom we call in our parts the chief priest, as they did in the olden time, and who is the bishop of Montluçon. The chief priest, who has a right to be heard by the chief judges, said and did things we know nothing about. Then he sent for my brother and said to him, 'My son, confess yourself to me as you would to God.' When Huriel had told him the whole truth, from end to end, the bishop said: 'Repent and do penance, my son. The matter is settled before men; you have nothing to dread in future; but you must appease the wrath of God, and in order to do that, I desire you to leave the company and brotherhood of the muleteers, who are men without religion and whose secret practices are contrary to the laws of heaven and earth.' My brother having humbly remarked to him that there were honest folk among them, the chief priest replied: 'So much the worse; if those honest folk refused to take the oaths they require, the society would cease to do evil, and would become a corporation of working-men as respectable as any other.' My brother thought over these words of the chief priest, and would have wished to reform the practices of his fraternity rather than do away with them altogether. He went to meet an assembly of muleteers and talked to them very sensibly,—so they told me; but after listening to him quietly, they answered that they neither could nor would change any of their customs. Whereupon he paid his forfeit and sold his mules, keeping only the *clairin* for our use. So Brulette, you are not going to see a muleteer, but a good, steady wood-cutter who works for his father."

"And who may find it very hard to get accustomed to such work," said Brulette, hiding the pleasure this news gave her.

"If he did find it hard to change his ways of life," answered Thérence, "he is well consoled when he remembers how afraid you were of the muleteers, and that in your country they are looked upon as an abomination. But now that I have satisfied your impatience to know how my brother got out of his troubles, I must tell you something more about Joseph, which may make you angry, Brulette, though it will also astonish you."

As Thérence said that with a spice of malice and a laugh, Brulette showed no uneasiness, and told her to explain.

"You must know," continued Thérence, "that we have spent the last three months in the forest of Montaigu, where we met Joseph, in good health, but serious as usual, and still wrapped up in himself. If you want to know where he now is, I will tell you that we have left him there with my father, who is helping him to get admitted to the association of bagpipers; for you know, or you don't know, that they too, are a fraternity, and have secret practices which others know nothing about. At first Joseph was rather embarrassed at seeing us. He seemed ashamed to speak to me and might have avoided us altogether if my father, after reproaching him for his want of confidence and friendship, had not pressed him to remain,—for he knew he could still be useful to him. When Joseph perceived that I was quite at my ease and had no unkind recollections, he made bold to ask for the return of our friendship, and he even tried to excuse his conduct; but my father, who would not let him lay a finger on my wound, turned the matter into a joke, and made him go to work, both in the woods and at his music, so as to bring the matter to an end as soon as possible. I was a good deal astonished that he never mentioned any of you, and I questioned him without getting a word out of him. Neither my brother nor I had heard anything of you (until last week, when we came through the village of Huriel). We were much worried about you, and my father told Joseph rather sharply that if he had letters from his own people he ought at least to tell us whether you were dead or alive. Joseph answered shortly, in a voice that sounded very hollow: 'Everybody is well, and so am I.' My father, who never beats about the bush, told him to speak out, but he answered stiffly, 'I tell you, master, that our friends over there are well and quite contented, and if you will give me your daughter in marriage I shall be contented too.' At first we thought he was crazy, and tried to make a joke of it, though his manner made us rather uneasy. But he returned to the subject two days later, and asked me if I had any regard for him. I took no other revenge for his tardy offer than to say, 'Yes, Joseph, I have as much regard for you as Brulette has.' He drew in his lips, lowered his head, and did not say another word. But my brother, having questioned him later, received this reply: 'Huriel, I no longer think of Brulette, and I beg you never to mention her to me again.' We could get nothing more out of him except that he was resolved, as soon as he should be received into the fraternity of bagpipers, to begin his service for a time in his own country, and prove to his mother that he was able to support her; after which he intended to take her to live with him in La Marche or the Bourbonnais, provided I would become his wife. This brought about a grand explanation between my father, my brother, and myself. Both tried to make me own that I might be induced to consent. But Joseph had come back too late for me, and I had made too many reflections about him. I quietly refused, feeling no longer any regard for him, and conscious also that he had none for me. I am too proud a girl to be taken as a remedy for disappointment. I supposed you had written him to put an end to his hopes."

"No," said Brulette, "I did not, and it is only by the mercy of God that he has forgotten me. Perhaps it was that he began to know you better, my Thérence."

"No, no," cried the girl of the woods, resolutely, "If it was not disappointment at your refusal, it was pique at my cure. He only cared for me because I had ceased to care for him. If that is his love, it is not mine, Brulette. All or nothing; yes for life, in all frankness; or no for life, with all freedom. There's that child waking up," she continued, interrupting herself, "and I want to take you to my new abode for a moment; it is in the old castle of Chassin."

"But won't you tell us," said Brulette, who was very much puzzled by all she heard, "how and why you are in this part of the country?"

"You are in too much of a hurry to know," replied Thérence; "I want you to see first."

Taking Brulette round the neck with her beautiful bare arm, well browned by the sun, she led her away without giving her time to take Charlot, whom she herself caught up like a bundle under her other arm, although he was now as heavy as a little calf.

The fief of Chassin was once a castle, as I have heard say, with seignorial rights and laws; but at the time of which I am telling, nothing remained of the building but the porch, which was a structure of some importance, heavily built, and so arranged that there were lodging-rooms on both sides of it. It seemed that the part of the building which I have called a porch, the use of which is difficult to explain at the present time (on account of its peculiar construction), was really a vaulted chamber leading to other buildings; for as to those that still remain around the courtyard, which are only miserable stables and dilapidated barns, I don't know what uses they could have been put to, or what comfort could have been found in them. There were still, at the time of which I am speaking, three or four unfurnished rooms which seemed quite ancient, but if any great lord ever took his pleasure in them he must have wanted very little of that article.

And yet it was among these ruins that happiness was awaiting some of those whose history I am telling you; and, as if there were something within each human being which tells him in advance of coming blessings, neither Brulette nor I saw anything sad or ugly in this old place. The grassy courtyard, surrounded on two sides by the ruins and on the other two by the moat and the little wood through which we passed; the great hedge, where I saw with surprise shrubs which are seen only in the gardens of the wealthy (showing that the place had once known care and beauty); the clumsy gateway, choked up with rubbish, where stone benches could still be seen, as if in former days some warder had had charge of this barrack then considered precious; the long brambles which ran from end to end of this squalid enclosure,—all these things, which made the whole place resemble a prison, closed, deserted, and forgotten, seemed as cheerful to our eyes as the springtide sun which was forcing its way in through the crevices and drying up the dampness. Perhaps, too, the sight of our old acquaintance, the *clairin*, who was feeding on the turf, gave us warning of the coming of a true friend. I think he recognized us, for he came up to be stroked, and Brulette could not refrain from kissing the white star on his forehead.

"This is my château," said Thérence, taking us into a room where her bed and other bits of furniture were already installed; "and there you see Huriel's room and my father's on the other side."

"Your father! then he is coming!" I cried, jumping for joy. "I am so glad, for there is no man under the sun I like better."

"And right you are," said Thérence, tapping my ear in sign of friendship. "And he likes you. Well, you will see him if you come back next week, and even—but it is too soon to speak of that. Here is the master."

Brulette blushed, thinking it was Huriel that Thérence meant; but it was only the foreign dealer who had bought the timber of the forest of Chassin.

I say "forest" because, no doubt, there were forests there once, which joined the small but beautiful growth of lofty trees that we saw beyond the river. As the name remains, it is to be supposed it was not bestowed for nothing. The conversation which ensued between Thérence and the wood-merchant explained to us very quickly the whole thing. He came from the Bourbonnais, and had long known the Head-Woodsman and his family as hard-working people who kept their word. Being in quest, through his business, of some tall masts for the king's navy, he had discovered these remains of a virgin forest (very rare indeed in our country), and had given the work of felling and trimming the trees to Père Bastien; and the latter had taken it all the more willingly because his son and daughter, knowing the place to be in our neighborhood, were delighted with the idea of spending the whole summer and perhaps part of the winter near us.

The Head-Woodsman was allowed the selection and management of his workmen under a contract with forfeiture between himself and the purchaser of the timber; and the latter had induced the owner of the estate to cede him the use, gratis, of the old castle, where he, a well-to-do tradesman, would have thought himself very ill-lodged, but where a family of wood-cutters might be far better off as the season grew late than in their usual lodges of logs and heather.

Huriel and his sister had arrived that morning; the one had immediately begun to install herself, the other had been making acquaintance with the wood, the land, and the people of the neighborhood.

We overheard the purchaser reminding Thérence, who talked business as well as any man, of a condition in his agreement with Père Bastien,—namely, that he would employ none but Bourbonnais workmen to prepare the trunks, inasmuch as they alone understood the work and would not spoil the finest pieces, like the laborers of our part of the country. "Very good," replied the woodland girl; "but for the branches and light-wood we shall employ whom we please. We do not think it wise to take all the work away from the people of the neighborhood, who might be annoyed and molest us in consequence. They are already ill-inclined to all who are not of their parish."

"Now listen, my dear Brulette," she said, when the dealer had departed, "it is my opinion that, if nothing detains you in your village, you might persuade your grandfather to employ his time very pleasantly here this summer. You have told me that he is still a good workman, and he would have to do with a good master,—I mean my father, who would let him work at his ease. You could lodge here at no expense and we would share the housekeeping together."

Then, while Brulette was burning with the desire to say yes, but not daring to betray herself, Thérence added, "If you hesitate, I shall think your heart is given in your own village and that my brother has come too late."

"Too late!" cried a ringing voice which came from the ivy-covered window. "God grant that those words be false!"

And Huriel, handsome and fresh-looking as he always was when the charcoal no longer concealed him, sprang into the room and caught Brulette in his arms to kiss her on the cheeks; for he wouldn't stand on ceremony, and he had no notion of the rather icy behavior of the people in our parts. He seemed so glad, and talked so loud, and laughed so heartily that she could not be angry with him. He kneaded me like a bit of dough and jumped about the room as if joy and friendship had the effect of new wine.

All of a sudden he spied Charlot and stopped short, tried to look away, forced himself to say a few words which had no connection with the child, then sat down on his sister's bed and turned so pale that I thought he was going to faint away.

"What's the matter with him?" cried Thérence, amazed. Then, touching his head, she said, "Good heavens, it is a cold sweat! Do you feel ill?"

"No, no," said Huriel, rising and shaking himself. "It is joy—the sudden excitement—it is nothing."

Just then the mother of the bride came to ask why we had left the wedding, and whether Brulette or the child were ill. Seeing that we were detained by the company of strangers, she very politely invited Huriel and Thérence to come with us to the feast and to the dance. This woman, who was my aunt, being the sister of my father and Brulette's deceased father, seemed to me to know the secret of Charlot's birth; for she had asked no questions and had taken great care of him when brought to her house. I had even heard of her saying that he was a relative, and the people of Chassin had no suspicion about the child.

As Huriel, who was still troubled in mind, merely thanked my aunt without giving any decided answer, Thérence roused him with the remark that Brulette was obliged to go back to the wedding, and that if he did not go he might lose his opportunity of bringing about what they both desired. Huriel, however, was still uneasy and hesitating, when Brulette said to him, "Do you really not wish to dance with me to-day?"

"Do you speak true, Brulette?" he said, looking her in the eye. "Do you wish me for a partner?"

"Yes," she said, "for I remember how well you dance."

"Is that the only reason why you wish for me?"

Brulette was embarrassed, thinking that the fellow was too much in a hurry, yet not daring to play off her former coquettish little airs, so fearful was she of seeing him hurt or disappointed again. But Thérence tried to help her out by reproaching Huriel for asking too much the first day.

"You are right, sister," he answered. "And yet I cannot behave differently. Hear me, Brulette, and forgive me. You must promise to have no other partner but me at this wedding, or I cannot go at all."

"What a funny fellow!" cried my aunt, who was a lively little woman and took all things for the best. "A lover of yours, my Brulette? I see that plainly; and no half-hearted one either! But, my lad," she added, turning to Huriel, "I would have you know that it is not the custom in these parts to show all you feel; and no one dances several times running with a girl unless there has been promise of heart and hand."

"It is here as it is with us, my good dame," replied Huriel; "nevertheless, with or without promise of her heart, Brulette must now promise me her hand for the whole dance."

"If she wishes it, I shall not prevent her," said my aunt, "she is a sensible girl, who knows very well how to behave. I have done my duty in warning her that she will be talked about."

"Brother," said Thérence, "I think you are crazy. Is that the way to do with Brulette, whom you know to be so reserved, and who has never yet given you the rights you claim?"

"Yes, I may be mad, and she may be shy," said Huriel, "but all the same my madness must gain the day and her shyness lose it, and at once. I ask nothing more of her than to allow me to dance with her to the end of this wedding. If after that she does not wish to hear of me again, she is mistress of her actions."

"That is all very well," said my aunt, "but the harm will then have been done, and if you withdraw from her then who will repair it?"

"She knows that I shall not withdraw," said Huriel.

"If you know that," said my aunt to Brulette, "why don't you explain yourself? I really can't understand this matter at all. Did you engage yourself to this lad in the Bourbonnais?"

"No," said Huriel, without giving Brulette time to answer. "I have never asked her, never! What I now ask of her she, and she alone, without consulting any one, must decide to grant or not, as she chooses."

Brulette, trembling like a leaf, had turned to the wall and was hiding her face in her hands. If she was glad to find Huriel so resolute about her, she was also annoyed that he had no compassion for her natural hesitation and timidity. She was not made, like Thérence, to speak out a noble "yes" before all the world; so being, and not knowing how else to get out of the matter, she took refuge in her eyes and began to cry.

TWENTY-THIRD EVENING.

"You are a downright bashaw, my friend," said my aunt to Huriel, giving him a push away from Brulette, whom he had approached in much excitement. Then, taking her niece's hands, she soothed her and asked her very gently to tell her the real meaning of it all.

"If your grandfather were here," she said, "he would explain what there is between you and this stranger lad, and we could then leave the matter to his judgment; but since I am here now as father and mother both, you must confide in me. Do you wish me to put an end to this pursuit? Shall I, instead of inviting this brute, or this rogue,—for I don't know which to call him,—tell him that he must let you alone?"

"Exactly," said Huriel, "that's what I want. I want her to say what she wishes, and I will obey her without anger, and she shall still retain my friendship and respect. If she thinks me a brute or a rogue let her pack me off. Speak, Brulette; I shall always be your friend and servant,—you know that very well."

"Be what you will," said Brulette at last, rising and giving him her hand; "you protected me in danger, and you have suffered such troubles on my account that I neither can nor will refuse so little a thing as to dance with you as much as you like."

"But think what your aunt has said," replied Huriel, holding her hand. "You will be talked of, and if nothing good comes of it between us, which on your side may still be, any plan you may have for another marriage would be destined or delayed."

"Well, that is a less danger than the one you threw yourself into on my account," said Brulette. "Aunt, please excuse me," she added, "if I cannot explain matters just now; but believe that your niece loves and respects you, and will never give you reason to blush for her."

"I am certain of that," said my aunt; "but what answer am I to give to the questions they will be sure to ask?"

"None at all, aunt," said Brulette, resolutely. "I can afford to put up with all their talk; you know I am in the habit of doing so."

"Thank you, darling of my heart!" cried Huriel, kissing her hand six or seven times. "You shall never repent what you have granted to me."

"Are you coming, you obstinate fellow?" said my aunt; "I can't stay away any longer, and if I don't carry Brulette down there at once, the bride is capable of leaving the wedding and coming after her."

"Go down, Brulette!" cried Thérence, "and leave the baby with me; I promise I will take care of him."

"Won't you come, too, my handsome Bourbonnaise?" said my aunt, who could not keep her eyes off Thérence, "I count upon you."

"I will go later, my good woman," replied Thérence. "But just now I want to give my brother suitable clothes in which to do honor to your invitation; for, as you see, we are still in our travelling things."

My aunt carried off Brulette, who wanted to take Charlot; but Thérence insisted on keeping him, wishing to leave her brother free with his darling without the trouble and annoyance of a small child. This was not at all satisfactory to Charlot, who set up a yell when he saw that Brulette was leaving him, and fought with all his strength in Thérence's arms; but she, looking at him with a grave and determined manner, said quietly:—

"You must be quiet, my boy; you must, you know."

Charlot, who had never been ordered in his life, was so astonished at her tone that he gave in immediately; but as I saw that Brulette was distressed at leaving him with a girl who had never in her life touched a baby, I promised to bring him to her myself if there should be the least trouble, and persuaded her to go with our good little aunt who was getting impatient.

Huriel, urged by his sister, went off to his room to shave and dress, and I, left alone with Thérence, helped her to unpack her boxes and shake out the clothes, while Charlot, quite subdued, stood, with open mouth, looking on. When I had carried Huriel the clothes which Thérence piled on my arms, I returned to ask if she didn't mean to dress herself too, and to offer to take the child to walk while she did so.

"As for me," she said, laying out her finery on her bed, "I will go if Brulette worries after me; but I will admit that if she would only forget me for a time, I would prefer to stay quietly here. In any case, I can be ready in a minute, and I need no one to escort me. I am accustomed to hunt up and get ready our lodgings in travelling, like a regular quartermaster on a campaign, and nothing disturbs me wherever I am."

"Then you don't like dancing?" I said; "or is it shyness at making new acquaintances that makes you wish to stay at home?"

"No, I don't like dancing," she replied; "nor the racket, nor the suppers, and particularly not the waste of time which brings weariness."

"But one doesn't love dancing for dancing's sake only. Do you fear, or dislike, the attentions the young men pay to the girls?"

"No, I have neither fear nor repugnance," she said, simply. "It does not amuse me, that is all. I am not witty, like Brulette. I don't know how to answer patly, nor how to make other people talk, and I can't be amusing. I am stupid and dreamy, and I am as much out of place in a lively company as a wolf or a fox at a dance."

"You don't look like a wolf nor any other villanous beast, and you dance as gracefully as the willow branches when the breeze caresses them—"

I don't know what more I was going to say, when Huriel came out of his room, handsome as the sun and more in a hurry to get off than I was, for I should have been just as satisfied to stay with his sister. She kept him a moment to straighten his cravat and to tie his garters at the knee, apparently not thinking him jaunty enough to dance through the wedding with Brulette, and as she did so she said: "Tell me, why were you so jealous of her dancing with any one but you? Were not you afraid of frightening her with such masterful orders?"

"Tiennet!" exclaimed Huriel, stopping short in what he was doing, and taking Charlot, whom he placed on the table and gazed at with all his eyes, "Whose child is this?"

Thérence, astonished, first asked him what he meant by the question, and then asked me why I did not answer it.

We looked each other in the eyes, like three dolts, and I would have given all I had to know how to answer, for I saw that a sword was hanging over our heads. At last, recollecting the virtue and truth I had seen that very afternoon in my cousin's eyes when I had pretty nigh asked her the same question, I plucked up courage and going straight to the point I said to Huriel, "Comrade, if you ask that question in our village many persons will tell you he is Brulette's child—"

He did not let me say more; but picking up the boy, he felt him and turned him over as a hunter examines a head of game. Fearing his anger, I tried to take the child from him; but he held him firmly, saying:—

"No fear for the poor innocent thing; my heart is not bad, and if I saw any resemblance to her I might not be able to refrain from kissing him, though I should hate the fate that brought me to it. But there is no such resemblance; my blood runs neither the hotter nor the colder with this child in my arms."

"Tiennet, Tiennet, answer him," cried Thérence, as if waking from a dream. "Answer me, too, for I don't know what all this means, and it makes me wild to think of it. There is no stain on our family and if my father believed—"

Huriel cut her short. "Wait, sister," he said; "a word too much is soon said. It is for Tiennet to speak. Come, Tiennet, you who are an honest man, tell me—one—two—whose child is that?"

"I swear to God I don't know," I answered.

"If it were hers, you would know?"

"I think she could not have hidden it from me."

"Did she ever hide anything else?"

"Never."

"Does she know the parents of the child?"

"Yes, but she will not even let me question her about them."

"Does she deny the child is hers?"

"No one has ever dared to ask her."

"Not even you?"

Thereupon I related in a few words what I knew, and what I believed, and finished by saying: "I can find no proof for or against Brulette; but, for the life of me, I cannot doubt her."

"Nor I either!" said Huriel, and kissing Charlot, he set him on the floor.

"Nor I either!" exclaimed Thérence, "but why should this idea have come into people's heads? Why into yours, brother, as soon as you looked at the child? I did not even think of asking whether it were Brulette's nephew or cousin; I thought it must belong to the family, and seeing it in her arms made me wish to take it in mine."

"I see I must explain," said Huriel, "though the words will scorch my mouth. But no," he added, "I would rather tell it! it will be the first and the last time, for my mind is made up, whatever the truth may be, and whatever happens. You must know, Thérence, that three days ago, when we were parting with Joseph at Montaigu—and you know with what a light heart I left him! he was cured, he gave her up, he asked you in marriage, and

Brulette was still free! He knew she was, and said so, and when I spoke of her he answered, 'Do what you like, I no longer love her; you can love her without hurting me.' Well, sister, at the very moment we were parting, Joseph caught me by the arm as you were getting into the cart, and said, 'Is it true, Huriel, that you are going into our parts; and that you mean to court the girl I loved so well?'"

"Yes," I answered, "since you ask me, that is my intention; and you have no right to change your mind, or I shall think you were tricking us when you asked for my sister in marriage."

"'I was not,'" replied Joseph, "'but I should feel I was deceiving you now if I allowed you to leave without telling you a miserable thing. God is my witness that these words should never have left my lips against a person whose father brought me up, if you were not on the point of taking a false step. But your father has also brought me up, educating my mind just as the other fed and clothed my body, and I am forced to tell you the truth. Huriel, at the time when I left Brulette with my heart full of love, she had already, without my knowledge, loved another man, and to-day there is a living proof of it which she does not even take the trouble to hide. Now, then, do as you please; I shall think no more about her.' So saying, Joseph turned his back on me and went into the woods. He looked so wild that I, with my heart full of faith and love, accused him in my thoughts of madness and wicked anger. You remember, sister, that you thought me ill as we drove that day to the village of Huriel. When we got there you found two letters from Brulette, and I found three from Tiennet, which our friends there had neglected to send on in spite of their promises. Those letters were so simple, so affectionate, and showed such truth in every word, that I said to myself, 'I will go!' and Joseph's words went out of my mind like a bad dream. I was ashamed for him, and would not remember them. And then, just now, when I saw Brulette, with that look of hers, so gentle, so modest, that charmed me so in the old days, I swear to God I had forgotten all as though it had never happened. The sight of the child killed me! And that was why I was resolved to know if Brulette were free to love me. She is; because she has promised to expose herself for my sake to the criticisms and neglect of others. Well, as she is now tied to no one— even if there be a fault in her—whether I believe it a little or not at all— whether she confesses or explains it—it is all one; I love her!"

"Would you love a degraded girl?" cried Thérence. "No, no, think of your father, of your sister! Don't go to this wedding; wait till we know the truth. I don't distrust Brulette, I don't believe in Joseph. I am sure that Brulette is spotless, but she must say so; she must do more, she must prove it. Go and fetch her, Tiennet. Let her explain this thing at once, before my brother takes one of those steps from which an honest man cannot back down."

"You shall not go, Tiennet," said Huriel, "I forbid you. If, as I believe, Brulette is as innocent as my sister Thérence, she shall not be subjected to the insult of that question before I have openly pledged my word to her."

"Think it over, brother," said Thérence, again urging him.

"Sister," said Huriel, "you forget one thing; if Brulette has done a wrong thing, I have committed a crime; if love betrayed her into bringing a child into the world, anger betrayed me into sending a man out of it." Then as Thérence still remonstrated, he added, kissing her and pushing her aside, "Enough, enough; I need pardon before I judge of others; did I not kill a man?"

So saying he rushed off without waiting for me, and I saw him running towards the bride's house, where the smoke of the chimney and the uproar within bespoke the wedding feast.

"Ah!" said Thérence, following him with her eyes, "My poor brother cannot forget his misfortune, and perhaps he will never be comforted."

"He will be comforted, Thérence," I replied, "when he sees how the girl he loves loves him; I'll answer for her loving him, and in times past, too."

"I think so too, Tiennet; but suppose she were unworthy of him?"

"My beautiful Thérence, are you so stern that you would think it a mortal sin if a misfortune happened to a mere child,—and, who knows? perhaps ignorantly or by force?"

"It is not the misfortune or the fault I should blame so much as the lies told and acted, and the behavior that followed. If at the first your cousin had said openly to my brother, 'Do not court me, for I have been betrayed,' I could understand that he might have forgiven all to such an honest confession. But to let him court her and admire her so much without saying a word! Come, Tiennet, tell me, do you really know nothing about it? Can't you at least guess or imagine something to set my mind at ease? I do so love Brulette that I haven't the courage to condemn her. And yet, what will my father say if he thinks I might have saved Huriel from such a danger?"

"Thérence, I know nothing and can tell you nothing, except that now, less than ever, do I doubt Brulette; for, if you wish me to tell you the only person whom I could possibly suspect of abusing her, and on whom public suspicion fell with some slight appearance of reason, I must honestly say it was Joseph, who now seems to me, after what your brother told us, to be as white as the driven snow. Now there is but one other person who, to my knowledge, was, I will not say capable, but in a position to use his friendship for Brulette to lead her wrong. And that is I. Do you believe I did, Thérence? Look me in the eyes before you answer. No one has accused me of it, that I know of, but I might be the sinner all the same, and you don't know me well enough yet to be sure of my honesty and good faith. That is why I say to you, look in my face and see if falsehood and cowardice are at home there."

Thérence did as I told her, and looked at me, without showing the least embarrassment; then she said:—

"No, Tiennet, it is not in you to lie like that. If you are satisfied about Brulette, I will be too. Come, my lad, now go off to the dance; I don't want you here any longer."

"Yes, you do," I said; "that child is going to plague you. He is not amiable with persons he does not know, and I would like either to carry him off or help you to take care of him."

"Not amiable, isn't he?" said Thérence, taking him on her knee. "Bah! what difficulty is therein managing a little monkey like that? I never tried, but I don't believe there is much art in it. Come, my young man, what do you want? Don't you want something to eat?"

"No," said Charlot, who was sulky without daring to show it.

"Well, just as you like. When you want your broth you can ask for it. I'll give you all you want, and even play with you, if you get tired. Say, do you want me to play with you?"

"No," said Charlot, frowning fiercely.

"Very good; then play alone," said Thérence, quietly, setting him on the floor. "I am going into the courtyard to see the pretty little black horse."

She moved to go; Charlot wept; Thérence pretended not to hear him till he came to her. "Dear me! what's the matter?" she said, as if surprised; "make haste and tell me, for I am going,—I can't wait."

"I want to see the pretty little black horse," sobbed Charlot.

"Then come along; but stop crying, for he runs away when he hears children cry."

Charlot choked down his sobs, and went off to stroke and admire the *clairin*.

"Should you like to get on him?" asked Thérence.

"No, I'm afraid."

"I'll hold you."

"No, I'm afraid."

"Very good, then don't get on."

In a minute more he wanted to.

"No," said Thérence, "you'll be afraid."

"No."

"Yes, you will."

"No, no!" said Charlot.

She put him on the horse and led it along, holding the child very carefully. After watching them a little while, I saw that Charlot's whims could not hold out against so quiet a will as Thérence's. She had discovered the way to manage a troublesome child at her first attempt, though it had taken Brulette a year of patience and weariness; but it really seemed as if the good God had made Thérence a mother without an apprenticeship. She had guessed the astuteness and decision needed, and practised them without worrying herself, or feeling surprised or impatient at anything.

Charlot, who had thought himself master of everybody, was much astonished to find that with her he was only master of the power to sulk, and as she did not trouble herself about that, he soon saw it was trouble wasted. At the end of half an hour he became quite pleasant, asking for what he wanted, and making haste to accept whatever was offered to him. Thérence gave him something to eat; and I admired how, out of her own judgment, she knew just what quantity to give him, not too much nor yet too little, and how to keep him occupied beside her while she was occupied in her own affairs, talking with him as if he were a reasonable being, and treating the imp with such confidence that, without seeming to question him, he soon ran over all his little tales, which he usually required much begging to do when others tried to make him. He even took such pleasure in her and was so proud of knowing how to converse that he got impatient at not knowing the words he wanted, and so invented some to express his meaning,—and they were not at all silly or meaningless either.

"What are you doing here, Tiennet?" she said to me suddenly, as if to let me know she thought I had been there long enough.

As I had already invented about fifty little reasons for staying on, her question took me short, and I could think of nothing to say except that I was occupied in looking at her. "Does that amuse you?" she exclaimed.

"I don't know," I answered; "You might as well ask the wheat if it likes to grow in the sunshine."

"Oh, oh! so you are getting mischievous and turning compliments, are you? but please remember it is lost time with me, for I know nothing about them and can't make any reply."

"I don't know anything about them either, Thérence. All that I meant to say was that to my mind there is nothing so beautiful and saintly as a young girl taking pleasure in a child's prattle."

"Is not that natural?" said Thérence. "It seems to me that I get to the truth of the things of the good God when I look at that little fellow and talk with him. I feel that I do not live, usually, as a woman ought to like to live; but I did not choose my own lot, and the wandering life I lead is my duty, because I am the support and happiness of my dear father. Therefore I never complain, and never wish for a life which would not be his; only I can understand the happiness of others; for instance, that of Brulette with her Charlot, whether he be her own or just the good God's, would be very sweet to me. I have not often had a chance to enjoy such amusement, so I take it when I find it. Yes, I like the company of this little man, and I had no idea he was so clever and knew so much."

"And yet, dear, Charlot is only tolerable because Brulette has taken such pains with him; he will have to improve very much before he is as amiable as the children God sends good into the world."

"You surprise me," said Thérence. "If there are nicer children than he it must be very pleasant to live with them. But now, that's enough, Tiennet. Go away; or they will send after you, and then they will ask me to go too; and that would, I confess, annoy me, for I am tired, and would much rather stay quietly here with the little one."

I had to obey; and I departed with my heart full, and topsy-turvy with ideas that suddenly came into my head about that girl.

TWENTY-FOURTH EVENING.

It was not only Thérence's extreme beauty which filled my thoughts, but a something, I don't know what, which made her seem to be above all others. I was surprised that I had loved Brulette, who was so unlike her, and I kept asking myself if the one were too frank, or the other too coy. I thought Brulette the most amiable; for she had always something kind to say to her friends, and she knew how to keep them about her with all sorts of little orders; which flatter young fellows, for they like to fancy themselves of use. On the other hand, Thérence showed you frankly that she did not want you, and even seemed surprised and annoyed if you paid her any attention. Both knew their own value, however; but whereas Brulette took the trouble to make you feel it, the other seemed only to wish for the same sort of regard as that she gave you. I don't know how it was that the spice of pride hidden under all this seemed to me an allurement which brought temptation as well as fear.

I found the dance at its height, and Brulette was skimming like a butterfly in Huriel's arms. Such ardor was in their faces, she was so intoxicated within and he without, that it really seemed as if neither could hear or see anything about them. The music carried them away, and I do believe that their feet did not touch the earth and that their souls were dancing in paradise. Now, among those who lead a reel, there are seldom any who have neither love nor some other wild fancy in their heads, and therefore no attention was paid to this pair; and there was so much wine, noise, dust, music, and lively talk in the heated air of the wedding feast that night came on before any one took much notice of the actions of others.

Brulette merely asked me about Charlot, and why Thérence did not come and dance; my answers satisfied her, and Huriel did not give her time to say much about the boy.

I did not feel inclined to dance, for I could not see any pretty girls; I believe there were plenty, but not one that compared with Thérence; and I could not get Thérence out of my head. I stood in a corner to watch her brother, so as to have something to tell her if she questioned me. Huriel had so completely forgotten his troubles that he was all youth and happiness. He was well-mated with Brulette, for he loved pleasure and racket as much as she did when he was in it, and he carried the day against the other lads, for he never got tired of dancing. All the world knows, for it is so in all lands, that women can floor the men at a reel, and can keep themselves going while we poor fellows are dying of heat and thirst. Huriel never cared for eating or drinking, and you would really have thought he had sworn to surfeit Brulette with her choice amusement; but I could see beneath the surface that he was doing it for his own pleasure, and that he would gladly have gone round the world on one foot could he have kept his airy partner in his arms.

At last, however, some of the youths, beginning to get annoyed that Brulette refused them, took notice that a stranger had cut them out, and talk began about it round the tables. I must tell you that Brulette, not expecting much amusement, and rather inclined to despise the young men of that neighborhood on account of their ill-natured speeches, was not dressed with her usual daintiness. She looked more like a little nun than the queen of our parts; and as others had come to the wedding in gala costumes, she did not produce the great effect of former days. Still, she was so animated in dancing that the company were forced to admit that no one compared with her; and as those who did not know her questioned those who did, a great deal of evil as well as good was talked around me.

I listened, wishing to make sure of what was being said, and not revealing that she was my relation. I heard the whole story of the monk and the child, and of Joseph and the Bourbonnais; it was also told that Joseph was probably not the father of the child, but more likely that tall fellow, who seemed so sure of his rights that no one else was allowed to approach her.

"Well," said one, "if it was he and he comes to make reparation, better late than never."

"Faith!" cried another, "she didn't choose badly. He is a splendid fellow, and seems good company."

"After all," said a third, "they make a fine couple, and when the priest has said his say, their home will be as good as any."

All of which let me know that a woman is never lost if she has good protection; but it must be the honest and lasting protection of one man, not the support of hundreds, for the more who meddle in the matter, the more there are to pull her down.

Just then my aunt took Huriel apart, and bringing him close into my neighborhood said to him, "I want you to drink a glass of wine to my health, for it does my heart good to see your fine dancing, which stirred up the company and made the wedding go off so well."

Huriel seemed not to like to leave Brulette even for a moment, but the mistress of the house was very peremptory, and he could not help showing her civility. They sat down at an empty table, with a candle between them, face to face. My aunt Marghitonne was, as I told you, a very small woman who had never been a fool. She had the drollest little face you ever saw, very fair and very rosy, though she was in the fifties and had brought fourteen children into the world. I have never seen such a long nose as hers, with very small eyes sunken each side of it, sharp as gimlets, and so bright and mischievous that one couldn't look into them without wishing to laugh and chatter.

I saw, however, that Huriel was on his guard and was cautious about the wine she poured out for him. He seemed to feel there was something quizzical and inquisitive about her, and without knowing why, he put himself on the defence. My aunt, who since early morning had not stopped talking and moving about, had a very pretty taste for good wine, and had scarcely drunk a glass or two when the end of her long nose grew as red as a haw, and her broad mouth, with its rows of narrow white teeth (enough to furnish three ordinary mouths), began to smile from ear to ear. However, she was not at all upset as to judgment, for no woman could be gay without freedom and mischievous without spite better than she.

"Well, now, my lad," she said, after some general talk which served only to lead up to her object, "here you are, for good and all, pledged to our Brulette. You can't go back now, for what you wished has happened; everybody is talking, and if you could hear, as I do, what is being said on all sides you would find that they have saddled you with the past as well as the future of my pretty niece."

I saw that the words drove a knife into Huriel's heart, and knocked him from the stars into the brambles; but he put a good face upon the matter and answered, laughing: "I might wish, my good lady, to have had her past, for everything about her is beautiful and good; but as I can have her future only I expect to share it with the good God."

"And right you are," returned my aunt, laughing still and looking closely at him with her little green eyes, which were very near-sighted, so that she seemed about to prick his forehead with the sharp end of her nose. "When people love they should love right through, and not be repelled by anything."

"That is my intention," said Huriel, in a curt tone, which did not disconcert my aunt.

"And that's all the more to your credit," she continued, "because poor Brulette has more virtue than property. You know, I suppose, that you could put her dowry into that glass, and there are no louis d'or to her account."

"Well, so much the better," said Huriel, "the reckoning is the sooner made; I don't like to spend my time doing sums."

"And besides," said my aunt, "a child already weaned is less trouble in a household, especially if the father does his duty, as I'll warrant he will in this case."

Poor Huriel went hot and cold; but thinking it was meant as a test, he stood it well, and answered:—

"I'll warrant, too, that the father will do his duty; for there will be no other father than I for all the children born or to be born."

"Oh! as for that!" she returned, "you won't be the master, I give you my word."

"I hope I shall," he said, clenching his glass as though he would crush it in his hand. "He who abandons his property has no right to filch it back; and I am too faithful a guardian to allow marauders about."

my aunt stretched out her skinny little hand and passed it over Huriel's forehead. She felt the sweat, though he was very pale, and then, suddenly changing her look of elfish mischief to one that expressed the goodness and kindness of her heart, she said: "My lad, put your elbows on the table and bring your face quite close to my mouth; I want to give you a good kiss upon your cheek."

Huriel, surprised at her softened manner, obeyed her fancy. She raised his thick hair and saw Brulette's token, which he still wore and which she probably recognized. Then, bringing her big mouth close to his ear as if she meant to bite him, she whispered three or four words into its orifice, but so low that I couldn't catch a sound. Then she added out loud, pinching his ear:—

"Here's a faithful ear! but you must admit, it is well-rewarded."

Huriel made but one bound right over the table, knocking over the glasses and candle before I had time to catch them; in a second he was sitting by my little aunt and kissing her as if she had been the mother that bore him; in short, he behaved like a crazy man, shouting, and singing, and waving his glass, while my aunt, laughing like a jack-daw, cried as she clinked her glass to his:—

"To the health of the father of your child! All of which proves," she said, turning to me, "that the cleverest folk are often those who are thought the greatest fools; just as the greatest fools are those who have thought themselves so clever. You can say that too, my Tiennet,—you with your honest heart and your faithful cousinship; I know that you behaved to Brulette as if you had been her brother. You deserve to be rewarded, and I rely on the good God to see that you get your dues; some day or other he will give you, too, your perfect contentment."

Thereupon she went off, and Huriel, clasping me in his arms, cried out: "Your aunt is right; she is the best of women. You are not in the secret, but that's no matter. You are only the better friend for it. Give me your word, Tiennet, that you will come and work here all summer with us; for I have got an idea about you, and please God to help me, you shall thank me for it fine and good."

"If I understand what you mean," I replied, "you have just been drinking your wine pure, and my aunt has taken the fly out of your cup; but any idea of yours about me seems more difficult to carry out."

"Friend Tiennet, happiness can be earned; and if you have no ideas contrary to mine—"

"I am afraid they are only too like; but ideas won't suffice."

"Of course not; but nothing venture nothing have. Are you such a Berrichon that you dare not tempt fate?"

"You set me too good an example to let me be a coward," I answered, "but do you think—"

Brulette here came up and interrupted us, and we saw by her manner that she had no suspicion of what had occurred.

"Sit here," said Huriel, drawing her to his knee, as we do in our parts without any thought of harm, "and tell me, my dear love, if you have no wish to dance with some one besides me? You gave me your word and you have kept it. That was all I needed to take a bitterness out of my heart; but if you think people will talk in a way to hurt your feelings, I will submit to your pleasure and not dance with you again till you command me."

"Is it because you are tired of my company, Maître Huriel," replied Brulette, "and that you want to make acquaintance with the other girls at the wedding?"

"Oh! if you take it that way," cried Huriel, beside himself with joy, "so much the better! I don't even know if there are other girls here besides you, and I don't want to know."

Then he offered her his glass, begging her to touch it with her lips and then drinking its contents with a full heart; after which he dashed it to pieces, so that no one should use it again, and carried off his betrothed, leaving me to think over the matter he had suggested, about which I felt I'm sure I don't know how.

I had not yet felt myself all over about it; and it had never seemed to me that my nature was ardent enough to fall in love lightly, especially with so grave a girl as Thérence. I had escaped all annoyance at not being able to please Brulette, thanks to my lively nature, which was always willing to be diverted; but somehow, I could not think of Thérence without a sort of trembling in the marrow of my bones, as if I had been asked to make a sea-voyage,—I, who had never set foot on a river boat!

"Can it be," thought I, "that I have fallen in love to-day without knowing it? Perhaps I ought to believe it, for here is Huriel urging me on, and his eye must have seen it in my face. Still I am not certain, because I feel half-suffocated, and love certainly ought to be a livelier thing than that."

Thinking over all this, I reached, I couldn't tell you how, the ruined castle. That old heap of stones was sleeping in the moonlight as mute as those who built it; but a tiny light, coming from the room which Thérence occupied on the courtyard, showed that the dead were not the only guardians of the building. I went softly to the window, which had neither glass nor woodwork, and looking through the leaves that shaded it, I saw the girl of the woods on her knees saying her prayers beside the bed, where Charlot was sleeping soundly with his eyes tightly closed.

I might live a thousand years and I should never forget her face as it was at that moment. It was that of a saint; as peaceful as those they carve in stone for the churches. I had just seen Brulette, radiant as the summer sun, in the joy of her love and the whirl of the dance; and here was Thérence, alone, content, and white as the moonlight of the springtide sky. Afar I heard the wedding music; but that said nothing to the ear of the woodland girl; I think she was listening to the nightingale as it sang its tender canticle in the neighboring covert.

I don't know what took place within me; but, all of a sudden, I thought of God,—a thought that did not often come to me in those days of youth and carelessness; but now it bent my knees, as by some secret order, and filled my eyes with tears which fell like rain, as though a great cloud had burst within my head.

Do not ask me what prayer I made to the good angels of the sky. I know it not myself. Certainly I did not dare to ask of God to give me Thérence, but I think I prayed him to make me worthier of so great an honor.

When I rose from the ground I saw that Thérence had finished her prayer and was preparing for the night. She had taken off her cap, and I noticed that her black hair fell in coils to her feet; but before she had taken the first pin from her garments, believe me if you will, I had fled as though I feared to be guilty of sacrilege. And yet I was no fool either, and not at all in the habit of making faces at the devil. But Thérence filled my soul with respect as though she were cousin of the Holy Virgin.

As I left the old castle, a man, whom I had not seen in the shadow of the great portal, surprised me by saying:

"Hey, friend! tell me if this is, as I think it is, the old castle of Chassin?"

"The Head-Woodsman!" I cried, recognizing the voice. And I kissed him with such ardor that he was quite astonished, for, naturally, he did not remember me as I did him. But when he did recollect me he was very friendly and said:—

"Tell me quick, my boy, if you have seen my children, or if you know whether they are here."

"They came this morning," I said, "and so did I and my cousin Brulette. Your daughter Thérence is in there, very quiet and tranquil, and my cousin is close by, at a wedding with your dear good son Huriel."

"Thank God, I am not too late!" said Père Bastien. "Joseph has gone on to Nohant expecting to find them there together."

"Joseph! Did he come with you? They did not expect you for five or six days, and Huriel told us—"

"Just see how matters turn out in this world," said Père Bastien, drawing me out on the road so as not to be overheard. "Of all the things that are blown about by the wind, the brains of lovers are the lightest! Did Huriel tell you all that relates to Joseph?"

"Yes, everything."

"When Joseph saw Thérence and Huriel starting for these parts, he whispered something in Huriel's ear. Do you know what he told him?"

"Yes, I know, Père Bastien, but—"

"Hush! for I know, too. Seeing that my son changed color, and that Joseph rushed into the woods in a singular way, I followed him and ordered him to tell me what secret he had just told Huriel. 'Master,' he replied, 'I don't know if I have done well or ill; but I felt myself obliged to do it; this is what it is, for I am also bound to tell you.' Thereupon he told me how he had received a letter from friends telling him that Brulette was bringing up a child that could only be her own. After telling me all this, with much suffering and anger, he begged me to follow Huriel and prevent him from committing a great folly and swallowing a bitter shame. When I questioned him as to the age of the child and he had read me the letter he carried with him, as though it were a remedy for his wounded love, I did not feel at all sure that it was not written to plague him,—more especially as the Carnat lad, who wrote the letter (in answer to a proposal of Joseph's to be properly admitted as a bagpiper in your parts), seemed to have an ill-natured desire to prevent his return. Besides, remembering the modesty and proper behavior of that little Brulette, I felt more and more persuaded that injustice was being done her; and I could not help blaming and ridiculing Joseph for so readily believing such a wicked story. Doubtless I should have done better, my good Tiennet, to have left him in the belief that Brulette was unworthy of his love; but I can't help that; a sense of justice guided my tongue, and prevented me from seeing the consequences. I was so displeased to hear an innocent young girl defamed that I spoke as I felt. It had a greater effect upon Joseph than I expected. He went instantly from one extreme to the other. Bursting into tears like a child, he let himself drop on the ground, tearing his clothes and pulling out his hair, with such anger and self-reproach that I had great trouble in pacifying him. Luckily his health has grown nearly as strong as yours; for a year sooner such despair, seizing him in this manner, would have killed him. I spent the rest of the day and all that night in trying to compose his mind. It was not an easy thing for me to do. On the one hand, I knew that my son had fallen in love with Brulette in a very earnest way from the day he first saw her, and that he was only reconciled to life after Joseph had given up a suit which thwarted his hopes. On the other hand, I have always felt a great regard for Joseph, and I know that Brulette has been in his thoughts since childhood. I had to sacrifice one or the other, and I asked myself if I should not do a selfish deed in deciding for the happiness of my own son against that of my pupil. Tiennet, you don't know Joseph, and perhaps you have never known him. My daughter Thérence may have spoken of him rather severely. She does not judge him in the same way that I do. She thinks him selfish, hard, and ungrateful. There is some truth in that; but what excuses him in my eyes cannot excuse him in those of a young girl like Thérence. Women, my lad, only want us to love them. They take into their hearts alone the food they live on. God made them so; and we men are fortunate if we are worthy to understand this."

"I think," I remarked to the Head-Woodsman, "that I do now understand it, and that women are very right to want nothing else of us but our hearts, for that is the best thing in us."

"No doubt, no doubt, my son," returned the fine old man; "I have always thought so. I loved the mother of my children more than money, more than talent, more than pleasure or livery talk, more, indeed, than anything in the world. I see that Huriel is tarred with the same brush, for he has changed, without regret, all his habits and tastes so as to fit himself to be worthy of Brulette. I believe that you feel in the same way, for you show it plainly enough. But, nevertheless, talent is a thing which God likewise values, for he does not bestow it on everybody, and we are bound to respect and help those whom he has thus marked as the sheep of his fold."

"But don't you think that your son Huriel has as much mind and more talent for music than José?"

"My son Huriel has both mind and talent. He was received into the fraternity of the bagpipers when he was only eighteen years old, and though he has never practised the profession, he has great knowledge and aptitude for it. But there is a wide difference, friend Tiennet, between those who acquire and those who originate; there are some with ready fingers and accurate memory who can play agreeably anything they learn, but there are others who are not content with being taught,—who go beyond all teaching, seeking ideas, and bestowing on all future musicians the gift of their discoveries. Now, I tell you that Joseph is one of them; in him are two very remarkable natures: the nature of the plain, as I may say, where he was born, which gives him his tranquil, calm, and solid ideas, and the nature of our hills and woods, which have enlarged his understanding and brought him tender and vivid and intelligent thoughts. He will one day be, for those who have ears to hear, something more than a mere country minstrel. He will become a true master of the bagpipe as in the olden time,—one of those to whom the great musicians listened with attention, and who changed at times the customs of their art."

"Do you really think, Père Bastien, that José will become a second Head-Woodsman of your craft?"

"Ah! my poor Tiennet," replied the old minstrel, sighing, "you don't know what you are talking about, and I should have hard work to make you understand it."

"Try to do so, at any rate," I replied; "you are good to listen to, and it isn't good that I should continue the simpleton that I am."

TWENTY-FIFTH EVENING.

"You must know," began Père Bastien, very readily (for he was fond of talking when he was listened to willingly), "that I might have been something if I had given myself wholly up to music. I could have done so had I made myself a fiddler, as I thought of doing in my youth. I don't mean that one improves a talent by fiddling three days and nights at a wedding, like that fellow I can hear from here, murdering the tune of our mountain jig. When a man has no object before his mind but money, he gets tired and rusty; but there's a way for an artist to live by his body without killing the soul within him. As every festival brings him in at least twenty or thirty francs, that's enough for him to take his ease, to live frugally, and travel about for pleasure and instruction. That's what Joseph wants to do, and I have always advised him to do it. But here's what happened to me. I fell in love, and the mother of my dear children would not hear of marrying a fiddler without hearth or home, always a-going, spending his nights in a racket and his days in sleeping, and ending his life with a debauch; for, unhappily, it is seldom that a man can keep himself straight at that business. She kept me tied to the woodsman's craft, and that's the whole story. I never regretted my talent as long as she lived. To me, as I told you, love is the divinest music. When I was left a widower with two young children, I gave myself wholly to them; but my music got very rusty and my fingers very stiff by dint of handling axe and shears; and, I confess to you, Tiennet, that if my two children were happily married, I should quit this burdensome business of slinging iron and chopping wood, and I would be off, happy and young again, to live as I liked, seeking converse with angels, until old age brought me back, feeble but satisfied, to my children's hearth. And then, too, I am sick of felling trees. Do you know, Tiennet, I love them, those noble old companions of my life, who have told me so many things by the murmur of their leaves and the crackling of their branches. And I, more malignant than the fire from heaven, I have thanked them by driving an axe into their hearts and laying them low at my feet like so many dismembered corpses! Don't laugh at me, but I have never seen an old oak fall, nor even a young willow, without trembling with pity or with fear, as an assassin of the works of God. I long to walk beneath their shady branches, repulsed no longer as an ingrate, and listening at last to the secrets I was once unworthy to hear."

The Head-Woodsman, whose voice had grown impassioned, stopped short and thought a moment; and so did I, amazed not to think him the madman I should have thought another in his place,—perhaps because he had managed to put his ideas into me, or possibly because I myself had had some such ideas in my own head.

"No doubt you are thinking," he resumed, "that we have got a long way from Joseph. But you are mistaken, we are all the nearer; and now you shall understand how it was that I decided, after some hesitation, to treat the poor fellow's troubles sternly. I have often said to myself, and I have seen, in the way his grief affected him, that he could never make a woman happy, and also that he would never be happy himself with any woman, unless she could make him the pride of her life. For it must be admitted that Joseph has more need of praise and encouragement than of love and friendship. What made him in love with Brulette in the first instance was that she listened to his music and urged him on; what kept him from loving my daughter (for his return to her was only pique) was that Thérence requires affection more than knowledge, and treated him like a son rather than a man of great talent. I venture to say that I have read the lad's heart, and that his one idea has been to dazzle Brulette some day with his success. So long as Brulette was held to be the queen of beauty and dignity in her own country he would, thanks to her, enjoy a double royalty; but Brulette smirched by a fault, or merely degraded by the suspicion of one, was no longer his cherished dream. I, who knew the heart of my son Huriel, I knew he would never condemn Brulette without a hearing, and that if she had not done anything wrong he would love her and protect her all the more because she was misjudged. So that decided me, finally, to oppose Joseph's love, and to advise him to think no longer of marriage. Indeed, I tried to make him understand that Brulette prefers my son, which is what I believe myself. He seemed to give in to my arguments, but it was only, I think, to get rid of them; for yesterday morning, before it was light, I saw him making his preparations for departure. Though he thought himself cleverer than I, and expected to get off without being seen, I kept with him until, losing patience, he let out the whole truth. I saw then that his anger was great, and that he meant to follow Huriel and quarrel with him about Brulette, if he found that Brulette was worth it. As he was still uncertain on the latter point, I thought best to blame him and even to ridicule a love like his which was only jealousy without respect,—gluttony, as one might say, without appetite. He confessed I was right; but he went off all the same, and by that you can judge of his obstinacy. Just as he was about to be received into the guild of his art (for an appointment was made for the competition near Auzances) he abandoned everything, though certain to lose the opportunity, saying he could get himself admitted willingly or unwillingly in his own country. Finding him so determined that he even came near getting angry with me, I decided to come with him, fearing some bad action on his part and some fresh misfortune for Huriel. We parted only a couple of miles from here at the village of Sarzay, where he took the road to Nohant, while I came on here, hoping to find Huriel and reason with him, thinking that if necessary my legs could still take me to Nohant to-night."

"Luckily, you can rest them to-night," I said; "to-morrow will be time enough to discuss matters. But are you really anxious for what may happen if the two gallants meet? Joseph was never quarrelsome, to my knowledge; in fact, I have always seen him hold his tongue when people showed him their teeth."

"Yes, yes," answered Père Bastien; "but that was in the days when he was a sickly child and doubted his strength. There is no more dangerous water than still water; it is not always healthy to stir the depths."

"Don't you want to come in to your new abode and see your daughter?"

"No, you said she was resting; I am not anxious about her, I am much more desirous to know the truth about Brulette; for, though my heart defends her, still my reason tells me that there may have been some little thing in her conduct which lays her open to blame; and I feel I ought to know more before going too far."

I was about to tell him what had happened an hour before, under my very eyes, between Huriel and my aunt, when Huriel himself appeared, sent by Brulette, who was afraid Thérence might be unable to get Charlot to sleep. Father and son had an explanation, in which Huriel, begging his father not to ask for a secret he was bound not to tell, and which Brulette herself was not aware that he knew, swore on his baptism that Brulette was worthy of his father's blessing.

"Come and see her, dear father," he added; "you can do it very easily because we are now dancing out of doors, and you need no invitation to be present. By the very way she kisses you, you will know that no girl so sweet and amiable was ever more pure in heart."

"I do not doubt it, my son; and I will go to please you, and also for the pleasure of seeing her. But wait a moment, for I want to speak to you of Joseph."

I thought I had better leave them alone, so I went off to tell my aunt of Père Bastien's arrival, knowing she would welcome him heartily and not let him stay outside. But I found no one in the house but Brulette. The whole wedding party, with the music at their head, had gone to carry the roast to the newly married couple, who had retired to a neighboring house, for it was past eleven o'clock at night. It is an ancient custom, which I have never thought very nice, to shame a young bride by a visit and joking songs.

Though the other girls had all gone, with or without malicious intention, Brulette had had the decency to stay in the chimney-corner, where I found her sitting, as if keeping watch in the kitchen, but really taking the sleep she so much needed. I did not care to disturb her nor to deprive her of the fine surprise she would feel on waking, at sight of the Head-Woodsman.

Very tired myself, I sat down at a table, laid my arms on it and my head on my arms, as you do when you mean to take a five minutes' nap; but I thought of Thérence and did not sleep. For a moment only my thoughts were hazy, and just then a trifling noise made me open my eyes without lifting my head, and I saw a man enter and walk up to the chimney. Though the candles had all been carried off for the visit to the bride, the fire of fagots which flamed on the hearth gave light enough to enable me to recognize at once who it was. It was Joseph, who no doubt had met some of the wedding guests on his way to Nohant, and finding where we were, had retraced his steps. He was dusty with his journey and carried a bundle on the end of his stick, which he threw into a corner and then stood stock still like a mile-stone, looking at Brulette asleep, and taking no notice of me.

The year during which I had not seen him had made as great a change in him as it had in Thérence. His health being better than it ever was, it was safe to call him a handsome man, whose square shoulders and wiry figure were more muscular than thin. His face was sallow, partly from a bilious constitution and partly from the heat of the sun; and this swarthy tint went singularly well with his large light eyes, and his long straight hair. It was still the same sad and dreamy face; but something bold and decided, showing the harsh will so long concealed, was mingled in it.

I did not move, wishing to observe the manner in which he approached Brulette and so judge of his coming meeting with Huriel. No doubt he did study the girl's face seeking for truth; and perhaps beneath the eyelids, closed in quiet slumber, he perceived her peace of heart; for the girl was sweetly pretty seen at that moment in the blaze from the hearth. Her complexion was still bright with pleasure, her mouth smiled with contentment, and the silken lashes of her closed eyes cast a soft shadow on her cheeks, which seemed to quiver beneath them like the sly glances that girls cast on their lovers. But Brulette was sound asleep, dreaming no doubt of Huriel, and thinking as little of alluring Joseph as of repelling him.

I saw that he felt her beauty so much that his wrath hung by a thread, for he leaned over her and, with a courage I did not give him credit for, he put his lips quite close to hers and would have touched them if I, in a sudden rage, had not coughed violently and stopped the kiss on its way.

Brulette woke up with a start; I pretended to do the same, and Joseph felt a good deal of a fool between the pair of us, who both asked what he was doing, without any appearance of confusion on Brulette's part or of malice on mine.

TWENTY-SIXTH EVENING.

Joseph recovered himself quickly, and showing plainly that he did not mean to be put in the wrong, he said to Brulette, "I am glad to find you here. After a year's absence don't you mean to kiss an old friend?"

He approached her again, but she drew back, surprised at his singular manner, and said, "No, José, it is not my way to kiss any lad, no matter how old a friend he is or how glad I am to see him."

"You have grown very coy!" he said, in an angry and scoffing tone.

"I don't think I have ever been coy with you, Joseph; you never gave me any reason to be; and as you never asked me to be familiar, I never had occasion to forbid your kissing me. Nothing is changed between us and I do not know why you should now lay claim to what has never entered into our friendship."

"What an amount of talk and wry faces, all about a kiss," said Joseph, his anger rising. "If I never asked for what you were ready enough to give others it was because I was a young fool. I thought you would receive me better now that I am neither a ninny nor a coward."

"What is the matter with him?" asked Brulette, surprised and even frightened, and coming close up to me. "Is it really he, or some one who looks like him? I thought I saw our José, but this is not his speech nor his face nor his friendship."

"How have I changed, Brulette?" began José, a little disconcerted and already repentant. "Is it that I now have the courage I once lacked to tell you that you are to me the loveliest in the world, and that I have always longed for your good graces? There's no offence in that, I hope; and perhaps I am not more unworthy of them than others whom you allow to hang round you."

So saying, with a return of his vexation, he looked me in the face, and I saw he was trying to pick a quarrel with whoever would take him up. I asked nothing better than to draw his first fire. "Joseph," I said, "Brulette is right in thinking you changed. There is nothing surprising in that. We know how we part, but not how we meet again. You need not be surprised, either, if you find a little change in me. I have always been quiet and patient, standing by you in all your difficulties and consoling your vexations; but if you have grown more unjust than you used to be, I have grown more touchy, and I take it ill that you should say to my cousin before me that she is prodigal of her kisses and allows too many young men about her."

Joseph eyed me contemptuously, and put on a really devilish look of malice as he laughed in my face. Then he said, crossing his arms, and looking at me as though he were taking my measure, "Well, is it possible, Tiennet? Can this be you? However, I always did doubt you, and the friendship you professed—to deceive me."

"What do you mean by that, José?" said Brulette, much affronted and fancying he had lost his mind. 'Where did you get the right to blame me, and why are you trying to see something wrong or ridiculous between my cousin and me? Are you ill or drunken, that you forget the respect you owe me and the affection that you know I deserve?"

Joseph drew in his horns, and taking Brulette's hand in his, he said to her, with his eyes full of tears. "I am to blame, Brulette; yes, I'm irritable from fatigue and the desire to get here; but I feel nothing but devotion for you, and you ought not to take it in bad part. I know very well that your manners are dignified and that you exact the respect of everybody. It is due to your beauty, which, I see, is greater, not less, than ever. But you surely will allow that you love pleasure, and that people often kiss each other when dancing. It is the custom, and I shall think it a very good one when I profit by it; which will be now, for I have learned how to dance like others, and for the first time in my life I am going to dance with you. I hear the bagpipes returning. Come, you shall see that all my ill-humor will clear off under the happiness of being your sweetheart."

"José," replied Brulette, not more than half pleased at this speech, "you are very much mistaken if you think I still have sweethearts; I may have been coquettish,—that's my way, and I am not bound to give account of my actions; but I have also the right and the will to change my ways. I no longer dance with everybody, and to-night I shall not dance again."

"I should have thought," said Joseph, piqued, "that I was not 'everybody,' as you say, to an old friend with whom I made my first communion, and under whose roof I lived."

The music and the wedding guests returning with a great racket, cut short their words, and Huriel, also entering, full of eagerness and taking no notice of Joseph, caught Brulette on his arm and carried her like a feather to his father, who was waiting outside, and who kissed her joyously, to the great annoyance of Joseph, who clenched his fists as he watched her paying the old man the filial attentions of a daughter.

Creeping up to the Head-Woodsman I whispered that Joseph was there, in a bad temper, and I proposed that he should draw Huriel aside while I persuaded Brulette to go to bed. Joseph, who was not invited to the wedding, would thus be obliged to go off and sleep at Nohant or at some other house in Chassin. The Head-Woodsman thought the suggestion good, and pretending not to see Joseph, who kept in the background, he talked apart with Huriel, while Brulette went away to see in what part of the house she could stow herself for the night. But my aunt, who had counted on lodging us, did not expect that Brulette would take it into her head to go to bed before three or four in the morning. The young men never go to bed at all on the first night of a wedding, and do their best to keep up the dance for three days and three nights running. If one of them gets tired, he goes into the hayloft and takes a nap. As to the girls and women, they all retire into one room; but generally it is only the old women and the ugly ones who abandon the dance.

So, when Brulette went up to the room where she expected to find a place next to some of her relatives, she came upon a crowd of snorers, among whom not a corner as big as the palm of her hand was vacant; and the few who woke up told her to come again towards morning, when they would be ready to go down and serve the tables. She came back to us and told her difficulty.

"Well, then," said Père Bastien, "you must go and sleep with Thérence. My son and I will spend the night here so that no talk can be made about it."

I declared that in order to avoid giving a pretext for Joseph's jealousy Brulette could easily slip out with me without saying a word; and Père Bastien going up to him and plying him with questions, I took my cousin to the old castle by a back way through my aunt's garden.

When I returned I found the Head-Woodsman, Joseph, and Huriel at table together. They called me, and I sat down to supper with them, eating, drinking, talking, and singing to avoid an explosion of anger which might follow on any talk about Brulette. Joseph, seeing us determined to keep the peace, controlled himself at first, and even seemed gay; but he could not help biting as he caressed, and every joke he made had a sting at the end of it. The Head-Woodsman tried to keep down his bile with a measure of wine, and I think Joseph might willingly have yielded in order to forget himself, if it were not that wine never affected him. He drank four times as much as the rest of us, who had no reason to wish to drown our intelligence, and yet his ideas were all the clearer and his speech, too.

At last, after some particularly spiteful remarks on the slyness of women and the treachery of friends, Huriel, striking his fist on the table and grasping his father's elbow, which for some time past had been nudging him to keep quiet, said in a decided tone:—

"No, father, excuse me, but I cannot stand any more of this, and it is much better to say so openly. I know very well that Joseph's teeth will be as sharp a year hence as they are now, and though I have closed my ears to his sayings up to this time, it is right that they should open now to his unjust remarks and reproaches. Come, Joseph, for the last hour I have seen what you mean; you have wasted a great deal of wit. Talk plain, I'm listening; say what you have on your mind, with the whys and the wherefores. I will answer you frankly."

"Well, so be it; come to an explanation," said the Head-Woodsman, reversing his glass and deciding the situation, as he well knew how to do when it became necessary; "we will have no more drinking if it is not to be in friendship, for it is ill mixing the devil's venom with the good God's wine."

"You surprise me, both of you," said Joseph, who had grown yellow to the whites of his eyes, though he still continued to laugh vindictively. "What the devil are you angry about, and why do you scratch yourselves when nothing is biting you? I have nothing against anybody; only I happen to be in the humor to jeer at everything, and I don't think you are likely to rid me of it."

"Perhaps I could," said Huriel, provoked.

"Try," said Joseph, sneering.

"That's enough!" said the Head-Woodsman, striking the table with his heavy hand, "Hold your tongues, both of you, and as there is no frankness in you, Joseph, I shall have enough for the two. You misjudged in your heart the woman you wished to love; that is a wrong that God can pardon, for it is not always easy for a man to be trustful or distrustful in his friendships; but it is, unfortunately, a wrong that cannot be repaired. You fell into that blunder; you must accept the consequences and submit to them."

"Why so, master?" said Joseph, setting up his back like an angry cat, "who will tell the wrong to Brulette? she has not known or suffered from it."

"No one," said Huriel, "I am not a blackguard."

"Then who will tell it?" demanded Joseph.

"Yourself," said Père Bastien.

"What can make me?"

"The consciousness of your love for her. Doubt never comes singly. You may get over the first twinge, but there comes a second, which will issue from your lips at the first words you say to her."

"In fact, I think it has happened already, Joseph," said I, "for this very evening you offended the person we are speaking of."

"Perhaps I did," he said haughtily, "but that is between her and me. If I choose that she shall return to me what makes you think she will not return? I remember my master's song,—the music is beautiful and the words are true,—'Gifts are for those who pray.' Well, Huriel, go ahead. Ask in words and I will ask in music, and we will see whether or no I can't win her back again. Come, play fair, you who blame what you call my crooked ways. The game is between us, and we'll have no shuffling. A fine house has more than one door, and we'll each knock at the one that suits us."

"I am willing," said Huriel, "but you will please to remember one thing. I will stand no more fault-finding, whether in jest or earnest. If I overlook the past, my good-nature does not go so far as to allow any more of it."

"What do you mean by that?" demanded Joseph, whose bile interfered with his memory.

"I forbid you to ask," said the Head-Woodsman, "and I command you to bethink yourself. If you fight my son you will be none the more innocent for that, and it will not add to your credit if I withdraw the forgiveness which, without a word of explanation, my heart has already granted you."

"Master!" cried Joseph, hot with excitement, "if you think you have anything to forgive I thank you for your forgiveness; but, in my opinion, I have done you no wrong. I never dreamed of deceiving you; and if your daughter had said yes, I should not have backed down from my offer. She is a girl without an equal for sense and uprightness; I should have loved her, ill or well, but at any rate sincerely and without betraying her. She might perhaps have saved me from much evil and much suffering; but she did not think me worthy of her. Therefore I am at liberty to court whom I will; and I consider that the man I trusted and who promised me his help has made haste to take advantage of my momentary pique to supplant me."

"Your momentary pique lasted a month, Joseph," said Huriel; "be fair about it,—one month, during which you asked my sister in marriage three times. I am forced to believe that you held her in derision; if you wish to clear yourself of that insult you must admit that I was not to blame in the matter. I believed your word; that is the only wrong I have done; don't give me reason to think it is one I must repent of."

Joseph kept silence; then, rising, he said, "Yes, you are good at argument; you are both cleverer than I at that; I have spoken and acted like a man who does not know what he wants; but you are greater fools than I if you don't know that, without being mad, we may wish for two opposite things. Leave me to be what I am, and I will leave you to be what you wish to be. If your heart is honest, Huriel, I shall soon know it, and if you win the game fairly, I will do you justice and withdraw without resentment."

"How can you tell if my heart is honest when you have been unable to judge it rightly hitherto??

"I can tell by what you now say of me to Brulette," replied Joseph. "You are in a position to prejudice her against me and I cannot do the same by you."

"Stop!" I said to Joseph, "don't blame any one unjustly. Thérence has already told Brulette that you asked her in marriage not a fortnight ago."

"But nothing further has been or will be told," added Huriel; "Joseph, we are better than you think us. We do not want to deprive you of Brulette's friendship."

The words touched Joseph, and he put out his hand as if to take Huriel's; but the good intention stopped half-way, and he went off without another word to any one.

"A hard heart!" cried Huriel, who was too kind himself not to suffer from this ingratitude.

"No, an unhappy one," said his father.

Struck by the words, I followed Joseph to either scold him or console him, for he looked as if death were in his eyes. I was quite as much displeased with him as Huriel was, but the old habit of pitying and protecting him was so strong that it carried me after him whether I would or no.

He walked so rapidly along the road to Nohant that I soon lost sight of him; but he stopped at the edge of the Lajon, a little pond on a barren heath. The place is very dreary, and without shade, except that of a few stunted trees ill-fed in the poor soil; but the swampy land around the pond abounded with wild-flowers, and as the white water-lily and other marsh plants were now in bloom, the place smelt as sweet as a garden.

Joseph had flung himself down among the reeds, and not knowing that he was followed but believing himself all alone, he was groaning and growling at the same time, like a wounded wolf. I called him, merely to let him know I was there, for I knew he would not answer me, and I went straight up to him.

"This is not the right thing at all," I said to him; "you ought to take counsel with yourself; tears are not reasons."

"I am not weeping, Tiennet," he answered, in a steady voice. "I am neither so weak nor so happy that I can find comfort that way. It is seldom, in my worst moments, that a tear gets out of my eyes, and it is fire, not water, that is forcing its way now, for it burns like live coal. But don't ask me why; I can't tell why, and I don't want to seek for the cause of it. The day of trusting in others is over with me. I know my strength, and I no longer need their help. It was only given out of pity, and I want no more of it; I can rely in future on myself. Thank you for your good intentions. Thank you, and please leave me."

"But where are you going to spend the night?"

"I am going to my mother's."

"It is very late, and it is so far from here to Saint-Chartier."

"No matter," he said, rising, "I can't stay here. We shall meet to-morrow, Tiennet."

"Yes, at home; we go back tomorrow."

"I don't care where," he said. "Wherever she is—your Brulette—I shall find her, and perhaps it will be seen that she has not made her final choice!"

He went off with a determined air, and seeing that his pride supported him I offered no further consolation. Fatigue, and the pleasure of seeing his mother, and a day or two for reflection might, I hoped, bring him to reason. I planned, therefore, to advise Brulette to stay at Chassin over the next day, and making my way back to the village with this idea in my head I came upon the Head-Woodsman and his son, in a corner of the field through which I was making a short cut. They were preparing what they called their bed-clothes; in other words, making ready to sleep on the ground, not wishing to disturb the two girls in the castle, and really preferring to lie under the stars at this sweet season of the year. I liked the idea, too, for the fresh grass seemed much nicer than the hay of a barn heated by the bodies of a score of other fellows. So I stretched myself beside Huriel, looked at the little white clouds in the clear sky, smelt the hawthorn odors, and fell asleep, thinking of Thérence in the sweetest slumber I ever had in my life.

I have always been a good sleeper, and in my youth I seldom wakened of myself. My two companions, who had walked a long distance the day before, let the sun rise without their knowing it, and woke up laughing to find him ahead of them, which didn't happen very often. They laughed still more to see how cautious I was not to tumble out of bed when I opened my eyes and looked about to see where I was.

"Come, up, my boy!" said Huriel; "we are late enough already. Do you know something? It is the last day of May, and it is the fashion in our parts to tie a nosegay to our sweetheart's door when there was no chance to do it on the first of the month. There is no fear that any one has got ahead of us, because, for one thing, no one knows where my sister and your cousin are lodging, and for another, it isn't the custom in this part of the country to leave, as we say, the *call-again* bunch. But we are so late I fear the girls are up, and if they leave their rooms before the May-bunch is hung to the door they will cry out upon us for laziness."

"As cousin," I answer, laughing, "I permit you to hang your bunch, and, as brother, I ask your permission to hang mine; but perhaps the father won't hear of it with your ears."

"Yes, he will," said Père Bastien. "Huriel said something to me about it. There's no difficulty in trying; succeeding is another thing. If you know how to manage it, so much the better, my lad. It is your affair."

Encouraged by his friendliness, I rushed into the adjoining copse with a light heart, and cut off the whole branch of a wild cherry-tree in full bloom, while Huriel, who had already provided himself with one of those beautiful silk and gold ribbons which the women of his country wear beneath their lace coifs, gathered a bunch of white hawthorn and a bunch of pink and tied them in a nosegay that was worthy of a queen.

We made but three strides from the field to the castle, where the silence assured us that the beauties still slept,—no doubt from having talked half the night. But imagine our amazement when, on entering the courtyard, our eyes lighted on a superb nosegay, decked with silver and white ribbons, hanging to the door we intended to garland.

"The devil!" cried Huriel, preparing to tear away the offending bunch, and looking askance at his dog whom he had stationed in the courtyard. "Is this the way you guard the house, master Satan? Have you made acquaintances already? why didn't you bite the legs of this Mayday prowler?"

"Stop," said the Head-Woodsman, preventing his son from taking down the nosegay. "There is but one person in these parts whom Satan knows and who also knows our custom of the call-again bunch, for he has seen it practised among us. Now, you pledged your word to that person not to interfere with him. You must be satisfied to make yourself acceptable and not undermine him; respect his offering, just as he, no doubt, would have respected yours."

"Yes, father," replied Huriel, "if I were sure it was he; but it may be some one else, and the bunch may be intended for Thérence."

I remarked that no one knew Thérence or had even seen her, and looking closer at the flowers I saw that a mass of white pond-lilies had been freshly gathered and tied in bunches, and I remembered that these plants were not common in the neighborhood and grew only in the Lajon, on the banks of which I had found Joseph lying. No doubt, instead of going to Saint-Chartier he had returned upon his steps; and he must even have waded into the water on the shifting sand of the pond, which is dangerous, before he could gather such an armful.

"Well, the battle has begun," said Huriel, sighing, as he fastened his May-bunch to the door with an anxious look that seemed to me very modest, for he might well have felt sure of success and feared no one. I wished I could feel as certain of his sister, and I hung up my cherry-bough with a beating heart, as if she were just behind the door all ready to fling it in my face.

And pale I was when the door opened; but it was Brulette who came first, and gave a kiss for good-morning to Père Bastien, a hand-shake to me, and a rosy blush of pleasure to Huriel, though she did not venture to speak to him.

"Oh, father!" cried Thérence, following her and clasping the Head-Woodsman in her arms; "have you been playing the young man all night? Come, come in, and let me give you some breakfast. But first, let me look at those nosegays. Three, Brulette! oh, what a girl you are! is the procession to last all day?"

"Only two for Brulette," said Huriel; "the third is for you, sister;" and he gave her my cherry-bough, so full of bloom that it had rained a white shower all round the door.

"For me?" said Thérence, surprised. "Then you did it, brother, to prevent my being jealous of Brulette?"

"Brothers are not so gallant," said Père Bastien. "Have you no suspicion of a timid and discreet lover who keeps his mouth shut instead of declaring himself?"

Thérence looked all round her as if she were trying to see some one beside me, and when at last her black eyes rested on my discomfited and idiotic face I thought she was going to laugh, which would have stabbed me to the heart. But she did nothing of the kind, and even blushed a little. Then, holding out her hand she said: "Thank you, Tiennet; you have shown that you remember me, and I accept the gift without giving it other meaning than belongs to a nosegay."

"Well," said Père Bastien, "if you accept it, my daughter, you must follow the usual custom, and fasten a spray of it to your coif."

"No," said Thérence, "that might displease some of the girls hereabouts, and I don't want my good Tiennet to repent of having done me a kindness."

"Oh, that won't displease anybody," I cried; "if it does not annoy you, it would hugely please me."

"So be it!" she said, breaking off a little twig of my flowers, which she fastened with a pin to her head. "We are here in the Chassin, Tiennet; if we were in your part of the country I should be more careful, for fear of getting you into trouble with some compatriot."

"You can get me into trouble with all of them, Thérence," I said; "I ask nothing better."

"As for that," she replied, "you go too fast. I don't know you well enough, Tiennet, to say if it would be well for either of us." Then changing the subject with that forgetfulness of herself which came so naturally to her, she said to Brulette: "It is your turn, darling; what return are you going to make for your two May bunches? which of them is to deck your cap?"

"Neither, till I know where they came from," replied my prudent cousin. "Tell me, Huriel, and keep me from making a mistake."

"I can't tell you," said Huriel, "except that this is mine."

"Then I shall carry it whole," she said, taking it down, "and as to that bunch of water-flowers, they must feel very much out of place on a door. I think they will be happier in the moat."

So saying, she adorned her cap and the front of her dress with Huriel's flowers, and took the rest into her room; then, returning, she was about to throw the lilies into the old moat which separated the courtyard from the park, when Huriel, unwilling that such an insult should be offered to his rival, stopped her hand. At this moment the sound of a bagpipe came from the shrubbery which closed the little court in front of us, and some one, who had been near enough to hear every word that had passed, played Père Bastien's air of the "Three Woodsmen."

He played it first as we knew it, next a little differently, in a softer and sadder way, then changing it throughout, varying the keys, adding music of his own, which was not less beautiful, and even seemed to sigh and to entreat in so tender a manner that we who heard it could hardly help being touched with compassion. At last the player took a stronger and louder tone,—as though it were a song of reproach and authority, and Brulette, who had gone to the edge of the moat intending to ding away the lilies, drew back as if terrified by the anger which was expressed in the sounds. Then Joseph, shoving aside the bushes with his feet and shoulders, appeared on the other side of the moat, still piping, his eyes blazing, and seeming, both by his looks and by his music, to threaten Brulette with some great disaster if she did not desist from the insult she was about to offer him.

TWENTY-SEVENTH EVENING.

"Noble music and a fine player," cried Père Bastien, clapping his hands when the sounds ceased. "That is both good and beautiful, Joseph; it is easy to console yourself for everything when you have the ball at your feet in that way. Come over here, and let us compliment you."

"Nothing consoles for an insult, master," replied Joseph; "and for the rest of my days there will be a ditch full of thorns between Brulette and me if she throws my offering into that moat."

"Heaven forbid," cried Brulette, "that I should make such an ill return for the beautiful nosegay. Come over here, José; there need be no thorns between us but those you plant yourself."

Joseph sprang into the courtyard, bursting like a wild boar through the line of thick-set brambles which divided him from the moat, and darting across the green slime which filled the bottom of it; then snatching the flowers from Brulette's hand, he pulled out several, which he tried to fasten on her head beside Huriel's pink and white hawthorn-blossoms. He did it with an air of authority, as though he had a right to exercise his will. But Brulette stopped him, saying:—

"One moment, Joseph; I have an idea of my own, and you must submit to it. You will soon be received into the bagpipers' guild; now God has given me a sense of music, enough to let me understand something of it without ever having learned. I've a fancy to have a competition here, and to reward the one who plays best. Give your bagpipe to Huriel, and let him make his trial just as you have now made yours."

"Yes, yes, I agree to that entirely," cried Joseph, whose face shone with defiance. "It is your turn, Huriel; make the buck-skin warble like the throat of a nightingale, if you can!"

"That was not in our agreement, Joseph," answered Huriel. "You agreed that I should speak, and I have spoken. I agreed to leave music, in which you excel me, to you. Take back your bagpipe, and speak again in your own language; no one here will weary of hearing you."

"As you own yourself vanquished," returned Joseph, "I shall play no more, unless Brulette requests it."

"Play," she said; and while he played in a marvellous way, she wove a garland of white lilies and tied it with the silver ribbon that bound the bunch. When the music ended she went up to Joseph and twisted the wreath about the pipe of his instrument, saying,—

"José, noblest piper, I receive thee into the guild, and give thee the prize. May this wreath bring thee happiness and glory, and prove to thee the high esteem in which I hold thy great talents."

"Yes, that's all very well," said Joseph. "Thank you, my Brulette; now complete my happiness and make me prouder still by wearing one of the flowers you give me. Select the finest and put it next your heart, if you will not wear it on your head."

Brulette smiled and blushed, beautiful as an angel; then she looked at Huriel, who turned pale, thinking it was all over with him.

"Joseph," she answered, "I have granted you the first of all triumphs, that of music. You must be satisfied, and cease to ask for that of love, which is not won by strength or knowledge, but by the will of the good God."

Huriel's face lighted, Joseph's darkened.

"Brulette," he cried, "God's will must be as my will!"

"Gently," she said, "He alone is master; and here is one of his little angels, who must not hear words against our holy religion."

As she spoke she took Charlot, who came bounding after her like a lamb to its mother, into her arms. Thérence, who returned to her room while Joseph was playing, had just taken him up, and the child, without letting himself be dressed, had run out half-naked to kiss his darling, as he called Brulette, with a jealous and masterful air which contrasted amusingly with that of the lovers.

Joseph, who had forgotten his suspicions, concluding he was duped by young Carnat's letter, drew back on seeing Charlot as though the child were a snake; and as he watched him kissing Brulette eagerly and calling her "mamma" and "Charlot's darling," a mist came over his eyes and he well-nigh swooned away; but almost immediately he sprang in a burst of anger toward the child, and clutching him brutally, cried out in a choking voice: "Here's the truth at last! This is the trick that has been played upon me, and the mastery of love that has defeated me!"

Brulette, frightened by Joseph's violence and Charlot's cries, tried to rescue the child; but Joseph, quite beside himself, pulled him away, laughing savagely and saying he wanted to look at him with all his eyes and see the resemblance; so doing he nearly choked the child, without meaning it, to

Brulette's horror, and she, not daring to add to the boy's danger by attempting to rescue him, turned back to Huriel, crying,—

"My child, my child! he is killing my poor child!"

Huriel made but one stride; catching Joseph by the nape of the neck, he held him so tightly and firmly that his arms relaxed and I caught Charlot from him and gave the half unconscious child back to Brulette.

Joseph nearly fainted too, as much from the violence of his anger as from the way in which Huriel had handled him. A fight would certainly have followed (and the Head-Woodsman had already flung himself between them) if Joseph had understood what was happening; but he was unable to consider anything except that Brulette was a mother, and that both she and we had deceived him.

"You no longer hide it?" he said to her, in a choking voice.

"What are you saying to me?" asked Brulette, who was sitting on the grass, all in tears, and trying to ease the bruises on Charlot's arms; "you are a wicked madman, I know that. Don't come near me, and never harm this child again or God will curse you."

"One word, Brulette," said Joseph; "if you are his mother, confess it. I will pity and forgive you; in fact, I will even defend you, if necessary. But if you can only deny it by a lie—I shall despise you, and forget you."

"His mother? I, his mother?" cried Brulette, springing up as if to cast off Charlot. "You think I am his mother?" she said again, taking back the poor child, the cause of all the trouble, and pressing him to her heart. Then she looked about her with a bewildered air, and her eyes sought Huriel. "Can it be possible," she cried, "that any one could think such a thing of me?"

"The proof that no one thinks it," cried Huriel, going up to her and kissing Charlot, "is that we love the child whom you love."

"Say something better than that, brother," cried Thérence, eagerly. "Say what you said to me yesterday: 'Whether the child is hers or not, he shall be mine, if she will be mine.'"

Brulette flung both arms round Huriel's neck and hung there like a vine to an oak.

"Be my master, then," she said; "I never had, and I never will have another than you."

Joseph watched this sudden understanding, of which he was the cause, with an anguish and regret that were terrible to see. The cry of truth in Brulette's words had convinced him, and he fancied he had dreamed the wrong he had just done her. He felt that all was over between them, and without a word he picked up his bagpipe and fled away.

Père Bastien ran after him and brought him back, saying:—

"No, no, that is not the way to part after a lifelong friendship. Bring down your pride, Joseph, and ask pardon of this honest girl. She is my daughter, their word is now pledged, and I am glad of it; but she must remain your sister. A woman forgives a brother for what she could never pardon in a lover."

"She may pardon me if she can and if she will," said Joseph; "but if I am guilty, I can receive no absolution but my own. Hate me, Brulette; that may be best for me. I see I have done the one thing that was needed to lose your regard. I can never get it back; but if you pity me, don't tell me so. I ask nothing further of you."

"All this would not have happened," said Brulette, "if you had done your duty, which was to go and see your mother. Go now, Joseph; but, above all, don't tell her what you have accused me of. She would die of grief."

"My dear daughter," said the Head-Woodsman, still detaining Joseph, "I think we do better not to scold children until their minds are quiet. Otherwise, they take things crookedly and do not profit by rebuke. To my thinking Joseph has times of aberration; and if he does not make honorable amends as readily as others do, it is perhaps because he feels his wrong-doing and suffers more from his own self-blame than from the blame of others. Set him an example of good sense and kindness. It is not difficult to forgive when we are happy, and you ought to be content to be loved as you are here. More love you could not have; for I now know things of you which make me hold you in such esteem that here are a pair of hands that will wring the neck of whoever insults you deliberately. But that was not the nature of Joseph's insult, which came from excitement, not reflection, and shame followed so swiftly that his heart is now making you full reparation. Come, Joseph, add your word to mine; I ask no more than that of you; and Brulette too, will be satisfied, will you not, my daughter?"

"You don't know him, father, if you think he will say that word," replied Brulette; "but I won't exact it, because I want, above all things, to satisfy you. And so, Joseph, I forgive you, though you don't care much about that. Stay and breakfast with us, and talk about something else; what has happened is forgotten."

Joseph said not a word, but he took off his hat and laid down his stick as if meaning to stay. The two girls re-entered the house to prepare the meal, and Huriel, who took great care of his horse, began to groom and currycomb him. I looked after Charlot, whom Brulette handed over to my keeping; and the Head-Woodsman, wishing to divert Joseph's mind, talked music, and praised the variations he had given to his song.

"Never speak to me of that song again," said Joseph; "it can only remind me of painful things, and I wish to forget it."

"Well then," said Père Bastien, "play me something of your own composition, here and now, just as the thought comes to you."

Joseph led the way into the park, and we heard him in the distance playing such sad and plaintive airs that his soul seemed really prostrate with contrition and repentance.

"Do you hear him?" I said to Brulette; "that is certainly his way of confessing, and if sorrow is a reparation, he gives you of his best."

"I don't think there is a very tender heart beneath that rough pride of his," replied Brulette. "I feel, just now, like Thérence; a little tenderness is more attractive to me than much talent. But I forgive him; and if my pity is not as great as Joseph wants to make it by his music, it is because I know he has a consolation of which my indifference cannot deprive him,—I mean the admiration which he and others feel for his talents. If Joseph did not care for that more than for love or friendship, his tongue would not now be dumb and his eye dry to the reproof of friendship. He is quite capable of asking for what he wants."

"Well," said the Head-Woodsman, returning alone from the park, "did you hear him, my children? He said all he could and would say, and, satisfied to have drawn tears from my old eyes, he has gone away tranquillized."

"But you could not keep him to breakfast," said Thérence, smiling.

"No," answered her father; "he played too well not to be three parts comforted; and he prefers to go away in that mood, rather than after some folly he might be led into saying or doing at table."

TWENTY-EIGHTH EVENING.

We ate our meal in peace, feeling relieved of the apprehensions of the night before as to the quarrel between Joseph and Huriel: and, as Thérence plainly showed, both in Joseph's presence and in his absence, that she had no feeling, good or ill, about the past, I indulged, as did Huriel and Fere Bastien, in tranquil and joyous thoughts. Charlot, finding that everybody petted him, began to forget the man who had frightened and bruised him. Every now and then he would start and look behind him at some trifling noise, but Thérence laughingly assured him the man was safely gone and would not return. We seemed like a family party, and I thought to myself, while courting Thérence with the utmost deference, that I would make my love less imperious and more patient than Joseph's.

Brulette seemed anxious and overcome, as though cut to the heart by a foul blow. Huriel was uneasy about her, but the Head-Woodsman, who knew the human soul in all its windings, and who was so good that his face and his words poured balm into every wound, took her little hands in his and drew her pretty head to his breast, saying, at the end of the meal:—

"Brulette, we have one thing to ask of you, and though you look so sad and distressed, my son and I will venture to make our request now. Won't you give us a smile of encouragement?"

"Tell me what it is, father, and I will obey you," answered Brulette.

"Well, my daughter, it is that you will present us to-morrow to your grandfather, so that he may be asked to accept Huriel as a grandson."

"Oh, it is too soon, father," cried Brulette, shedding a few more tears, "or rather, it is too late; if you had told me to do so an hour ago, before Joseph uttered those words, I would gladly have consented. But now, I confess, I should be ashamed to accept so readily the love of an honest man, when I find I am no longer supposed to be an honest girl. I knew I had been blamed for coquetry. Your son himself twitted me about it a year ago. Thérence blamed me,—though, for all that, she gave me her friendship. So, seeing that Huriel had the courage to leave me without asking for anything, I made a great many reflections in my own mind. The good God helped me by sending me this child, whom I did not like at first and might possibly have rejected, if my sense of duty had not been mixed with a sort of idea that I should be better worthy of being loved through a little suffering and self-denial than for my chatter and my pretty clothes. I thought I could atone for my thoughtless years and trample my love for my own little person underfoot. I knew that I was criticised and neglected, but

I consoled myself with the thought: 'If he comes back to me he will know that I do not deserve to be blamed for getting serious and sensible.' But now I have heard something very different, partly through Joseph's conduct, partly by Thérence's remark. It was not Joseph only who thought I had gone astray, but Huriel also, or his great heart and his strong love would have had no need to say to his sister yesterday: 'Guilty or not guilty, I love her, and will take her as she is.' Ah, Huriel! I thank you; but I will not let you marry me till you know me. I should suffer too much to see you blamed, as you doubtless would be, on my account. I respect you too much to let it be said that you take upon yourself the paternity of a foundling. I must indeed have been light in my behavior, or such an accusation could never have been made against me! Well, I wish you to judge me now by my every-day conduct; I want you to be sure that I am not only a gay dancer at a wedding but the good guardian of my duty in my home. We will come and live here, as you desire it; and in a year from now, if I am not able to prove to you that my care of Charlot need not cause me to blush, I shall at least have given you by my actions a proof that I am reasonable in mind and sound in conscience."

Huriel snatched Brulette from his father's arms, and reverently kissed the tears that were flowing from her beautiful eyes; then he gave her back to Père Bastien, saying:—

"Bless her, my father; for you can now judge if I told you false when I said she was worthy of your blessing. The dear golden tongue has spoken well, and there is no answer to make to it, unless it be that we want neither year nor day of trial, but desire to go this very evening and ask her of her grandfather; for to pass another night still doubtful of his consent is more than I can bear, and to get it is all I need to make me sovereign of the world."

"See what has happened to you by asking for a respite," said Père Bastien to Brulette. "Instead of asking your grandfather to-morrow, it seems it must be to-night. Come, my child, you must submit; it is the punishment of your naughty conduct in times gone by."

Contentment overspread her sweet face, and the hurt she had received from Joseph was forgotten. However, just as we left the table, another hesitation seized her. Charlot, hearing Huriel address the Head-Woodsman as father, called him so himself, and was kissed and fondled for it, but Brulette was a trifle vexed.

"Wouldn't it be best," she said, "to take the trouble to invent parents for the poor child; every time he calls me mother it seems like a stab to those I love."

We were beginning to reassure her on this point when Thérence said: "Speak low; some one is listening to us;" and following her glance toward the porch, we saw the end of a stick resting on the ground, and the bulging side of a full sack, showing that a beggar was there, waiting till some one took notice of him, and hearing things that he ought not to hear.

I went up to the intruder and recognized Brother Nicolas, who came forward at once and admitted without hesitation that he had been listening for the last quarter of an hour, and had been very well pleased with what he had heard.

"I thought I knew Huriel's voice," he said, "but I so little expected to find him on my rounds that I should not have been certain, my dear friends, that it was he, but for some things which you have been saying, in which, as Brulette knows, I have a right to intrude."

"We know it too," said Huriel.

"Do you?" exclaimed the monk. "Well, that's as it should be."

"And the reason is," said Huriel to Brulette, "that your aunt told me everything last night. So you see, dearest, I don't deserve all the credit you give me."

"Yes," said Brulette, much comforted, "but yesterday morning! Well, since everything is known," she added, turning to the monk, "what do you advise me to do, Brother Nicolas? You have been employed on Charlot's account; can't you find some story to spread about to cover the secret of his parentage and repair the harm done to my reputation?"

"Story?" said the friar. "I, advise and abet a lie? I am not one of those who damn their souls for the love of the young girls, my little one. I should gain nothing by it. You must be helped some other way; and I have already been working at it more than you think. Have patience; all will come out right, as it did in another matter, where, as Maître Huriel knows, I have not been a bad friend to him."

"I know that I owe you the peace and safety of my life," said Huriel. "People may say what they like of monks, I know one, at least, for whom I would be drawn and quartered. Sit down, Brother, and spend the day with us. What is ours is yours, and the house we are in is yours too."

Thérence and the Head-Woodsman were showing their hospitality to the good friar, when my aunt Marghitonne came hurrying up, and would not let us stay anywhere but with her. She said the wedding party were going to perform the "cabbage ceremony;" which is an old-fashioned foolery practised the day after the marriage; the procession, she said, was already forming and was coming round our way. The company drank, and sang, and danced at each stopping-place. It was impossible for Thérence now to keep aloof, and she accepted my arm to go and meet the crowd, while Huriel escorted Brulette. My aunt took charge of the little one, and the Head-Woodsman marched off with the monk, who was easily persuaded into joining a jovial company.

The fellow who played the part of gardener, or as we still say among us, the pagan, seated on a hand-barrow, was decorated in a style that astonished everybody. He had picked up near the park a beautiful garland of waterlilies tied with a silver ribbon, which he had bound about his flaxen poll. It didn't take us much time to recognize Joseph's bunch, which he had dropped or thrown away on leaving us. The ribbons were the envy of all the girls of the party, who deliberated how to get possession of them unspoiled; at last, flinging themselves on the pagan, they snatched them away from him and divided the booty, though in defending himself he managed to kiss more than one with a mouth that was covered with foam. So scraps of Joseph's ribbon glittered all day in the caps of the prettiest girls in the neighborhood, and came to a much better end than their owner thought for when he left his bunch in the dust of the road.

This farce, played from door to door through the village, was as crazy as usual, ending with a fine repast and dancing till twilight. After which, we all took leave, Brulette and I, the Head-Woodsman, Thérence, and Huriel, and started for Nohant, with the monk at our head, leading the *clairin*, on which Charlot was perched, tipsy with excitement at what he had seen, laughing like a monkey, and trying to sing as he had heard others do all that day.

Though the young people of the present age have degenerated wofully, you must often have seen girls in their teens tramping fifteen miles in the morning and as much more in the evening in the hottest weather, for a day's dancing, and so you can easily believe that we arrived at home without fatigue. Indeed, we danced part of the way along the road, we four; the Head-Woodsman playing his bagpipe, and the friar declaring we were crazy, but clapping his hands to excite us on.

We reached Brulette's door about ten at night, and found Père Brulet sound asleep in his bed. As he was quite deaf and slept hard, Brulette put the baby to bed, served us a little collation, and consulted with us whether to wake him before he had finished his first nap. However, turning over on his side, he saw the light, recognized his granddaughter and me, seemed surprised at the others, and sitting up in bed as sober as a judge, listened to a statement the Head-Woodsman made to him in a few words, spoken rather loud but very civilly. The monk, in whom Père Brulet had the utmost confidence, followed in praise of the Huriel family, and Huriel himself declared his wishes and all his good intentions both present and to come.

Père Brulet listened without saying a word, and I began to fear he had not understood; but no such thing; though he seemed to be dreaming, his mind was really quite clear, and he presently answered discreetly that he recognized in the Head-Woodsman the son of a former friend; that he held the family in much esteem, and considered Brother Nicolas as worthy of all confidence; and, above all, he trusted in the sense and good judgment of his granddaughter. Then he went on to say that she had not delayed her choice and refused the best offers of the neighborhood to commit a folly in the end, and that if she wished to marry Huriel, Huriel would certainly be a good husband.

He spoke in a collected manner: yet his memory failed him on one point, which he recalled soon after, as we were about to take leave, namely, that Huriel was a muleteer.

"That is the only thing that troubles me," he said. "My girl will be so lonely at home by herself for three-quarters of the year."

We satisfied him at once with the news that Huriel had left the craft and become a woodsman; and thereupon he readily agreed to the plan of working in the woods of Chassin during the summer months.

We parted, all well pleased with one another. Thérence stayed with Brulette, and I took the others to my own house.

We learned the next evening, through the monk, who had been begging about all day, that Joseph had not gone near the village of Nohant, but had spent an hour with his mother at Saint-Chartier, after which he started to go round the neighborhood and collect all the bagpipers for a meeting, at which he would demand a competition for admission to the craft and the right to practise the calling. Mariton was much troubled by this determination, believing that the Carnats, father and son, and all the bagpipers of the country round, who were already more in number than were needed, would oppose it and cause him both trouble and injury. But Joseph would not listen to her, still saying that he was resolved to get her out of service and take her to some distant place to live with him, though she seemed not as much inclined to that idea as he had hoped.

On the third day, all our preparations having been made, and Huriel and Brulette's first banns published in the parish church, we started to return to Chassin. It was like departing on a pilgrimage to the ends of the earth. We were obliged to carry furniture, for Brulette was determined that her grandfather should lack for nothing; so a cart was hired and the whole village opened its eyes very wide to see the entire contents of the house going off, even to the baskets. The goats and the hens went too, for Thérence was delighted at the idea of taking care of them; never having known how to manage animals, she wanted to learn, as she said, when the opportunity offered. This gave me the chance to propose myself in jest for her management, as the most docile and faithful animal of the flock. She was not annoyed, but gave me no encouragement to pass from jest to earnest. Only, it did seem to me that she was not displeased to find me cheerfully leaving home and family to follow her; and that if she did little to attract me she certainly did still less to repulse me.

Just as old Brulet and the women, with Charlot, were getting into the cart (Brulette very proud of going off with such a handsome lover, in the teeth of all the lovers who had misjudged her), the friar came up to say good-bye, adding for the benefit of inquisitive ears: "As I am going over to your parts, I'll ride a bit of the way with you."

He got up beside Père Brulet, and at the end of the third mile, in a shady road, he asked to be set down. Huriel was leading the *clairin*, which was a good draught horse as well as a pack horse, and the Head-Woodsman and I walked in front. Seeing that the cart lagged behind, we turned back, thinking there might have been an accident, and found Brulette in tears, kissing Charlot, who clung to her screaming because the friar was endeavoring to carry him off. Huriel interceded against it, for he was so troubled at Brulette's tears that he came near crying himself.

"What is the matter?" said Père Bastien. "Why do you wish to send away the child, my daughter? Is it because of the notion you expressed the other day?"

"No, father," replied Brulette, "his real parents have sent for him, and it is for his good to go. The poor little fellow can't understand that; and even I, though I do understand it, my heart fails me. But as there are good reasons why the thing should be done without delay, give me courage instead of taking it away from me."

Though talking of courage she had none at all against Charlot's tears and kisses, for she had really come to love him with much tenderness; so Thérence was called in to help her. Every look and tone of the woodland girl conveyed such a sense of her loving-kindness that the stones themselves would have been persuaded, and the child felt it, though he did not know why. She succeeded in pacifying him, making him understand that Brulette was leaving him for a short time only, so that Brother Nicolas was able to carry him off without using force; and the pair disappeared to the tune of a sort of rondo which the monk sang to divert his charge, though it was more like a church chant than a song. But Charlot was pleased, and when their voices were lost in the distance that of the monk had drowned his expiring moans.

"Come, Brulette, start on," said Père Bastien. "We love you so well we can soon console you."

Huriel jumped on the shaft to be near her, and talked to her so gently all the way that she said to him just before we arrived: "Don't think me inconsolable, my true friend. My heart failed me for a second; but I know where to turn the love I felt for that child, and where I shall find the happiness he gave me."

It did not take us long to settle down in the old castle and even to feel at home in it. There were several habitable chambers, though they hardly looked so, and at first we thought them likely to fall about our heads. But the ruins had so long been shaken by the wind without collapsing that we felt they might outlast our time.

Aunt Marghitonne, delighted to have us near her, furnished the household with the various little comforts to which we were accustomed, and which the Huriel family were coaxed with some difficulty into sharing with us, for they were not used to such things and cared very little for them. The Bourbonnais wood-cutters, whom the Head-Woodsman had engaged, arrived duly, and he hired others in the neighborhood. So that we made quite a colony, quartered partly in the village and partly in the ruins, working cheerfully under the rule of a just man, who knew what it was to spare over-work and to reward the willing workman, and assembling every night in the courtyard for the evening meal; relating stories and listening to them; singing and frolicking in the open air, and dancing on Sundays with all the lads and lasses of the neighborhood, who were glad enough to get our Bourbonnais music, and who brought us little gifts from all parts, showing us a deal of attention.

The work was hard on account of the steep slopes on which the forest grew, which rose straight from the river, and made the felling a very dangerous matter. I had had experience of the quick temper of the Head-Woodsman in the woods of Alleu. As he was employing none but choice workmen for the felling, and the choppers understood the cutting up, nothing happened to irritate him; but I was ambitious to become a first-class chopper in order to please him, and I dreaded lest my want of practice should once more make him call me unhandy and imprudent, which would have mortified me cruelly in presence of Thérence. So I begged Huriel to take me apart and show me how to work and to let me watch him at the business. He was quite willing to oblige me, and I went at it with such a will that before long I surprised the master himself by my ability. He praised me, and even asked me before his daughter why I took hold so valiantly of a business I had no occasion for in my own country. "Because," I replied, "I am not sorry to know how to earn my living wherever I am. Who knows what may happen? If I loved a woman who wanted me to live in the depths of the woods, I could follow her, and support her there as elsewhere."

To prove to Thérence I was not so self-indulgent as perhaps she thought, I practised sleeping on the bare ground, and living frugally; trying to become as hardy a forester as the rest of them. I did not find myself any the worse for it; in fact I felt that my mind grew more active and my thoughts clearer. Many things that I did not at first understand without long explanations, unravelled themselves little by little, of their own accord, so that Thérence had no longer any occasion to smile at my stupid questions. She talked to me without getting weary and appeared to feel confidence in my judgment.

Still, a full fortnight went by before I felt the slightest hope of success; though when I bemoaned myself to Huriel that I dared not say a word to a girl who seemed so far above me that she could never so much as look at me, he replied,—

"Don't worry, Tiennet; my sister has the truest heart in existence; and if, like all young girls, she has her fanciful moments, there is no fancy in her head which will not yield to the love of a noble truth and an honest devotion."

His father said the same, and together they lent me courage; and Thérence found me so good an attendant, I watched so closely that no pain, fatigue, or annoyance should touch her from any cause within my power to control, and I was so careful never to look at another girl,— indeed I had little desire to,—in short, I behaved myself with such honest respect, showing her plainly on what a pinnacle I set her, that her eyes began to open; and several times I saw her watch how I went beforehand of her wishes with a softened, reflective look, and then reward me with thanks of which, I can tell you, I was proud enough. She was not accustomed, like Brulette, to have her wishes anticipated, and would never have known, like her, how to encourage it prettily. She seemed surprised that any one thought of her; and when it did happen, she showed such a sense of obligation that I never felt at my ease when she said to me with her serious air and guileless frankness, "Really, Tiennet, you are too kind," or perhaps, "Tiennet, you take too much trouble for me; I wish I could take as much for you some day."

One morning she was speaking to me in this way before a number of woodcutters, and one of them, a handsome Bourbonnais lad, remarked in a low tone that she showed a deal of interest in me.

"Certainly I do, Leonard," she replied, looking at him with a confident air. "I feel the interest that is due to him for all his kindness and friendship to me and mine."

"Don't you know that every one would do as he does," remarked Leonard, "if they thought they would be paid in the same coin?"

"I would try to be just to everybody," she replied, "if I felt a liking or a need for everybody's attentions. But I don't; and to one of my disposition the friendship of one person suffices."

I was sitting on the turf beside her as she said this, and I took her hand in mine, without daring to retain it more than a second. She drew it away, but as she did so she let it rest a moment on my shoulder in sign of confidence and relationship of soul.

However, things still went on in this way, and I began to suffer greatly from the reserve between us,—all the more because the lovers Huriel and Brulette were so tender and happy, and the contrast grieved my heart and troubled my spirit. Their day of joy was coming, but mine was not within sight.

TWENTY-NINTH EVENING.

One Sunday—it was that of the last publication of Brulette's banns—the Head-Woodsman and his son, who had seemed all day to be consulting privately, went off together, saying that a matter connected with the marriage called them to Nohant. Brulette, who knew all about the arrangements for her wedding, was a good deal surprised at their sudden activity, and still more that they told her nothing about it. She was even inclined to pout at Huriel, who said he should be absent for twenty-four hours; but he would not yield, and managed to pacify her by letting her think he was only going on her business and planning to give her some pleasant surprise.

But Thérence, whom I watched narrowly, seemed to me to make an effort to hide her uneasiness, and as soon as her father and Huriel had started, she carried me off into the little park and said:—

"Tiennet, I am worried to death, and I don't know what can be done to remedy matters. Listen to what has happened, and tell me if we can do anything to prevent harm. Last night as I lay awake I heard my father and brother agreeing to go and protect Joseph, and from what they said I made out that Joseph, though very ill-received by the bagpipers of your parts, to whom he applied for admission to the guild, is determined to insist on admittance,—a thing that they dare not refuse him openly without having put his talents to the test. It appears that the younger Carnat has also applied for admittance in place of his father, who retires; and his trial was to take place before the corporation this very day; so that Joseph has put himself forward to interfere with a claim that was not to be contested, and which was promised and half-granted in advance. Now, some of our wood-cutters who frequent the wine-shops have overheard certain wicked plans which the bagpipers of your neighborhood are making; for they are resolved to eject Joseph, if they can, by sneering at his music. If there was no greater risk than his having to bear injustice and defeat, I should not be so uneasy as you see me; but my father and brother, who belong to the guild and have a voice in all proceedings, feel it their duty to be present at this competition solely to protect Joseph. And, more than that, there was something I could not make out, because the guild have certain secret terms among themselves which my father and brother used, and which I did not understand. But however one looks at it, I am sure they are going into danger, for they carried under their blouses those little single-sticks, the harm of which you have already seen, and they even sharpened their pruning-hooks and hid them under their clothes, saying to each other early this morning, 'The devil is in that lad; he can neither be happy himself nor let others be. We must protect him, however; though he is obstinately rushing among the wolves, without thinking of his own skin or that of others.' My brother complained, saying he did not want to break anybody's head or have his own broken just as he was going to be married. To which my father replied that there was no use in anticipating evil; what one had to do was to go where humanity required us to help our neighbor. As they named Leonard among those who had overheard the malicious talk, I questioned him hastily just now, and he told me that Joseph, and consequently those who support him, have been threatened for a week or more, and that your bagpipers talk of not only refusing him admittance at this competition, but also of depriving him of the wish and the power to try again. I know, from having heard it spoken of as a child when my brother was admitted, that the candidates must behave boldly and endure all sorts of trials of their strength and courage. With us, the bagpipers lead a wandering life and do not make their music so much of a business as yours do; therefore they don't stand in each other's way and never persecute the candidates. It seems, from what Leonard told me and from my father's preparations, that here it is different, and that such matters end in fights which last till one or the other side gives up. Help me, Tiennet, for I am half-dead with fear and anxiety. I dare not rouse our wood-cutters; if my father thought I had overheard and betrayed the secrets of the guild he would deny me all trust and confidence in future. He expects me to be as brave as any woman can be in danger; but ever since that dreadful Malzac affair, I own to you I have no courage at all, and that I am tempted to fling myself into the middle of the fight, so much do I dread the results for those I love."

"And you call that want of courage, my brave girl?" I replied. "Now don't be troubled and leave me to act. The devil will be very cunning if I can't discover for myself, without suspicion falling on you, what those bagpipers are about; and if your father blames me, if he even drives me away and refuses the happiness I have been hoping to win,—I shall not care, Thérence! So long as I bring him or send him safe back to you, and Huriel also, I shall have my reward even if I never see you again. Good-bye; don't give way to anxiety; say nothing to Brulette, for she would lose her head. I know what should be done. Look as if you knew nothing. I take it all on my shoulders."

Thérence flung herself on my breast and kissed me on both cheeks with the innocence of a pure girl; so, filled to the brim with courage and confidence, I went to work.

I began by finding Leonard, whom I knew to be a good fellow, very bold and strong, and much attached to Père Bastien. Though he was rather jealous of me on the score of Thérence, he entered into my scheme, and I questioned him as to the number of bagpipers who were to meet for the competition, and the place where we could watch the assembly. He could not tell me anything under the first head; as to the second he knew that the trial was not to be in secret, and the place appointed was Saint-Chartier, in Benoît's tavern, an hour after vespers. The deliberation on the merits of the candidates was all that was to be held in secret, and even that was to be in the same house, and the decision was to be rendered in public.

I thought of half a dozen resolute lads fully able to keep the peace if, as Thérence feared, the matter should end in a quarrel; and I felt that justice being on our side, plenty of other fellows would come forward to support us. So I chose four who consented to follow me,—making, with Leonard and myself, six in all. They hesitated only on one point,—the fear of displeasing their master, the Head-Woodsman, by giving him help he had never asked for; but I swore to them that he should never know that they gave it deliberately, for we could easily pretend we were there by accident, and then, if any one were blamed, they could throw it all on me, who had asked them there to drink without their knowing what was going on.

So it was all agreed, and I went to tell Thérence that we were fully prepared against every danger. After which we started, each carrying a stout cudgel, and reached Saint-Chartier at the hour named.

Benoît's wine-shop was so full there was no turning round in it, and we were obliged to take a table outside. Indeed I was not sorry to leave my contingent there (exhorting them not to get drunk), and to slip myself into the shop, where I counted sixteen professional bagpipers, without reckoning Huriel and his father, who were sitting at table in a dark corner with their hats over their eyes, and all the less likely to be recognized because few of those present had met them in our parts. I pretended not to see them, and speaking so that they could hear me, I asked Benoît what this meeting of bagpipers was for, as if I had not heard a word about it, and did not understand its object.

"Why, don't you know," said the host, who was getting over his illness but was pallid and much reduced, "that your old friend Joseph, the son of my housekeeper, is going to compete with Carnat's son? I must say it is great folly on his part," added Benoît, lowering his voice. "His mother is much distressed, and fears the ill-will that grows out of these competitions. Indeed, she is so troubled that she has lost her head, and the customers are complaining, for the first time, that she does not serve them properly."

"Can I help you?" I said, glad to get a reason for staying inside and going about among the tables.

"Faith, my boy," he replied, "if you really mean it, you can do me good service; for I don't deny that I am still pretty weak, and I can't stoop to draw the wine without getting giddy. Here is the key of the cellar. Take charge of filling and bringing in the jugs. I hope that Mariton and her scullions can do the rest."

I didn't need telling twice; I ran out for an instant to tell my companions of the employment I had taken for the good of the cause, and then I went to work as tapster, which enabled me to see and hear everything.

Joseph and the younger Carnat were at either end of a long table feasting the guild, each taking the guests half-way down. There was more noise than pleasure going on. The company were shouting and singing to avoid talking, for they were all on the defensive, and it was easy to feel the jealousies and self-interests heaving below. I soon observed that all the bagpipers were not, as I had feared, in favor of the Carnats against Joseph; for, no matter how well a guild is managed, there are always old grudges which set members by the ears. But I also saw, little by little, that there was no comfort for Joseph in this, because those who did not want his rival, wanted him still less, and hoped to get the number of professional bagpipers lessened by the retirement of old Carnat. I even fancied that the greater number thought in this way, and I concluded that both candidates would be rejected.

After feasting for about two hours, the competition began. Silence was not demanded; for bagpipes in a room are instruments that don't trouble themselves about other noises, and the shouters and talkers soon gave up the contest. A crowd of people pressed in from outside. My five comrades climbed on the open window sill, and I went and stood near them. Huriel and his father did not stir from their corner. Carnat, who drew the lot to begin, mounted the bread-box and, encouraged by his father, who could not restrain himself from beating time with his sabots, played for half an hour on the old-fashioned bagpipe of the country with its narrow wind-bag.

He played very badly, being much agitated, and I saw that this pleased the greater part of the bagpipers. They kept silence, as they always did, so as to seem solemn and important, but others present kept silence too. This hurt the poor fellow, who had hoped for a little encouragement, and his father began to growl, and to show his revengeful and malicious nature.

When Joseph's turn came, he tore himself away from his mother, who was still entreating him in a low voice not to compete. He, too, mounted the box, holding his great Bourbonnaise bagpipe with great ease, the which quite dazzled the eyes of all present with its silver ornaments, its bits of looking-glass, and the great length of its pipes. Joseph carried himself proudly, looking round contemptuously on those who were to hear him. Everyone noticed his good looks, and the young fellows about asked if he could really be "José the dullard," whom they had once thought so stupid, and seen so puny. But his haughty air disgusted everybody, and as soon as the sound of his instrument filled the room there was more fear than pleasure in the curiosity he excited.

Nevertheless, there were present persons who knew good music, particularly the choir of the parish church and the hemp-spinners, who are great judges, and even elderly women, guardians of the good things of the past; and among such as these Joseph's music was quickly accepted, as much for the easy manner in which he used his instrument as for the good taste he displayed and the correct rendering which he gave to the new and very beautiful airs he played. A remark being made by the Carnats that his bagpipe, having a fuller sound, gave him an advantage, he unscrewed it and used only the chanter, which he played so well that the music was even more delightful than before. Finally, he took Carnat's old fashioned bagpipe, and played it so cleverly that any one would have said it was another instrument than the one first used.

The judges said nothing; but all others present trembled with pleasure and applauded vehemently, declaring that nothing so fine had ever been heard in our parts; and old mother Bline de la Breuille, who was eighty-seven years old and neither deaf nor dumb, walked up to the table and rapping it with her distaff said to the bagpipers, with the freedom her age warranted:—

"You may make faces as much as you like and shake your heads, but there's not one of you can play against that lad; he'll be talked of two hundred years hence; but all your names will be forgotten before your carcasses are rotten in the earth."

Then she left the room, saying (as did all present) that if the bagpipers rejected Joseph it would be the worst injustice that was ever done, and the wickedest jealousy that could be confessed.

The conclave of bagpipers now ascended to an upper room, and I hurried to open the door, hoping to gather something by overhearing what they said to each other in going up the stairs. The last to enter were the Head-Woodsman and his son; as they did so, Père Carnat, who recognized Huriel from having seen him with us at the midsummer bonfire, asked what they wanted and by what right they came to the council.

"The right of membership in your guild," answered Père Bastien; "and if you doubt it, ask us the usual questions, or try us with any music you like."

On this they were allowed to enter and the door was shut. I tried to listen, but every one spoke in a low voice, and I could not be sure of anything, except that they recognized the right of the two strangers to be present, and that they were deliberating about the competition without either noise or dispute. Through a crack in the door I could see that they divided into parties of five or six, exchanging opinions in a low voice before they began to vote. But when the time for voting came, one of the bagpipers looked out to see if any one were listening, and I was forced to disappear in a hurry lest I should be caught in a position which would put me to shame without an excuse; for I certainly could not say that my friends were in danger in such a peaceful conclave.

I found my young fellows below, sitting at table with others of our acquaintance, who were toasting and complimenting Joseph. Carnat the younger was alone and gloomy in a corner,—forgotten and mortified. The monk was there, too, in the chimney-corner, inquiring of Mariton and Benoît what was going on. When told all about it he came up to the long table, where they were drinking with Joseph, and asking him where and from whom he had got his teaching.

"Friend Joseph," said he, "we know each other, you and I, and I wish to add my voice to the applause you are now, of good right, receiving. But permit me to point out that it is generous as well as wise to console the vanquished, and that in your place, I should make friendly advances to young Carnat, whom I see over there all alone and very sad."

The monk spoke so as to be heard only by Joseph and a few others who were near him, and I thought he did as much out of kind-heartedness as by instigation of Joseph's mother, who wanted the Carnats to get over their aversion to her son.

This appeal to Joseph's generosity flattered his vanity. "You are right, Brother Nicolas," he said; then, in a loud voice, he called to young Carnat:—

"Come, François, don't sulk at your friends. You did not play as well as you know how to, I am quite sure. But you shall have your revenge another time; besides, judgment is not given yet. So, instead of turning your back on us, come and drink, and let us be as quiet together as a pair of oxen yoked to a cart."

Everybody approved of this speech, and Carnat, fearing to seem jealous, accepted the offer and sat down near him. So far so good, but

Joseph could not keep from showing his opinion that his art was far above that of others, and in offering civilities to his rival he put on such a patronizing manner that Carnat was more hurt than ever.

"You talk as if you were already elected," he said, "and it is no such thing. It is not always for the skill of the fingers and the cleverest compositions that those who know what they are about select a man. Sometimes they choose him for being the best-known and most respected player in the country, for that makes him a good comrade to the rest of the guild."

"Oh! I expect that," returned Joseph. "I have been long absent, and though I pique myself on deserving as much respect as any man, yet I know they will try to fall back on the foolish reason that I am little known. Well, I don't care for that, François! I did not expect to find a company of good musicians among you, capable of judging me or my merits, and lovers enough of true knowledge to prefer my talent to their own interests and that of their acquaintances. All that I wanted was to be heard and judged by my mother and friends,—by intelligent ears and reasonable beings. For the rest, I laugh at your screaming and bellowing bagpipes, and I must say, God forgive me! that I shall be prouder of being rejected than accepted."

The monk remarked gently that he was not speaking judiciously. "You should not challenge the judges you demanded of your own free-will," he said; "pride spoils the highest merit."

"Leave him his pride," said Carnat; "I am not jealous of what he can show. He ought to have some talent, to cover his other misfortunes. Remember the old saying: 'Good player, good dupe.'"

"What do you mean by that?" said Joseph, setting down his glass and looking the other in the eye.

"I am not obliged to tell you," said Carnat; "all the others understand it."

"But I don't understand it, and as you are speaking to me I'll call you a coward if you dare not explain yourself."

"Oh, I can tell you to your face," returned Carnat; "it is something that need not offend you at all, for perhaps it is no more your fault to be unlucky in love than it is mine to be unlucky to-night in music."

"Come, come!" said one of the young men who were present; "let *Josette* alone. She has found some one to marry her, and that's enough; it is nobody's business."

"It is my opinion," said another, "that it was not Joseph who was tricked in that affair, but the other who is going to shoulder his work."

"Whom are you speaking of?" cried Joseph, as if his head were reeling. "Who is it you call *Josette*? What wicked nonsense are you trying on me?"

"Hold your tongues!" cried Mariton, turning scarlet with anger and grief, as she always did when Brulette was attacked. "I wish your wicked tongues were torn out and nailed to the church door."

"Speak lower," said one of the young men; "you know that Mariton won't allow a word against her José's fair friend. All beauties uphold each other, and Mariton is not yet so old but what she has a voice in the chapter."

Joseph was puzzling his brains to know whether they were blaming or ridiculing him.

"Explain it to me," he said, pulling me by the arm. "Don't leave me without a word to say."

I was just going to meddle, though I had vowed I wouldn't get into any dispute in which Père Bastien and his son were not concerned, when François Carnat cut me short. "Nonsense!" he said to Joseph, with a sneer; "Tiennet can't tell you more than what I wrote you."

"That is what you are talking of, is it?" said Joseph. "Well, I swear you lie! and that you have written and signed false witness. Never—"

"Bravo!" cried Carnat. "You knew how to make your profit out of my letter! and if, as people think, you are the author of that child, you have not been such a fool, after all, in getting rid of your property to a friend,—a faithful friend, too, for there he is upstairs, looking after your interests in the council. But if, as I now think, you came into these parts to assert your right to the child, which was refused, that accounts for a queer scene which I saw from a distance at the castle of Chassin—"

"What scene?" said the monk. "Let me tell you, young man, that I too may have witnessed it, and I want to know how truly you relate the things that you see."

"As you please," returned Carnat. "I will tell you what I saw with my own eyes, without hearing a word that was said; and you may explain it as you can. You are to know, the rest of you, that on the last day of last month Joseph got up early in the morning to hang his May bunch on Brulette's door; and seeing a baby about two years old, which of course was his, he wanted no doubt to get possession of it, for he seized it, as if to go off with it; and then began a sharp dispute, in which his friend the Bourbonnais wood-cutter (the same that is upstairs now with his father, and who is to marry Brulette next Sunday) struck him violently and then embraced the mother and child; after which Joseph was gently shoved out of the door and did not show his face there again. I call that one of the queerest histories I ever knew. Twist it as you will, it still remains the tale of a child claimed by two fathers, and of a girl who, instead of giving herself to the first seducer, kicks him away as unworthy or incapable of bringing up the child of their loves."

Instead of answering, as he had proposed to do, Brother Nicolas returned to the chimney, and talked in a low voice, but very eagerly, with Benoît. Joseph was so taken aback at the interpretation put upon a matter of which, after all, he did not know the real meaning, that he looked all round him for assistance, and as Mariton had rushed from the room like a crazy woman, there was no one but me to put down Carnat. The latter's speech had created some astonishment, but no one thought of defending Brulette, against whom they still felt piqued. I began to take her part; but Carnat interrupted me at the first word:—

"Oh! as for you," he said, "no one accuses you. I dare say you played your part in good faith, though it is known that you were used to deceive people by bringing the child from the Bourbonnais. But you are so simple, Tiennet, you may never have suspected anything.—The devil take me!" he continued, addressing the company, "if that fellow isn't as stupid as a basket. He is capable of being godfather to a child believing all the while they were christening a clock. He probably went into the Bourbonnais to fetch this godson of his, who, they told him, was found in a cabbage, and he brought it back in a pilgrim's sack. In fact he is such a slave and good cousin to the girl, that if she had tried to make him believe the boy was like him he would have thought so too."

THIRTIETH EVENING.

There was no use in protesting and getting angry; the company were more inclined to laugh than to listen, for it is always a great delight to misbehaving fellows to speak ill of a poor girl. They make haste to plunge her in the mire, reserving the right to deny it if they find she is innocent.

In the midst of their slanderous speeches, however, a loud voice, slightly weakened by illness but still capable of drowning every other in the room, made itself heard. It was that of the master of the tavern, long accustomed to quell the dissensions of wine and the hubbub of junketing.

"Hold your tongues," he said, "and listen to me, or I'll turn you out this moment, if I never open the house again. Be silent about an honest girl whom you decry because you have all found her too virtuous. As to the real parents of the child who has given rise to these tales, tell them to their face what fault you find with them, for here they are before you. Yes," he continued, drawing Mariton, who was holding Charlot in her arms and weeping, up to him, "here is the mother of my heir, and this is my son whom I recognize by my marriage to this good woman. If you ask me for exact dates, I shall tell you to mind your own business; nevertheless, to any who have the right to question me, I will show deeds which prove that I have always recognized the child as mine, and that his mother was my legitimate wife before his birth, though the matter was kept secret."

The silence of astonishment fell on everybody; and Joseph, who had risen at the first words, stood stock still like a stone image. The monk who noticed the doubt, shame, and anger in his eyes, thought best to add further explanations. He told us that Benoît had been unable to make his marriage public because of the opposition of a rich relative, who had lent him money for his business, and who might have ruined him by demanding it back. As Mariton feared for her reputation, specially on account of her son Joseph, they had concealed Charlot's birth and had put him to nurse at Saint-Sevère; but, at the end of a year Mariton had found him so ill-used that she begged Brulette to take charge of him, thinking that no one else would give him as much care. She had not foreseen the harm this would do to the young girl, and when she did find it out, she wished to remove the child, but Benoît's illness had prevented her doing so, and moreover Brulette had become so attached to Charlot that she would not part with him.

"Yes!" cried Mariton, "poor dear soul that she is, she proved her courage for me. 'You will have trouble enough,' she said to me, 'if you lose your husband; and, perhaps your marriage will be questioned by the family.

He is too ill to trouble him now about declaring it. Have patience; don't kill him by talking of your affairs. Everything will come right if God grant that he recovers.'"

"And if I have recovered,' added Benoît, "it is by the care of this good woman, my wife, and the kindheartedness of the young girl in question, who patiently endured both blame and insult rather than cause me injury at that time by exposing our secrets. And here is another faithful friend," he added, pointing to the monk,—"a man of sense, of action, and of honest speech, an old school friend of mine in the days when I was educating at Montluçon. He it was who went after my old devil of an uncle, and who at last, no later than this morning, persuaded him to consent to my marriage with my good housekeeper; and when my uncle had given his word to make me heir to his whole property, Brother Nicolas told him the priest had already joined Mariton and me, and showed him that fat Charlot, whom he thought a fine boy and very like the author of his existence."

Benoît's satisfaction revived the lost gayety of the party; every one was struck with the resemblance, which, however, no one had yet noticed,—I as little as any.

"So, Joseph," continued the innkeeper, "you can and ought to love and respect your mother, just as I love and respect her. I take my oath here and now that she is the bravest and most helpful Christian woman that ever a sick man had about him; and I have never had a moment's hesitation in my resolve to declare sooner or later what I have declared to-day. We are now very well off in our worldly affairs, thank God, and as I swore to her and to God that I would replace the father you lost, I will agree, if you will live here with us, to take you into partnership and to give you a good share of the profits.' So you needn't fling yourself into bagpiping, in which your mother sees all sorts of ills for you and anxieties for her. Your notion was to get her a home. That's my affair now, and I even offer to make hers yours. Come, you'll listen to us, won't you, and give up that damned music? Why can't you live in your own country and stay at home? You needn't blush at having an honest innkeeper for a step-father."

"You are my step-father, that's very certain," replied Joseph, not showing either pleasure or displeasure, but remaining coldly on the defensive; "you are an honest man, I know, and rich, I see, and if my mother is happy with you—"

"Yes, yes, Joseph, as happy as possible; above all to-day," cried Mariton, kissing him, "for I hope you will never leave me again."

"You are mistaken, mother," answered Joseph; "you no longer have any need of me, and you are contented. All is well. You were the only thing that brought me back into this part of the country; you were all I had to love, for Brulette—and it is well that all present should hear this from my own mouth—for Brulette never had any feeling but that of a sister for me. Now I am free to follow my destiny; which is not a very kindly one, but it is so plainly mine that I prefer it to all the money of innkeeping and the comfort of family life. Farewell, mother, God bless those who make you happy; as for me, I want nothing in these parts, not even admission to the guild which evil-intentioned fools are trying to deny me. My inward thoughts and my bagpipe go with me wherever I am; and I know I can always earn my living, for wherever my music is heard I shall be welcome."

As he spoke the door to the staircase opened and the whole company of bagpipers entered in silence. Père Carnat requested the attention of those present, and in a firm and cheerful manner, which surprised everybody, he said:—

"François Carnat, my son, after careful examination of your merits and full discussion of your rights, you are declared too much of a novice for present admission. You are advised to study a while longer, without discouragement, so as to present yourself for competition later when circumstances may be more favorable. And you, Joseph Picot, of the village of Nohant, the decision of the masters of this part of the country is that you be, by reason of your unparalleled talents, received into the first class of the guild; and this decision is unanimous."

"Well," replied Joseph, who seemed wholly indifferent to his victory and to the applause with which it was received, "as the matter has turned out this way, I accept the decision, although, not expecting it, I hardly care for it."

Joseph's haughty manner displeased everybody, and Père Carnat hastened to say, with an air which I thought showed disguised malignity: "Does that mean, Joseph, that you wish for the honor and the title, and do not intend to take your place among the professional bagpipers in these parts?"

"I don't know yet," said Joseph, evidently by way of bravado, and not wishing to satisfy his judges. "I'll think about it."

"I believe," said young Carnat to his father, "that he has thought about it already, and his decision is made, for he hasn't the courage to go on with the matter."

"Courage?" cried Joseph, "courage for what, if you please?"

Then the dean of the bagpipers, old Paillou of Verneuil, said to Joseph:—

"You are surely not ignorant, young man, that something more than playing an instrument is required, to be received into our guild; there is such a thing as a musical catechism, which you must know and on which you will be questioned, if you feel you have the knowledge and also the boldness to answer. Moreover, there are certain oaths to be taken. If you feel no repugnance to these things, you must decide at once to submit to them, so that the matter may be settled to-morrow morning."

"I understand you," said Joseph. "The guild has secret oaths, and tests and trials. They are all great folly, as far as I know, and music has no part in them, for I defy you to reply to any musical question which I might put to you. Consequently, the questions you address to me on a subject you know less about than the frogs in the pond, are no better than old women's gabble."

"If you take it that way," said Renet, the Mers bagpiper, "we are willing you should think yourself a great genius and the rest of us jackasses. So be it. Keep your secrets, and we will keep ours. We are not anxious to tell them to those who despise us. But remember one thing: here is your certificate as a master bagpiper, which we now hand to you, signed and sealed by all, including your friends the Bourbonnais bagpipers, who agree that all is done in good order. You are free to exercise your talents where you please and where you can; except in the parishes where we play and which number one hundred and fifty, according to the distribution we make among ourselves, the list of which will be handed to you; in those parishes you are forbidden to play. We give notice that if you break this rule it will be at your own risk and peril, for we shall put a stop to it, if need be, by main force."

Here Mariton spoke up.

"You needn't threaten him," she said, "it is safe to leave him to his own fancy, which is to play his music and look for no profit. He has no need to do that, thank God, and besides, his lungs are not strong enough for your business. Come, Joseph, thank them for the honor have done you, and don't keep them anxious about their interests. Let the matter be settled now, and here's my man who will pay the pipers with a good quartern of Sancerre or Issoudun wine, at the choice of the company."

"That's all right," said old Carnat. "We are quite willing the matter should end thus. It is best, no doubt, for your son; for one needn't be either a fool or a coward to shrink from the tests, and I do think the poor fellow is not cut out to endure them."

"We will see about that!" cried Joseph, falling into the trap that was set for him, in spite of the warnings Père Bastien was giving him in a low voice. "I demand the tests; and as you have no right to refuse them after delivering to me the certificate, I intend to practise your calling if I choose, or, at any rate, to prove that I am not prevented from doing so by any of you."

"Agreed!" said the dean, showing plainly, as did Carnat and several others, the malignant pleasure Joseph's words afforded them. "We will now prepare for your initiation, friend Joseph. Remember there is no going back, and that you will be considered a milk-sop or a braggart if you change your mind."

"Go on, go on!" cried Joseph. "I'll await you on a firm foot."

"It is for us to await you," said old Carnat in his ear, "at the stroke of midnight."

"Where?" said Joseph, coolly.

"At the gate of the cemetery," replied the dean, in a low voice. Then, without accepting the wine which Benoît offered them, or giving heed to the remonstrances of his wife, they went off in a body, threatening evil to all who followed them or spied upon their mysteries.

The Head-Woodsman and Huriel went with them without a word to Joseph, by which I plainly saw that, although the pair were opposed to the spirit of the other bagpipers, they thought it none the less their duty not to warn Joseph, nor to betray in the slightest degree the secrets of the guild.

In spite of the threats which were made, I was not deterred from following them at a distance, without other precaution than carelessly sauntering down the same road, with my hands in my pockets, and whistling as if I were paying no attention to them or their affairs. I knew they would not let me get near enough to overhear their plots, but I wanted to make sure in what direction they meant to lie in wait, so as to get there later, if possible, unobserved. With that notion in my head, I signed to Leonard to keep the others at the tavern until I returned to call them. But my pursuit was soon ended. The inn stood on a street which ran down-hill to the river, and is now the mail route to Issoudun. In those days it was a breakneck little place, narrow and ill-paved, lined with old houses with pointed gables and stone mullions. The last of these houses was pulled down a year ago. From the river, which ran along the wall below the inn of the Bœuf Couronné, a steep ascent led to the market-place, which was then, as it is now, that long unevenly paved space, planted with trees, bordered on the left by old houses, on the right by the broad moat, full of water, and the great wall (then unbroken) of the castle. The church closes the market-place at the further end, and two alleys lead down from it, one to the parsonage, the other past the cemetery. The bagpipers turned down the latter path. They were about a gunshot in advance of me, that is to say, just time enough to pass along the path by the cemetery and out into the open country by the postern of the English tower, unless they chose to stop at this particular spot; which was not very convenient, for the path—which ran between the moat of the castle on one side and the bank of the cemetery on the other—was only wide enough for one person at a time.

When I judged that the bagpipers must have reached the postern, I turned the corner of the castle under an arcade which in those days was used as a footpath by the gentry on their way to the parish church. I found I was all alone when I entered the path by the churchyard, a place few Christian men would set foot in alone after nightfall,—not only because it led past the cemetery, but because the north flank of the castle had a bad name. There was talk of I don't know how many persons drowned in the moat in the days of the English war; and some folks swore they had heard the cocadrillos whistle on that particular path when epidemics were about.

You know of course that the cocadrillo is a sort of lizard, which sometimes seems no bigger than your little finger, and sometimes swells to the size of an ox and grows five or six yards long. This beast, which I have never seen, and whose existence I couldn't warrant, is supposed to vomit a venom which poisons the air and brings the plague. Now, though I did not believe much of this, I was not over-fond of going along this path, where the high wall of the castle and the tall trees of the cemetery shut out every speck of light. On this occasion I walked fast, without looking to the right or left, and passed through the postern of the English gate, of which, by the bye, not one stone upon another remains to the present day.

Once there, and notwithstanding that the night was fine and the moon clear, I could not see, either far or near, the slightest trace of the eighteen persons I was after. I looked in every direction; I even went as far as Père Begneux's cottage, the only house they could have entered. The occupants were all asleep, and nowhere about was there any noise, or trace, or sign, of a living person. I therefore concluded that the missing bagpipers had entered the cemetery to perform some wicked conjuring, and—though far from liking to do so, but determined to risk all for Thérence's relations—I returned through the postern and along the accursed path, stepping softly, skirting the bank so close that I touched the tombstones, and keeping my ears open to the slightest sound. I heard the screech-owl hooting in the casemates, and the adders hissing in the black water of the moat, but that was all. The dead slept in the ground as tranquilly as the living in their beds. I plucked up courage to climb over the cemetery bank and to give a glance round the field of death. All was quiet,—no signs whatever of the bagpipers.

Then I walked all round the castle. It was locked up, and as it was after ten o'clock masters and servants slept like stones.

Then I returned to the inn, not being able to imagine what had become of the guild, but determined to station my comrades in the path leading to the English gate, from which we could see what happened to Joseph when he reached the rendezvous at midnight at the gate of the cemetery. I found them on the bridge debating whether or not they should start for home, and declaring they could see no danger to the Huriels, because it was evident they had agreed amicably with the other bagpipers in the matter of the competition. As for what concerned Joseph, they cared little or nothing, and tried to prevent me from interfering. I told them that to my thinking the danger for all three would be when the tests were applied, for the evil intentions of the bagpipers had been plainly shown, and the Huriels, I knew, were there to protect Joseph.

"Are you already sick of the enterprise?" I said. "Is it because we are only eight to sixteen, and you haven't a heart for two inside of you?"

"How do you count eight?" asked Leonard. "Do you think the Head-Woodsman and his son would go with us against their fellow-members?"

"I did count wrong;" I answered; "for we are really nine. Joseph won't let himself be fleeced if they make it too hot for him, and as both the Huriels carry arms, I feel quite sure they mean to defend him if they can't be heard otherwise."

"That's not the point," returned Leonard. "We are only six, and they are twenty; but there's another thing which pleases us even less than a fight. People have been talking in the inn, and each had a story to relate of these tests. The monk denounced them as impious and abominable; and though Joseph laughed at what was said, we don't feel certain there is nothing in it. They told of candidates nailed on a bier, and furnaces into which they were tripped, and red-hot iron crosses which they were made to clasp. Such things seem hard to believe; and if I were certain that that was all I'd like to punish the fellows who are bad enough to ill-treat a neighbor in that way. Unfortunately—"

"There, there!" said I, "I see you have let yourself be scared. What is behind it all? Tell the whole, and let's either laugh at it or take warning."

"This is it," said one of the lads, seeing that Leonard was ashamed to own his fears. "None of us have ever seen the devil, and we don't want to make his acquaintance."

"Ho, ho!" I cried, seeing that they were all relieved, now the words were out. "So it is Lucifer himself that frightens you! Well, I'm too good a

Christian to be afraid of him; I give my soul to God, and I'll be bound I'll take him by the horns, yes I myself, alone against the enemy of mankind, as fearlessly as I would take a goat by the beard. He has been allowed to do evil to those who fear him long enough, and it is my opinion that an honest fellow who dared to wrench off his horns could deprive him of half his power, and that would be something gained at any rate."

"Faith!" said Leonard, ashamed of his fears, "if you look at it that way I won't back down, and if you'll smash his horns I'll try to pull out his tail. They say it is fine, and we'll find out if it is gold or hemp."

There is no such remedy against fear as fun, but I don't deny that though I took the matter on that tone, I was not at all anxious to pit myself against "Georgeon," as we call the devil in our parts. I wasn't a bit more easy in mind than the rest, but for Thérence's sake I felt ready to march into the jaws of hell. I had promised her, and the good God himself couldn't have turned me back now.

But that's an ill way to talk. The good God, on the contrary, gave me strength and confidence, and the more anxiety I felt all that night, the more I thought on him and asked his aid.

When our other comrades saw that our minds, Leonard's and mine, were made up, they followed us. To make the affair safer, I went back to the inn to see if I could find other friends who, without knowing what we were after, would follow us for fun, and, if occasion came, would fight with us. But it was late, and there was no one at the Bœuf Couronné but Benoît, who was supping with the monk, Mariton, who was saying her prayers, and Joseph, who had thrown himself on a bed and was sound asleep with, I must own, a tranquillity that put us to shame.

"I have only one hope," said Mariton, as she got off her knees; "and that is that he will sleep over the time and not wake up till morning."

"That's just like all women!' cried Benoît, laughing, "they want life at the price of shame. But I gave my word to her lad to wake him before midnight, and I shall not fail to do so."

"Ah, you don't love him!" cried the mother. "We'll see if you push our Charlot into danger when his turn comes."

"You don't know what you are talking about, wife," replied the innkeeper; "go to bed and to sleep with my boy; I promise you I'll not fail to wake yours. You would not wish him to blame me for his dishonor?"

"Besides," said the monk, "what danger do you suppose there is in the nonsense they are going to perform? I tell you you are dreaming, my good woman. The devil doesn't get hold of anybody; God doesn't allow it, and you have not brought your boy up so ill that you need fear that he will get himself damned for his music. I tell you that the villanous tests of the bagpipers are really nothing worse than impious jokes, from which sensible people can easily protect themselves; and Joseph need only laugh at the demons they will set upon him, to put them all to flight."

The monk's words heartened up my comrades wonderfully.

"If it is only a farce," they said to me, "we will tumble into the middle of it and thrash the devil well; but hadn't we better take Benoît into our confidence? He might help us."

"To tell you the truth," I said, "I am not sure that he would. He is thought a worthy man; but you never know the secrets of a family, especially when there are children by a first marriage. Step-fathers don't always like them, and Joseph has been none too amiable this evening with his. Let's get off without a word to anyone; that's best, and it is nearly time we were there."

Taking the road past the church, walking softly and in single file, we posted ourselves in the little path near the English gate. The moon was so low we could creep in the shadow of the cemetery bank and not be seen, even if any one passed quite close to us. My comrades, being strangers, had no such repugnance to the place as the villagers, and I let them go in front while I hid within the cemetery, near enough to the gate to see who entered, and also near enough to call to them when wanted.

THIRTY-FIRST EVENING.

I waited a good long time,—all the longer because the hours go so slow in company with dead folks. At last midnight struck in the church steeple and I saw the head of a man rising beyond the low wall of the cemetery quite near the gate. Another quarter of an hour dragged along without my seeing or hearing anything but that man, who, getting tired of waiting, began to whistle a Bourbonnais tune, whereby I knew it was Joseph, who no doubt betrayed the hopes of his enemies by seeming so cool in presence of the dead.

At last, another man, who was stuck close to the wall inside the gate, and whom I hadn't seen on account of the big box-trees which hid him, popped his head quickly over the wall as if to take Joseph by surprise; but the latter did not stir, and said, laughing: "Well, Père Carnat, you are rather late; I came near going to sleep while waiting. Will you open the gate, or must I enter that 'nettle-field,' by the breach?"

"No," said Carnat, "the curate would not like it; we mustn't openly offend the church people. I will go to you."

He climbed over the wall and told Joseph he must let his head and arms be covered with a very thick canvas sack, and then walk wherever he was led.

"Very good," said Joseph in a contemptuous tone. "Go on."

I watched them from over the wall, and saw them enter the little path to the English gate; then I made a short cut to the place where I had left my comrades and found only four of them; the youngest had slipped off without a word, and I was rather afraid the others would do the same, for they found the time long and told me they had heard very queer noises, which seemed to come from under the earth.

Presently Joseph came along, with his head covered and led by Carnat. The pair got close upon us, but turned from the path about twenty feet off. Carnat made Joseph clamber down to the edge of the moat, and we thought he meant to drown him. At once we were on our legs to stop such treachery, but in a minute more we saw they were both walking in the water, which was shallow at that place, until they reached a low archway in the wall of the castle which was partly in the water of the moat. They passed through it, and this explained to me what had become of the others whom I had hunted for.

It was necessary to do as they did; which didn't seem to me very difficult, but my comrades were hard to persuade. They had heard that the vaults of the castle ran nine miles out into the country, as far as Deols, and that persons who did not know their windings had been lost in them. I was forced to declare that I knew them very well, though I had never set foot there in my life, and had no idea whether they were common wine-cellars or a subterraneous town, as my friends declared.

I walked first, without seeing where I set my feet, feeling the walls, which inclosed a narrow passage where one's head very nearly touched the roof. We advanced in this way for a short time, when a hullaballoo sounded beneath us like forty thunder-claps rolling round the devil's cave. It was so strange and alarming that I stopped short to try and find out what it meant; then I went quickly forward, not to let myself get chilled with the idea of some devil's caper, telling my companions to follow me. But the noise was so loud they did not hear me and I, thinking they were at my heels, went on and on, till, hearing nothing more, I turned to speak to them and got no answer. Not wishing to call aloud, I went back four or five steps; it was all dark. I stretched out my hands, and called cautiously; good-bye to my valiant contingent,—they had deserted me!

I thought I must be pretty near the entrance and could surely catch up with them within or without. I returned through the arch by which we had entered, and searched carefully along the little path beside the cemetery; but no! my comrades had disappeared just like the bagpipers; it seemed as if the earth had opened and swallowed them up.

I had a moment of horrid worry, thinking I must either give up the whole thing or return to those devilish caverns and take myself all alone into the traps and terrors they were preparing for Joseph. But I asked myself whether, even if the matter concerned only him, I could quietly leave him in danger. My soul answered no, and then I asked my heart if love for Thérence wasn't quite as real a thing as one's duty to one's neighbor, and the answer I received sent me back through the dark and slimy archway and along the subterranean passages—I won't say as gayly, but at any rate as quickly as if I were going to my own wedding.

While I was feeling my way forward I found, on my right, an opening to another passage, which I had not found before because I then felt to my left; and I thought to myself that my comrades in going out had probably found it and turned that way. I followed the passage, for there was no sign that the other way would bring me any nearer to the bagpipers. I did not find my comrades, but as for the bagpipers, I had not taken twenty steps before I heard their din much nearer than it sounded the first time; and presently a quivering kind of light let me see that I was entering a large round cave which had three or four exits, black as the jaws of hell.

I was surprised to see so clearly in a vault where there wasn't any light, but I presently noticed that gleams were coming from below through the ground I trod upon. I noticed that this ground seemed to swell up in the middle, and fearing it was not solid, I kept close to the wall, and getting near to a crevice, I lay down with my eye close to it and saw very plainly what was going on in another cavern just below the one I was in. It was, as I afterwards learned, a former dungeon, adjoining an oubliette or black hole, the mouth of which could still be seen thirty years ago in the upper hall of the castle. I thought as much when I saw the remains of human bones at the lower end of the cave, which the bagpipers had set up in rows to terrify the candidate, with pine torches inside their skulls. Joseph was there all alone, his eyes unbound, his arms crossed, just as cool as I was not, listened contemptuously to the uproar of eighteen bagpipes, which all brayed together, prolonging a single note into a roar. This crazy music came from an adjoining cave where the bagpipers were hidden, and where, as they doubtless knew, a curious echo multiplied the sound. I, who knew nothing about it then, fancied at first that all the bagpipes of Berry, Auvergne, and the Bourbonnais were collected together in that cave.

When they had had enough of growling with their instruments, they began to squeal and squall themselves, and the walls echoed them, till you would have fancied they were a great troop of furious animals of all kinds. But Joseph, who was really an unusual kind of man among our peasantry,—indeed, I hardly ever knew his like,—merely shrugged his shoulders and yawned, as if tired with such fool's play. His courage passed into me, and I began to think of laughing at the farce, when a little noise at my back made me turn my head. There I saw, at the entrance of the passage by which I had come, a figure which froze my senses.

It was that of a lord of the olden time, carrying a lance and wearing an iron breastplate and leathern garments of a style no longer seen. But the most awful part of him was his face, which was actually like a death's head.

I partly recovered myself, thinking it was only a disguise some of the enemy had put on to frighten Joseph; but on reflection I saw the danger was really mine, because, finding me on the watch, he would surely do me some damage. However, though he saw me as plain as I could see him, he did not stir, but remained stock-still like a ghost, half in shadow, and half in the light that came up from below; and as this light flickered according as it was moved about, there were moments when, not seeing him, I thought he was a notion of my own brain,—until suddenly he would reappear, all but his legs, which remained in darkness behind a sort of step or barrier, which made me fancy he was as it were floating on a cloud.

I don't know how long I was tortured with this vision, which made me forget to watch Joseph, and scared me lest I was going mad in trying to do more than it was in me to perform. I recollected that I had seen in the hall of the castle an old picture which they said was the portrait of a wicked warrior whom a lord of the castle in the olden time, who was the warrior's brother, had flung into the dungeon. The garments of leather and iron which I saw before me on that skeleton figure, were certainly like those in the picture, and the notion came into my head that here was a ghost in pain, watching the desecration of his sepulchre, and waiting to show his displeasure in some way or other.

What made this idea the more probable was that the ghost said nothing to me, and evidently took no notice of my presence,—apparently aware that I had no evil intentions against his poor carcass.

At last a noise different from all others attracted my eyes away from him. I looked back into the cave below me, where stood Joseph, and something near him very ugly and very strange.

Joseph stood boldly in front of an abominable creature, dressed in the skin of a dog, with horns sticking out of his tangled hair, and a red face, and claws and tail; the which beast was jumping about and making faces like one possessed of the devil. It was vile to see, and yet I wasn't the dupe of it very long, for though the creature tried to disguise his voice I thought I recognized that of Doré-Fratin, the bagpiper of Pouligny, one of the strongest and most quarrelsome men in our neighborhood.

"You may sneer as you please," he was saying to Joseph, "at me and at hell, but I am the king of all musicians, and you shall not play your instrument without my permission unless you sell me your soul."

Joseph answered, "What can such a fool of a devil as you do with the soul of a musician? You have no use for it."

"Mind what you say," returned the other. "Don't you know that down here you must either give yourself to the devil or prove that you are stronger than he?"

"Yes, yes, I know the proverb," said Joseph: "'Kill the devil or the devil will kill you.'"

As he spoke, I saw Huriel and his father come from a dark opening into the vault and go up to the devil as if to speak to him; but they were pulled back by the other bagpipers who now showed themselves, and Carnat the elder addressed Joseph.

"You have proved," he said, "that you don't fear witchcraft, and we will let you go free if you will now conform to the usual custom, which is to fight the devil, in proof that you, a Christian man, refuse to submit to him."

"If the devil wants to be well thrashed," replied Joseph, "let me go at him at once, and we'll see if his skin is any tougher than mine. What weapons?"

"None but your fists," replied Carnat.

"It is fair play, I hope," said the Head-Woodsman.

Joseph took no time to inquire; his temper was up. Enraged by the tricks that were played on him, he sprang on the devil, tore off his horns and head-dress, and caught him so resolutely round the body that he brought him to earth and fell on top of him.

But he instantly got up, and I fancied he gave a cry of surprise and pain; but the bagpipers all began to play, except Huriel and his father, who stood watching the encounter with an expression of doubt and uneasiness.

Joseph, meantime, was tumbling the devil about and seeming to get the better of him; but his rage seemed to me unnatural, and I feared he might put himself in the wrong through too much violence. The bagpipers seemed to help him, for instead of rescuing their comrade, who was knocked down three times, they marched round and round the fight, piping loudly, and beating with their feet to excite him.

Suddenly the Head-Woodsman separated the combatants by levelling a blow with his stick on the devil's paws, and threatening to strike harder the second time if he was not listened to. Huriel ran to his father's side, raising his stick also, while all the others stopped walking round and round and piping; and a moment's silence and stillness fell on all.

Then I saw that Joseph, overcome with pain, was wiping his torn hands and his face, which was covered with blood, and that he would have fainted if Huriel had not caught him in his arms, while Doré-Fratin merely threw aside his trappings, panting with heat, and wiping the sweat from his forehead with a grin.

"What does this mean?" cried Carnat, coming up to the Plead-Woodsman with a threatening air, "Are you a traitor to the guild? By what right do you interfere with the tests?"

"I interfere at my own risk and to your shame," replied the Head-Woodsman. "I am not a traitor, and you are evil-doers, both treacherous and cruel. I suspected that you were tricking us to lead this young man here and wound him, perhaps dangerously. You hate him because you know that every one will prefer him to you, and that wherever he is heard no one will listen to your music. You have not dared to refuse him admission to the guild, because the whole country would blame you for such a crying injustice; but you are trying to frighten him from playing in the parishes you have taken possession of, and you have put him through hard and dangerous tests which none of you could have borne as long as he."

"I don't know what you mean," said the old dean, Pailloux de Verneuil; "and the blame you cast upon us here, in presence of a candidate, is unheard-of insolence. We don't know how you practise initiation in your part of the country, but here we are following our customs and shall not allow you to interfere."

"I shall interfere," said Huriel, who was sopping Joseph's blood with his handkerchief, and had brought him back to consciousness, as he held him on his knee. "I neither can nor will tell of your conduct away from here, because I belong to the brotherhood, but at least I will tell you to your faces that you are brutes. In our country we fight with the devil in jest, taking care to do no one any harm. Here you choose the strongest among you and furnish him with hidden weapons, with which he endeavors to put out the eyes and stab the veins of your victims. See! this young man is exhausted, and in the rage which your wickedness excited in him, he would have let you kill him if we had not stopped the fight. And then what would you have done? You would have flung his body into that vault, where so many other unfortunates have perished, whose bones ought to rise and condemn you for being as cruel as your former lords."

These words reminded me of the apparition I had forgotten, and I turned round to see if it was still there. I could not see it, and then I bethought me of finding my way to the lower cave, where, as I began to think, I might be useful to my friends. I found the stairway at once and went down to the entrance of the vault, not trying to conceal myself, for such disputing and confusion were going on that no one paid any attention to me.

The Head-Woodsman had picked up the devil's skin-coat and showed that it was covered with spikes like a comb for currying oxen; and also the mittens which the sham devil wore on his hands, in which strong nails were fastened with the points outside. The bagpipers were furious. "Here's a pretty fuss about a few scratches," cried Carnat. "Isn't it in the order of things that a devil should have claws? And this young fool, who attacked him so imprudently, why didn't he know how far he could play at that game without getting his snout scraped? Come, come, don't pity him so much; it's a mere nothing; and since he has had enough of it, let him confess he can't play at our games, and is not fit to belong to our guild in any way."

"I shall belong to it!" cried Joseph, wrenching himself from Huriel's arms and showing as he did so his torn shirt and bleeding breast. "I shall belong to it in spite of you! I insist that the fight shall go on, and one of us be left in this cavern."

"I forbid it!" said the Head-Woodsman, "and I insist that this young man shall be proclaimed victor, or I swear to bring into this place a company of bagpipers who shall teach you how to behave, and who will see justice done."

"You?" said Doré-Fratin, drawing a sort of boar-knife from his belt. "You can do so if you choose, but you shall carry with you some marks on your body, so that people may believe your reports."

The Head-Woodsman and Huriel put themselves in an attitude of defence. Joseph flung himself upon Fratin to get away his knife, and I made one bound in amongst them. But before any of us could strike a blow the figure that startled me so in the upper cavern appeared at the opening of the lower one, stretched forth his lance, and slowly advanced in a way to strike terror to the minds of the evil-doers. Then, as they all paused, dumbfounded with fear and amazement, a piteous voice was heard from the depths of the dungeon, reciting the prayers for the dead.

This routed the whole brotherhood. One of the pipers cried out: "The dead! the dead are rising" and they all fled, pell-mell, yelling and pushing through the various openings except that to the dungeon, where stood another figure wrapped in a winding-sheet, chanting the most dismal sing-song that anybody ever heard. A minute later all our enemies had disappeared, and the warrior flinging off his helmet and mask, we beheld the jovial face of Benoît, while the monk, getting out of his winding sheet, was holding his sides in convulsions of laughter.

"May God forgive me for masquerading," he said. "I did it with the best intentions; those rascals deserve a good lesson, if it is only to teach them not to laugh at the devil, of whom they are really more afraid than those whom they threaten with him."

"For my part, I felt quite certain," said Benoît, "that our comedy would put an end to theirs." Then, noticing Joseph's wounds, he grew very uneasy, and showed such feeling for him that all this, together with the succor he had brought in so timely a manner, proved to my mind his regard for his step-son, and his good heart, which I had hitherto doubted.

While we examined Joseph and convinced ourselves he was not very seriously hurt, the monk told us how the butler at the castle had once said to him that he allowed the bagpipers and other societies to hold their secret meetings in the cellars of the castle. Those in which we found ourselves were too far from the inhabited parts of the castle to disturb the lady mistress of Saint-Chartier, and, indeed, if it had, she would only have laughed, not imagining that any mischief could come of it. But Benoît, who suspected some evil intent, had got the same butler to give him a key to the cellars, and a disguise; and that was how it was that he got these in time to avert all danger.

"Well," said the Head-Woodsman, addressing him, "thank you for your assistance; but I rather regret you came, for those fellows are capable of declaring that I asked you to do so and consequently that I betrayed the secrets of the guild. If you will take my advice we had better get away noiselessly, at once, and leave them to think you were really ghosts."

"All the more," added Benoît, "that their wrath may deprive me of their custom, which is no slight matter. I hope they did not recognize Tiennet—but how the devil was it that Tiennet got here in the nick of time?"

"Didn't you bring him?" asked Huriel.

"That he didn't," said I. "I came on my own account, because of the stories they tell of your deviltries. I was curious to see them; but I swear to you those fellows were too scared and the sight of their eyes was too wide of the mark ever to have recognized me."

We were about to leave when the sound of angry voices and an uproar like that of a fight was heard.

"Dear, dear!" cried the monk, "what's that now? I think they are coming back and we have not yet done with them. Quick, let's get back into our disguises!"

"No," said Benoît, listening, "I know what it is. I met, as I came along through the castle cellars, four or five young fellows, one of whom is known to me; and that is Leonard, your Bourbonnais wood-chopper, Père Bastien. These lads were there from curiosity no doubt; but they had got bewildered in the caverns, and I lent them my lantern, telling them to wait for me. The bagpipers must have met them and they are giving chase."

"It is more likely that they are being chased themselves if there are not more than five of them," said Huriel. "Let us go and see."

We were just starting when the noise and the footsteps approached, and Carnat, Doré-Fratin, and eight others returned to the cave, having, in fact, exchanged a few blows with our comrades, and finding that they had to do with real flesh and blood instead of spectres, were ashamed of their cowardice and so came back again. They reproached the Huriels for having betrayed them and driven them into an ambush. The Head-Woodsman defended himself, and the monk tried to secure peace by taking it all upon himself, telling the bagpipers to repent of their sins. But they felt themselves in good force, for others kept coming back to their support; and when they found their numbers nearly complete they raised their voices to a roar, and went from reproaches to threats and from threats to blows. Seeing there was no way to avoid an encounter, all the more because they had drunk a good deal of brandy while the tests were going on and were more or less intoxicated, we put ourselves in an attitude of defence, pressing one against the other, and showing front to the enemy on all sides, like oxen when a troop of wolves attack them at pasture. The monk, having already lost his morality and his Latin, now lost his patience also, and seizing the pipe of an instrument which had got broken in the scrimmage, he laid about him as hard as a man well could, in defence of his own skin.

Unluckily, Joseph was weakened by the loss of blood, and Huriel, who bore upon his heart the recollection of Malzac's death, was more fearful of giving blows than of receiving them. Anxious to protect his father, who sprang into the fray like an old lion, he put himself in great danger. Benoît fought very well for a man who was just out of an illness; but the truth is we were only six against fifteen or sixteen, and as the blood rose anger came, and I saw our enemies opening their knives. I had only time to fling myself before the Head-Woodsman, who, still unwilling to draw his blade, was the object of their bitterest anger. I received a wound in the arm, which I hardly felt at the moment, but which hindered my fighting on, and I thought the day was lost, when, by great good luck, my four comrades decided to come and see what the noise was about. The reinforcement was sufficient, and together we put to flight, for the second time and the last, our exhausted enemies, taken in the rear and ignorant how many were upon them.

I saw that victory was ours and that none of my friends were much hurt; then, suddenly perceiving that I had got more than I wanted, I fell like a log and neither knew nor felt another thing.

THIRTY-SECOND EVENING.

When I came to my senses I found myself in the same bed with Joseph, and it took me some time to recover full consciousness. When I did, I saw I was in Benoît's own room, that the bed was good, the sheets very white, and my arm bound up after a bleeding. The sun was shining through the yellow bed-curtains, and, except for a sense of weakness, I felt no ill. I turned to Joseph, who was a good deal cut about the head, but in no way to disfigure him, and who said, as he kissed me: "Well, my Tiennet, here we are, as in the old days, when we fought the boys of Verneuil on our way back from catechism, and were left lying together at the bottom of a ditch. You have protected me to your hurt, just as you did then, and I can never thank you as I ought; but you know, and I think you always knew, that my heart is not as churlish as my tongue."

"I have always known it," I replied, returning his kiss, "and if I have again protected you I am very glad of it. But you mustn't take too much for yourself. I had another motive—"

Here I stopped, fearing I might give way and let out Thérence's name; but just then a white hand drew back the curtain, and there I saw a vision of Thérence herself, leaning towards me, while Mariton went round between the bed and the wall to kiss and question her son.

Thérence bent over me, as I said; and I, quite overcome and thinking I was dreaming, tried to rise and thank her for her visit and assure her I was out of danger, when there! like a sick fool and blushing like a girl, I received from her lips the finest kiss that ever recalled the dead.

"What are you doing, Thérence?" I cried, grasping her hands, which I could almost have eaten up. "Do you want to make me crazy?"

"I want to thank you and love you all my life," she answered, "for you have kept your word to me; you have brought my father and my brother back to me safe and sound, and I know that all that you have done, all that has happened to you, is because you loved them and loved me. Therefore I am here to nurse you and not to leave you as long as you are ill."

"Ah, that's good, Thérence!" I said, sighing; "it is more than I deserve. Please God not to let me get well, for I don't know what would become of me afterwards."

"Afterwards?" said Père Bastien, coming into the room with Huriel and Brulette. "Come, daughter, what shall we do with him afterwards?"

"Afterwards?" said Thérence, blushing scarlet for the first time.

"Yes, Thérence the Sincere," returned her father, "speak as becomes a girl who never lies."

"Well, father, then afterwards, I will never leave him, either," she said.

"Go away, all of you!" I cried; "close the curtains; I want to get up and dress and dance and sing. I'm not ill; I have paradise inside of me—" and so saying I fell back in a faint, and saw and knew nothing more, except that I felt, in a kind of a dream, that Thérence was holding me in her arms and giving me remedies.

In the evening I felt better; Joseph was already about, and I might have been, too, only they wouldn't let me; and I was made to spend the evening in bed, while the rest sat and talked in the room, and my Thérence, sitting by my pillow, listened tenderly to what I said, letting me pour out in words all the balm that was in my heart.

The monk talked with Benoît, the pair washing down their conversation with several jorums of white wine, which they swallowed under the guise of a restorative medicine. Huriel and Brulette were together in a corner; Joseph with his mother and the Head-Woodsman in another.

Huriel was saying to Brulette: "I told you, the very first day I saw you, when I showed you your token in my earring, that it should stay there forever unless the ear itself came off. Well, the ear, though slit in the fight, is still there, and the token, though rather bent, is in the ear—see! The wound will heal, the token can be mended, and everything will come all right, by the grace of God."

Mariton was saying to Père Bastien: "What is going to be the result of this fight? Those men are capable of murdering my poor boy if he attempts to play his bagpipe in this region."

"No," replied Père Bastien, "all has happened for the best; they have had a good lesson, and there were witnesses enough outside of the brotherhood to keep them from venturing to attack Joseph or any of us again. They are capable of doing harm when, by force or persuasion, they have brought the candidate to take an oath. But Joseph took none; he will, however, be silent because he is generous. Tiennet will do the same, and so will our young woodsmen by my advice and order. But your bagpipers know very well that if they touch a hair of our heads all tongues will be loosened and the affair brought to justice."

And the monk was saying to Benoît: "I can't laugh as you do about the adventure, for I got into a passion which compels me to confess and do penance. I can forgive them the blows they tried to give me, but not those they forced me to give them. Ah! the prior of my convent is right enough to taunt me with my temper, and tell me I ought to combat not only the old Adam in me but the old peasant too,—that is, the man within me who loves wine and fighting. Wine," continued the monk, sighing, and filling his glass to the brim, "is conquered, thank God! but I discovered this night that my blood is as quarrelsome as ever, and that a mere tap could make me furious."

"But weren't you in a position of legitimate defence?" said Benoît. "Come, come; you spoke to those fellows in a proper manner, and you didn't strike till you were obliged to."

"That's all very true," replied the friar, "but my evil genius the prior will ask me questions,—he'll pump the truth out of me; and I shall be forced to confess that instead of doing it regretfully, I was carried away with the pleasure of striking like a sledge-hammer, forgetting I had a cassock on my back and thinking of the days when, keeping my flocks in the Bourbonnais pastures, I went about quarrelling with the other shepherds for the mere earthly vanity of proving I was the strongest and most obstinate of them all."

Joseph was silent; no doubt he felt badly at seeing two such happy couples without the right to sulk at them, after receiving such good support from Huriel and me. The Head-Woodsman, who had a tender spot in his heart for the fellow on account of his music, kept talking to him of glory. Joseph made great efforts to witness the happiness of others without showing jealousy; and we had to admit that, proud and cold as he was, there was in him an uncommon force of will for self-conquest. He remained hidden, as I did, for some time in his mother's house, till the marks of the fray were effaced; for the secret of the whole affair was very well kept by my comrades, though Leonard, who behaved very boldly and yet judiciously, threatened the bagpipers to reveal all to the authorities of the canton, if they did not conduct themselves peacefully.

When we all got about again it was found that no one was seriously damaged, except Père Carnat, whose wrist, as it proved, I had dislocated, and a parley and settlement ensued. It was agreed that Joseph should have certain parishes; and he had them assigned to him, though with no intention of using his privilege.

I was rather more ill than I thought for; not so much on account of my wound, which was not severe, nor yet of the blows that had been rained on my body, but because of the bleeding the monk had done to me with the best intentions. Huriel and Brulette had the charming amiability to put off their marriage till ours could take place; and a month later, the two weddings were celebrated,—in fact, there were three, for Benoît wished to acknowledge his publicly, and to celebrate the occasion with us. The worthy man, delighted to have had his heir so well taken care of by Brulette, tried to get her to accept a gift of some consequence, but she steadily refused, and throwing herself into Mariton's arms she said: "Remember that this dear woman was a mother to me for more than a dozen years; do you think I can take money when I am not yet out of her debt?"

"That maybe," said Mariton, "but your bringing up was nothing but honor and profit to me, whereas that of my Charlot brought you trouble and insult."

"My dear friend," replied Brulette, "that very fact is all that evens our account. I would gladly have made your José happy in return for all your goodness to me; but that did not depend on my poor heart, and so to compensate you for the grief I caused him, I was bound to suffer all I did for your other child."

"There's a girl for you!" cried Benoît, wiping his big round eyes, which were not used to shed tears. "Yes, yes, indeed, there's a girl!—" and he couldn't say any more.

To get even with Brulette, he was determined to pay all the costs of her wedding, and mine into the bargain. As he spared nothing and invited at least two hundred guests, it cost him a pretty sum, which he paid without a murmur.

The monk promised faithfully to be present, all the more because the prior had kept him on bread and water for a month and the embargo on his gullet was raised the very day of the wedding. He did not abuse his liberty, however, and behaved in such a pleasant way that we all became as fast friends with him as Huriel and Benoît had previously been.

Joseph kept up his courage till the day of the wedding. In the morning he was pale, and apparently deep in thought; but as we left the church he took the bagpipe from my father-in-law's hand, and played a wedding march which he had composed that very night in our honor. It was such a beautiful piece of music, and was so applauded, that his gloom disappeared, and he played triumphantly his best dance airs all the evening, and quite forgot himself and his troubles the whole time the festivities lasted.

He followed us back to Chassin, and there the Head-Woodsman, having settled his affairs, addressed us one and all, as follows:—

"My children, you are now happy, and rich for country folks; I leave you the business of this forest, which is a good one, and all I possess elsewhere is yours. You can spend the rest of the season here, and during that time you can decide on your plans for the future. You belong to different parts of the country; your tastes and habits are not alike. Try, my sons, both of you, to find what kind of life will make your wives happy and keep them from regretting their marriages now so well begun. I shall return within a year. Let me have two fine grandchildren to welcome me. You can then tell me what you have decided to do. Take your time; a thing that seems good to-day may seem worse, or better, to-morrow."

"Where are going, father?" said Thérence, clasping him in her arms in fear.

"I am going to travel about with Joseph, and play our music as we go," answered Père Bastien. "He needs it; and as for me, I have hungered for it these thirty years."

Neither tears nor entreaties could keep him, and that evening we escorted them half way to Saint Sevère. There, as we embraced Père Bastien with many tears, Joseph said to us: "Don't be unhappy. I know very well he is sacrificing the sight of your happiness to my good, for he has a father's heart for me and knows I am the most to be pitied of his children; but perhaps I shall not need him long; and I have an idea you will see him sooner than he thinks for." Then he added, kneeling before my wife and Huriel's, "Dear sisters, I have offended both of you, and I have been punished enough by my own thoughts. Will you not forgive me, so that I may forgive myself and go away more peacefully?"

They both kissed him with the utmost affection, and then he came to each of us, and said, with surprising warmth of heart, the kindest and most affectionate words he had ever said in his life, begging us to forgive his faults and to hold him in remembrance.

We stood on a hill to watch them as long as possible. Père Bastien played vigorously on his bagpipe, turning round from time to time to wave his cap and blow kisses with his hand.

Joseph did not turn round; he walked in silence, with his head down as if in thought or in grief. I could not help saying to Huriel that I saw on his face as he left us that strange look I had seen in his childhood, which, in our parts, is thought the sign of a man doomed to evil.

Our tears were dried, little by little, in the sunshine of happiness and hope. My beautiful dear wife made a greater effort than the rest of us, for never before being parted from her father, she seemed to have lost a portion of her soul in losing him; and I saw that in spite of her courage, her love for me, and the happiness she felt in the prospect of becoming a mother, there was always something lacking for which she sighed in secret.

So my mind was constantly turning on how to arrange our lives to live in future with Père Bastien, were it even necessary to sell my property, give up my family, and follow my wife wherever she wished to live.

It was just the same with Brulette, who was determined to consult only her husband's tastes, specially when her old grandfather, after a brief illness, died quietly, as he had lived, protected by the care and love of his dear daughter.

"Tiennet," she often said to me, "I see plainly that Berry must give way to the Bourbonnais in you and me. Huriel is too fond of this free, strong life and change of air to endure our sleepy plains. He makes me so happy I will never let him feel a secret pain. I have no family now in our parts; all my friends there, except you, have hurt me; I live only for Huriel. Where he is happy there I am happiest."

The winter found us still in the forest of Chassin. We had stripped that beautiful region of its beauty, for the old oak wood was its finest feature. The snow covered the prostrate bodies of the noble trees, flung head-foremost into the river, which held them, cold and dead, in its ice. One morning Huriel and I were lunching beside a fire of brushwood which our wives had lighted to warm our soup, and we were looking at them with delight, for both were in a fair way to keep the promise they had made to Père Bastien to give him descendants, when suddenly they both cried out, and Thérence, forgetting she was not so light as she once was, sprang almost across the fire to kiss a man whom the smoke of damp leaves had hidden from our sight. It was her good father, who soon had neither arms nor lips enough to reply to our welcome. After the first joy was over, we asked him about Joseph, and then his face darkened and his eyes filled with tears.

"He told you that you would see me sooner than I expected," said Père Bastien, sadly; "he may have had a presentiment of his fate, and God, who softened the hard shell of his heart at that moment, no doubt counselled him to reflect upon himself."

We dared not inquire further. Père Bastien sat down, opened his sack and drew forth the pieces of a broken bagpipe.

"This is all that remains of that poor lad," he said. "He could not escape his star. I thought I had softened his pride, but, alas! in everything connected with music he grew daily more haughty and morose. Perhaps it was my fault. I tried to console him for his love troubles by proving to him the happiness of his art. From me, at least, he got the sweets of praise, but the more he sucked them the greater his thirst. We went far,—as far even as the mountains of the Morvan, where there are many bagpipers as jealous as those in these parts, not so much for their selfish interests as for their conceit in their talents. Joseph was imprudent; he used language that offended them at a supper to which they hospitably invited him with the kindest intentions. Unhappily, I was not there; not feeling very well, and having no reason to fear a misunderstanding, I stayed away. He was absent all night, but that often happened, and as I had noticed he was rather jealous of the applause people were pleased to give to my old ditties, I was apt not to go with him. In the morning I went out, still not feeling well, and I heard in the village that a broken bagpipe had been picked up at the edge of a pond. I ran to see it, and knew it at a glance. Then I went to the place where it was found, and breaking the ice of the pond, I found his poor body, quite frozen. There were no marks of violence on it, and the bagpipers swore that they had parted from him, soberly and without a quarrel, about a league from the spot. I searched in vain for the cause of his death. The place was in a very wild region, where the law fears the peasant and the peasant fears nought but the devil. I was forced to content myself with their foolish remarks and reasons. In those parts they firmly believe a great deal that we should laugh at here; for instance, they think you can't be a musician without selling your soul to hell; and that Satan tears the bagpipe from the player's hands and breaks it upon his back, which drives him wild and maddens him, and then he kills himself. That is how they explain the revenge which bagpipers often take upon each other; and the latter never contradict, for it suits them to be feared and to escape all consequences. Indeed, all musicians are held in such fear and disrepute that I could get no attention to my complaints, and if I had remained in the neighborhood I might even have been accused of summoning the devil to rid me of my companion."

"Alas!" said Brulette, weeping, "my poor José, my poor dear companion! Good God, what are we to say to his mother?"

"We must tell her," said Père Bastien, sadly, "not to let Charlot take a fancy to music. It is too harsh a mistress for folks like us; we have not head enough to stand on the heights to which it leads without turning giddy."

"Oh, father!" cried Thérence, "if you would only give it up! God knows what misfortunes it may yet bring upon you."

"Be comforted, my darling," said Père Bastien, "I have given it up! I return to live with my family, to be happy with my grandchildren, whom I dream of already as they dance at my knee. Where shall we settle ourselves, my dear children?"

"Where you wish," said Thérence.

"Where our husbands wish," said Brulette.

"Where my wife wishes," I cried.

"Where you all wish," said Huriel.

"Well," said Père Bastien, "as I know your likings and your means, and as, moreover, I bring you back a bit of money, I've been thinking; as I trudged along that we could all be satisfied. When you wish the peach to ripen you mustn't pull out the stone. The peach-stone is the property which Tiennet owns at Nohant. We will buy other land that adjoins it, and build a good house for all of us. I shall be content to watch the wheat-fields,—glad not to fell God's noble trees, but to make my little songs in the olden fashion, at evening, by my door, among mine own, instead of drinking the wine of others and making jealousies. Huriel likes to roam, and his wife, just now, is of the same turn of mind. They can undertake such enterprises as we have now finished in this forest (where I see you have worked well), and they can spend the fine season in the woods. If their young family is in the way, Thérence has strength and heart enough to manage a double nest, and you will all meet together in the autumn with increased pleasure, until my son, long after he has closed my eyes, will feel the need of resting all the year round, as I feel it now."

All that my father-in-law said came to pass, just as he advised and prophesied. The good God blessed our obedience; and as life is a pasty mixed of sadness and content, poor Mariton often came to us to weep, and the worthy monk, as often, came to laugh.

THE END.